The University as a Critical Institution?

HIGHER EDUCATION RESEARCH IN THE 21ST CENTURY SERIES

Volume 10

Series Editors

Pedro Teixeira, *CIPES and University of Porto, Portugal*
Jussi Välimaa, *University of Jyväskylä, Finland*

International Editorial Advisory Board

Mari Elken, *University of Oslo, Norway*
Gaële Goastellec, *University of Lausanne, Switzerland*
Manja Klemenčič, *Harvard University, USA*
Simon Marginson, *University College London, United Kingdom*
Emanuela Reale, *Institute for Research on Firm and Growth CERIS – CNR Rome, Italy*
Creso Sá, *University of Toronto, Canada*

Scope

This series provides overviews about state of the art research in the field of higher education studies. It documents a selection of papers from the annual conferences of the Consortium of Higher Education Researchers (CHER), the world organisation of researchers in the field of higher education. This object and problem related field of studies is by nature interdisciplinary and theoretically as well as methodologically informed by disciplines such as sociology, political science, economics, history, philosophy, law and education. Each book includes an introduction by the editors explaining the thematic approach and criteria for selection as well as how the book can be used by its possible audience which might include graduate students, policy makers, researchers in the field, and practitioners in higher education administration, leadership and management.

Please email queries to Pedro Teixeira: pedrotx@fep.up.pt

The University as a Critical Institution?

Edited by

Rosemary Deem
Royal Holloway, University of London, UK

and

Heather Eggins
Lucy Cavendish College, University of Cambridge, UK

SENSE PUBLISHERS
ROTTERDAM/BOSTON/TAIPEI

A C.I.P. record for this book is available from the Library of Congress.

ISBN: 978-94-6351-114-8 (paperback)
ISBN: 978-94-6351-115-5 (hardback)
ISBN: 978-94-6351-116-2 (e-book)

Published by: Sense Publishers,
P.O. Box 21858,
3001 AW Rotterdam,
The Netherlands
https://www.sensepublishers.com/

All chapters in this book have undergone peer review.

Printed on acid-free paper

TABLE OF CONTENTS

ACKNOWLEDGEMENTS

This book is the tenth in the series produced from selected papers presented at the annual conferences of the Consortium of Higher Education Researchers (CHER). It could not have been produced without the assiduity of its authors who have been under considerable pressure to finalise their chapters for publication to meet the publication date before the 2017 conference. We also wish to acknowledge the help of members of the Conference Organising Committee in reviewing these chapters, and particularly Jurgen Enders, Terri Kim, Ye Liu, Lisa Lucas, Simon Marginson, Peter Scott and Patrick Clancy. We wish to thank Jack Simmons and Emma Berndt for their help with the preparation of the manuscript. We also wish to acknowledge the ongoing support of Lucy Cavendish College, University of Cambridge, whose sponsorship enabled the conference and its publication to be successfully undertaken. We thank all colleagues drawn from 26 countries who attended the 29th CHER conference in Cambridge, and contributed to the lively and informative event which has enabled this volume to be produced.

INTRODUCTION

ROSEMARY DEEM AND HEATHER EGGINS

1. THE UNIVERSITY AS A CRITICAL INSTITUTION?
AN INTRODUCTION

The notion of the university as a critical institution is far from new but the twentieth and twenty-first centuries have provided many profound challenges for higher education institutions, both in Europe and beyond, from the growth of a globalised context and massification of their undergraduate education cohorts (Altbach, 2015) and dealing with diversity and social inequality (Smith, 2009; Eggins, 2017; Deem, 2018), through audits of their research and teaching and league tables/rankings (Cheng, 2009; Shore & Wright, 2015), to funding regimes (Jongbloed & Vossensteyn, 2016), the changing meaning of the 'public good' (Marginson, 2016), academic capitalism (Rhoades & Slaughter, 2004), new managerialism (Deem & Hillyard et al., 2007), student consumerism (Budd, 2016) and student employability (Rooney & Rawlinson, 2016). Whether universities can survive as critical organisations in the current time is an open question, as digitalisation challenges the monopoly of knowledge, MOOCS question the necessity of university campuses and would-be students in countries where higher education fees are high start to consider more carefully whether they really want or need a degree. Universities are also affected by contemporary concerns such as what happens to higher education in war-zones and the impact of migration, anti-migrant ideologies, political populism, the post-truth era and the rejection of 'experts'. A great variety of authors have written critiques of the changing nature of the university from Lyotard in the 1980s (Lyotard, 1984) to Collini in the 2000s (Collini, 2012) but that is somewhat different from encouraging criticality within universities among both students and staff and thinking about the organisational nature of contemporary universities and whether there are alternatives to the forms, governance and management we have now.

In the call for papers for the 2016 CHER Conference, this was our opening gambit on the university as a critical institution:

> The capacity of higher education to contribute to society, policy, economy and cultural formation depends above all on its capacity to sustain open and critical thought; to relentlessly scrutinise society, the natural world and the human/ nature interface using a range of different lenses; to continually develop and explore alternative ways of thinking and social organization; and to prepare graduates with capacities in critical thought and reconstructive practices. If the gift of Europe to the world is that of the university centred on critical thought and imagination, that gift can never be taken for granted. Nurturing

R. Deem & H. Eggins (Eds.), The University as a Critical Institution?, 3–14.

the conditions for open critical thinking and autonomous discussion and communication are part the permanent remit of higher education institutions. In a more instrumental period, with rapidly growing obligations of and pressures on higher education, the vision of the university as a critical institution needs to be renewed—just as it has been periodically renewed throughout its history.

The chapters in this volume are a selection of those presented at the Conference in Cambridge in September 2016. We have tried to choose a variety of papers illustrative of the main strands from the much larger number of papers given at the original event, some offering overviews of a number of different HE systems, others focused on developments in a particular context and system but all in some way related to the notion of the critical (or in some cases uncritical) university. Each paper concerns itself either with some aspect of a broad research-informed critique of universities, takes a critical perspective on some aspect of current practice in higher education institutions or system or explores the potential for the future of universities as organisations. The chapters will be of interest not only to academics and students studying higher education themes but also to HE leaders, managers and policy makers.

There are four papers in the first section on 'The Contemporary University: Governance and Organisational Futures', the first one a theoretical and philosophical overview of how universities might be organized in a different way to the current neo-liberal and managerialist model, the second a detailed analysis of staff responses to different varieties and dimensions of managerial narratives and discourses in Portuguese universities, the third a comparison of the different recent paths of universities in the Ukraine and Poland in respect of management and governance and finally a comparison of academic freedom in one Italian and one Singaporean university in very contrasting situations. The opening paper in the first section, based on a plenary address given at the conference by Susan Wright, asks a provocative and extremely critical question about what is happening to higher education in the Anthropocene, an epoch in which humans largely shape the planet, in conjunction with what Wright calls the Capitalocene (a reference to the huge extent to which capitalism now defines what happens in the world). She enquires as to whether it is possible to conceptualise a more liveable university than those we have today, driven as the latter are by key features such as 'world class universities', entrepreneurial universities, marketised university systems and competition states, where universities are given a special role to support and trigger knowledge-economy competitiveness. Wright notes how universities are now positioned alongside businesses and industries and other organisations, conceptualized as an externalized economy. She wonders if an alternative conception of universities as an ecology could offer some plausible and original alternatives to the current position of higher education institutions by disrupting existing power relations and supply chains and putting academics back in the institutional driving seat. This, she observes, has already happened with some powerful Danish professor 'project barons' who determine for themselves how they run their research activities. It might also involve encouraging those who work or study in public higher education institutions to be both critically reflexive *and* willing to act politically on changing the organizational, cultural, social and political basis of higher education. This could include protests and other what she calls 'system disturbances' which question the current way in which particular universities are organized and run. Wright mentions that the Marie Curie International Training Network Universities in the Knowledge Economy (UNIKE) she directed, has produced, first in Auckland, then in Copenhagen, a declaration of six principles of the organization of public universities [Public Good, Social Responsibility, Academic Freedom, Educational Autonomy, University Independence and Humane Workplace] which have already been discussed at various European and international gatherings. It is intimated that the declaration could form the basis of a new ecology for higher education, thus providing a form of liveable university that could be along co-operative or Trust-type lines whereby all staff and students would have a genuine financial and organizational stake in their institution and the university could not be sold to a private venture capitalist. This would transform the organizational basis of universities and also offer an escape from managerialism (the dominance of management), neo-liberalism (the rise of markets) and 'boardism', the emphasis on external stakeholders having a say in how universities are run (Veiga & Magalhães et al., 2015).

The other papers in this first section on 'Governance and Organisational Futures' explore through a critical lens what is happening to governance, or to related concerns such as academic freedom, in individual countries. Magalhães, Veiga and Videira note that New Public Management in European universities often exists alongside other governance narratives and practices such as 'new governance' and 'networked governance'. They explore, using a 2014–2015 on-line survey of staff, including managers, administrators and academics, in all Portuguese higher education institutions (both public and private), respondents' views on governance and management held in those organisations after the 2007 reforms to HE governance in Portugal. These reforms have encouraged a shift away from academic collegiality towards a greater emphasis on strong rectorates and deans, a private-sector type of Human Resource Management, managerialism and 'boardism', which is where outside people from business are brought in to oversee institutional governance, with matching rhetorics (Veiga & Magalhães et al., 2015). Government narratives about managerialism, it is suggested, may have reinforced institutional autonomy in Portugal by drawing on and interacting with both networked governance and collegial governance in order to invest in and fix the meanings of core concepts of governance and management. The authors note that their respondents had experienced a range of forms of managerialism and governance narratives, on a continuum from hard to soft managerialism. The authors argue that the influence of managerialism does not happen with the same intensity in different governance dimensions, such as management hierarchies, how academic work and outputs are managed, strategic goal setting and the relative strength of competitiveness versus collaboration. Hard managerialism emphasizes managerial skills and sharp hierarchies, objectives linked to measurable outputs and performance indicators, commodification of activities and competition within and outside the institution, whereas soft managerialism, by contrast, puts much more emphasis on distributed leadership and interpersonal networks, the relationship of organizational goals to organizational mission statements, collaboration and cooperation, and uses negotiation and persuasion and seeks to empower staff. The findings of the study showed that non-academic staff working in higher education for less than 8 years, as well as those high up the institutional decision-making hierarchy, were more likely to perceive a growing influence of external stakeholders on governing bodies but regarded this as soft managerialism. Whilst those new to academic work tended to take managerialism for granted, staff who had worked in academe for longer periods saw the creeping influence of hard managerialism. In the public universities and amongst teaching staff, there was a greater perception of the influence of hard managerialism than amongst administrators and those who worked in private universities.

Hladchenko, Antonowitch and de Boer's chapter documents and compares some of the recent changes in university governance in two former Communist regimes, Poland and the Ukraine. The two systems are compared using the public sector governance equalizer model (de Boer & Enders et al., 2006) utilizing the five dimensions, viz state regulation, stakeholder guidance, academic self-governance, managerial-self- governance, and competition. Whilst Poland joined the EU in 2004, the Ukraine experienced two revolutions (2004 and 2013–2014) as well as retaining some of the power hierarchies of the former Communist regime. After 1990, Poland initially gave universities a high degree of freedom but in 2010 the government tried to regain its steering role. University leaders were initially administrator-academics and whilst rectors' roles have changed, they and deans are still elected by and accountable to their peers, but with their powers limited by central regulations. Since 2005 the Conference of Rectors of Academic Schools has had a legal monopoly in representing HE institutions at the national policy level. Competition has developed for students between public and private institutions, and also for research funding. The influence of the EU and the Bologna process on Poland's HE system is very evident. In the Ukraine, the inherited division between teaching-oriented higher education institutions and research-only institutions has remained in place. State regulation of higher education is still strong but weakened through the development of a private higher education sector after 1991. Public universities now also charge fees. A National Agency of Quality Assurance of Higher Education (established in 2015) was rocked by a series of scandals about allegations of plagiarism by candidates seeking election to it, which did not aid its legitimacy amongst universities. Steps have been taken to extend financial autonomy to public universities, though student fees can only be used for academic salaries or improving teaching not for research purposes. There is little emphasis on competitive research funding. The lack of a common HE framework in the Ukraine and the absence of broader international practice is very evident. The authors conclude that both countries have come somewhat closer to New Public Management with less state regulation, more stakeholder guidance, more managerial self-governance and increased competition for students and/or for research funding but both systems, it is claimed, still remain less embedded in NPM than is the case for management and governance regimes in most European countries, with state regulation still substantial, as well as limited stakeholder guidance and academic self-governance (the latter particularly so in Poland). Also in both systems, academics who are openly critical of their higher education system still appear to make themselves vulnerable to attack or dismissal.

Finally in this section, Westa examines the contested and complex phenomenon of academic freedom, which has close links to criticality and institutional autonomy and which is a hot topic in many countries now like China and Turkey, where politicians have attempted to significantly limit academic freedom of speech and political activity. The author develops her arguments in the context of two very different higher education systems, Italy and Singapore. In Italy, academic freedom is a constitutional right. But there have been some recent reforms to Italian higher education in 2010 (the Gelmini Reforms) which on the one hand have given universities more autonomy in financial and material ways but on the other hand have restricted how many faculties are allowed and how many particular types of appointments may be made and for how long. Italian universities are also increasingly dependent on external evaluation of both teaching and research, which can hinder academic freedom in relation to research topics and even teaching. Academic freedom is not a constitutional right in Singapore (even though a general freedom of speech exists for citizens of the country, in practice this is restricted when security concerns arise) and regulations and laws relating to academics make no mention of the term. Westa notes a history of informal bans about academics mentioning certain topics connected to religion, local corruption, governmental policies and politics etc in their teaching. The research focusses on two institutions, the university of Bologna (formed in 1088) and the National University of Singapore, formed as a medical school in 1908 in Malaysia and becoming a full university in 1962 on Singapore's independence. As part of her research, Westa conducted a series of interviews with academics in both universities in relation to academic freedom. She found some similar ties of views in both countries, with both sets of respondents seeing connections between academic freedom and responsibility for students and society and in addition many observing that not all academics took the latter seriously. Interviewees from both countries mentioned the stress connected with the requirement to publish their research outputs (which could be interpreted as limiting freedom to publish when they wished and on a topic of their own choice) but even in Singapore there seemed some signs that academic freedom in other respects was opening up.

In Section 2 on 'Widening Participation, Curricular Innovation and Research Policy', there are three papers which focus on critiquing the practice of elite UK universities dealing with widening participation, the growth of student centred liberal arts degree programmes in private universities in Germany and how two Portuguese polytechnics are responding to current government policy on research activity by academics. The first chapter by Boliver, Gorard and Siddiqui critiques, underpinned by a considerable amount of quantitative evidence, some of the limitations of English universities' responses to the current government policy requirement to widen participation to universities by students from disadvantaged households and/or first generation university applicants. Like Wright's opening piece in Section 1, this paper is based on a plenary address originally given in Cambridge by Boliver. The authors examine what universities in England have done to date to encourage non-traditional and disadvantaged household students to apply to universities, particularly to what have become known as 'selective' universities which have many more applicants than places (mostly but not exclusively members of the elite Russell mission Group), as contrasted with 'recruiting' universities that have more places than applicants. Efforts to date have largely consisted of two main strategies. One is trying to improve the pre-application attainments of would-be applicants from disadvantaged backgrounds, by devices such as summer schools, workshops, and even universities taking over the running of secondary schools in less well-off areas. The second strategy has been to endeavor to raise the aspirations of potential applicants from disadvantaged backgrounds, though the authors suggest that the aspirations of those who want to attend university may already be quite high. Experiments using contextualized admissions data which give information about the number of pupils going to university and socio-economic data about the typical pupil background have led some research- intensive universities to lower the entry grades for students from under resourced schools in areas of economic deprivation but in the case of Bristol University, which did this in the mid-2000s, it led to a backlash from angry private-school head-teachers. The authors suggest that considerably lower grade offers could be made to students from disadvantaged schools and areas but with the proviso that even this is not enough, as universities also have to give greater support, including changing their pedagogies, to such students when they are actually studying at university. It is perhaps the latter which elite universities may resist the most. But as the authors note, accepting students from disadvantaged backgrounds with lower grades is not in itself enough to ensure that those students succeed in their degree studies. Perhaps the message here is that elite institutions are insufficiently self-critical of their own attempts to widen participation and unwilling to change traditional pedagogic modes aimed at elite students. There would also be a cost factor to the university to provide the necessary support.

Kontowski and Kretz offer a very different focus on critical higher education institutions, examining a form of student-centred or progressive higher education in the shape of the liberal arts degree, which offers students considerable latitude and scope compared to many conventional and constrained bachelors degree programmes in much of mainland Europe (unlike the US where liberal arts universities are well established but perhaps on the basis of a somewhat different model). The authors chose to explore how a small number of private fee-paying higher education institutions in Germany have experimented with liberalizing the curriculum at first degree level, thus allowing students a greater choice of both what and how they study. Following such a path in a country with free comprehensive university programmes (but mostly mono-disciplinary) easily available almost everywhere is not straightforward and as the authors show, each of the three universities they investigated experienced crises of various kinds, particularly financial crises (since there is no tax relief regime for philanthropy in Germany comparable to that found in the USA for example) but also challenges to leadership as well as to the stability and continuity of the institutions concerned. The three institutions tend to emphasise teaching rather than research, though one of the case study institutions did attract some strong researchers. The authors point out that the advantages of these institutions lies in their small size and flexibility, factors that lend themselves to educational experimentation and offer an alternative to the now increasingly dominant neo-liberal institutions in which most European students find themselves studying. There is also an emphasis on non-vocational degrees. Highly structured programmes, the authors contend, merely reinforce existing inequalities and do not challenge social injustice in the same way as less structured degrees (Nussbaum, 1998). The preceding Boliver/Gorard/Siddiqui paper showed how elite universities in England tend to reproduce rather than challenge social inequalities. The full integration of egalitarian academic learning with no strong student/ teacher demarcation on campus-based communities can encourage student self-organization and help democratize university bureaucracies, though the importance of charismatic leaders in the case-study universities somewhat challenges this idea. However, even where financial help is made available at private liberal arts universities in Germany for students from lower income households (not easy given that all three institutions experienced financial difficulties including having to shed staff), it is difficult to see how this could become a mass model for higher education. But there is clearly much here for more conventional institutions to learn from and indeed liberal arts degrees are also now beginning to appear in public institutions outside North America.

Finally in section 2, Hasanefendic, Patricio and de Bakker examine how two different Portuguese polytechnics have responded to twenty-first century government policies in Portugal which require polytechnics to pursue applied rather than pure or 'blue skies' research, as well as teaching vocational education programmes or those that attend to the needs of society. Both attempt to differentiate their ethos significantly from that of the public universities. The authors argue that much research on universities and other higher education institutions tends to emphasise the cumulative effects of external policy drivers on organizational cultures and practices both within and across different countries, assuming that this induces a sense of similarity rather than difference in organizational responses and cultures. Furthermore, some interpretations of institutional theory, it is suggested, have focused our attention on how isomorphic many universities in different parts of the world have become (though often while theories do suggest this, the empirical evidence for identifying isomorphism is thin). By contrast, in this chapter the authors concentrate on how the two institutions studied have responded very differently to a uniform policy aimed at all polytechnics in a single higher education system, with actors using policy ambiguities, staff biographies and different institutional ambitions to move in different directions in the two institutions. The paper draws on views and responses from a wide range of actors including teaching staff, Deans, Programme Directors and the Presidents of the two polytechnics chosen for the study (we are not told whether the two institutions were selected because they were known to be different or whether that was accidental). The fieldwork included participant observation, interviews, documentary analysis and information drawn from websites. As the authors point out, many academic staff in both institutions themselves studied in Portuguese universities, not polytechnics and a good number of them can see no reason why their teaching and research should be any different from the place where they studied. Furthermore, some academics pointed out that they are required to publish research outputs at the same time as being told to collaborate with industry which does not often permit publicly available outputs as a research outcome. Additionally, nationally accredited Masters Programmes via the Portuguese higher education quality agency A3ES require academic staff to have a doctoral degree *and* research outputs. One institution wanted to be just like a university and so followed a course of action leading in this direction (a Wannabe approach), whereas the other aimed for a hybrid status mid-way between a university and a polytechnic (the Hybridizer approach), partly due to geographical location and a desire to serve the local community and its industry, whilst continuing to publish conventional scientific outputs. Both polytechnics emerge as critical institutions that are carefully considering their possible future path-dependency and exploiting policy inconsistencies to their own benefit.

In Section 3, on 'Higher Education Policies and Practices on Teaching Quality and Excellence and the Student Experience', there are four papers which cover quality assessment issues, different aspects of the student experience and how best to nurture and develop teaching excellence. Manatos, Rosa and Sarrico's chapter examines the effects on institutions and the views of internal stakeholders, including students and both academic and administrative staff in Portuguese universities after Portugal set up a new Higher Education Quality Agency, A3ES, in 2007. A3ES is a private foundation that validates teaching programmes in universities and audits institutional quality systems. Existing literature shows that university staff in general but particularly academics tend to distinguish between the development of quality assurance systems and actual improvements in quality, focusing more on their concerns and views about the processes put in place rather than considering how these are related to changes to the quality of teaching, learning and assessment. The literature also shows that academics are less favourably disposed towards quality assurance than are administrators and other staff who are not directly engaged in teaching. Academics have also been reported as regarding the idea of quality assurance as contradictory to academic cultures and values. The research study involved case studies of three different universities that were the first higher educational institutions in Portugal to establish internal quality management systems.

Semi-structured interviews were conducted with different stakeholder groups – students, academics and administrators in three academic fields: Engineering, Language and Literature, and Education, including both those closely involved with quality assurance and those less involved. Those staff closely involved with quality assurance tended to have more positive views about the processes and their links to improving quality, whilst those academics less involved were often the most resistant and some saw QA mechanisms as being more about controlling academic staff than the quality of teaching, learning and assessment. Staff resisters claimed they could detect no positive effects of QA procedures. Some student respondents were also very critical and did not understand the purpose of surveys linked to QA, as well as being somewhat cynical that universities would act upon the results of these surveys. A number of students also said not everyone could be bothered filling in these forms. The researchers suggest more staff development needs to be done and more work with students too, explaining why quality assurance is necessary and what it tries to achieve, thus ensuring that a higher proportion of academics are engaged in QA processes and so that students come to see themselves as critical but vital partners in the QA processes rather than sceptical and passive bystanders.

Horntvedt and Carm's work relates to both student experience and internationalization and particularly to what degree of intercultural competence and related criticality is acquired as a result of students going on international exchanges. The research they conducted was based in Norway in a single higher education institution that has a tradition of sending bachelors degree students to other countries in the global south as part of their programme. Most undertook a project whilst abroad. The researchers compared the views and attitudes of young students on full-time professional training programmes such as healthcare, social work and teaching with adults studying part-time to be teachers based on their previous occupations in which they all held vocational diplomas. International exchanges are in theory intended to give students experience of living and studying in another country and to develop their understanding of a different and unfamiliar culture, as well as learning to relate to people whose way of life is different from theirs, although some researchers question whether just going abroad is sufficient, as some exchangers may remain isolated from people in the country concerned and just stay with people from their own culture (de Wit, 2013). As part of the study, the researchers analysed dissertations and projects written as part of the exchange process to see how they discussed intercultural competence and also interviewed a sample of students from both groups before, during and after the exchange visits. The findings were perhaps somewhat surprising in that, of the responses to the exchanges, two groups exhibited either direct racism or zenophobia (dislike of people from other countries). A third group wanted to be assimilated in the new culture as quickly as possible and a fourth group did show real signs of both appreciating and trying to understand the new culture and relating it to their own culture and were beginning to develop intercultural competence. The only other difference was that the part-time adult students presented themselves abroad in relation to their previous occupation, not the one they were training for, whereas younger students wanted to connect their current training to the context they were in on exchange.

Anzivino and Rostan's paper also focuses on an aspect of the university student experience, this time using a study based in a research-intensive university in Italy, but in this case the lens is on another aspect of extra-curricular activity, not exchange visits as in Horntvedt and Carm's chapter but other outside-class events and activities which involve interaction with other students and university staff. The authors are not just interested in the activity *per se* but in the extent to which such non-curriculum activities affect the study career of individuals during their degree programme (do they finish on time or delay their studies?) and the level of academic achievement attained. The paper is an example of the critical university at work, as one of the authors is also a University Vice Rector for Student Affairs: using his management work to shape research is a strategy that he has consciously adopted (Deem, 2016). Previous research shows some positive effects arising from out of class activity but much of the context is in Anglo-Saxon countries and there is some uncertainty as to the effects on things like degree study regularity and attainment level. A large sample of undergraduate and postgraduate students at Pavia University were surveyed during the 2014–2015 academic year on their outside class activities and the responses linked to a range of information about their academic attainment and study lifecycle as well as to their individual characteristics as derived from the survey and institutional data. 2,186 students returned the survey, a response rate of 32.3%. Pavia has a system of halls of residence which also act as college-like organisations for those who obtain good grades but a high percentage of those not living in halls commute to the university from outside the city. The survey found some positive results connected to study regularity including studying together with peers, intense involvement in leisure activities and interaction with academic staff. Interaction with staff outside of formal classes is also linked to getting good grades, though interaction with other students outside of class isn't. So far as individual characteristics are concerned, being under 25, having a lot of family cultural capital, studying certain subjects, attending a second cycle course, passing from first to second year and staying in Pavia during term all favour studying with peers, taking part in leisure activities and interaction with Faculty members, though over 25s have the highest levels of interaction with Faculty. Some policy implications are suggested at the end of the paper. The chapter is a good example of how in a senior management role it is possible to take a critical lens to what is happening on your own doorstep.

Finally in this section, Kottman's chapter explores the idea of Centres of Excellence and their role in improving teaching in higher education institutions. This is a different kind of being critical, because it relates to the capacity of teachers in higher education to become involved in reflection upon and development of their own teaching, which as previous research on leading teaching demonstrates, is a complex task (Gibbs & Knapper et al., 2009). In the chapter, Kottman describes a study which compares a central Teaching unit based in a comprehensive German university and largely paid for by institutional funding but having one externally funded project, with what is effectively a teachers network funded by a national initiative and based in a very small specialist music college in Norway. The intention of the study was to examine the effects of both Centres on teachers' engagement with pedagogic and curricular practice, as well as to explore the micro-cultures surrounding teaching in each institution. It is probably no surprise that it was the teachers' network with its own staffing and project money, which seemed to have the greatest chance of making HE teachers develop a critical approach to their own teaching, because it was a collaborative entity, not a remote unit but also something localized and contextualized. In that setting, teachers can feel confident to share things, a finding replicated by researchers looking at different kinds of collaborative micro teaching cultures (Mårtensson & Roxå, 2016). The large central unit in the German university is largely disregarded by the majority of experienced teachers in the institution because it is not linked to any particular disciplinary schools or faculties, and does not seek out academics to invite them to take an active part (there are no incentives to do project work). Though it is run by those who are also teachers, perhaps teaching other teachers is not always seen as equivalent to teaching students. During interviews it became clear that in the German university there was little sharing of teaching practice: learning more about teaching for more experienced staff was a question of trial and error and there was little interest in or knowledge of the institution's learning and teaching strategy. In the small Norwegian teachers' network, in contrast, there were incentives to do projects, there was no real staff hierarchy, and the micro-culture was supportive of thinking about teaching (in effect becoming self-critical).

We hope that the volume will have something to help all our readers reflect on the 21st century concept of the university as a critical institution. If universities stop being a space where different views may be aired and if they are no longer able to encourage their staff and students to think and act critically, then the era of the university would truly be over.

REFERENCES

Altbach, P. (2015). Globalization and forces for change in higher education. *International Higher Education, 50*.

Budd, R. (2017). Undergraduate orientations towards higher education in Germany and England: Problematizing the notion of 'student as customer'. *Studies in Higher Education, 73*(1), 23–37.

Cheng, M. (2009). *Changing academics: Quality audit and its perceived impact*. Saarbrücken, Germany: VDM Verlag.

Collini, S. (2012). *What are universities for?* London: Penguin.

de Boer, H. F., Enders, J., & Schimank, U. (2006). On the way towards new public management? The governance of university systems in England, the Netherlands, Austria, and Germany. In D. Jansen (Ed.), *New forms of governance in research organizations – Disciplinary approaches, interfaces and integration* (pp. 137–154). Dordrecht, the Netherlands: Springer.

de Wit, H. (2013). Internationalisation of higher education, an introduction on the why, how and the what. In H. de Wit (Ed.), *An introduction to higher education internationalisation*. Milan: Vita e pensiero.

Deem, R. (2016). Higher education researchers as managers and leaders in universities: Contributing through co-production of academic knowledge? (Unpublished paper). *European Conference of Educational Researchers*. Dublin: University College.

Deem, R. (2018). The gender politics of higher education. In B. Cantwell, H. Coates, & R. King (Eds.), *Handbook on the politics of higher education*. Cheltenham: Edward Elgar.

Deem, R., Hillyard, S., & Reed, M. (2007). *Knowledge, Higher Education and the new managerialism: The changing management of UK Universities*. Oxford: Oxford University Press.

Eggins, H. (Ed.). (2010). *Access and equity: Comparative perspectives*. Rotterdam, the Netherlands: Sense Publishers.

Eggins, H. (Ed.). (2017). *The changing role of women in higher education*. Dordrecht, the Netherlands: Springer.

Gibbs, G., et al. (2009). *Departmental leadership of teaching in research-intensive environments*. London: Leadership Foundation for HE (UK).

Jongbloed, B., & Vossensteyn, H. (2016). University funding and student funding: International comparisons. *Oxford Review of Economic Policy, 32*(4), 576–595.

Lyotard, J. F. (1984). *The postmodern condition: A report on knowledge*. Manchester: Manchester University Press.

Marginson, S. (2016). Public/private in higher education: A synthesis of economic and political approaches. *Studies in Higher Education,* 1–16

Mårtensson, K., & Roxå, T. (2016). Working with networks, micro cultures and communities: The staff and educational development series. In D. Baume & C. Popovic (Eds.), *Advancing practice in academic development* (pp. 174–187). London: Routledge.

Nussbaum, M. C. (1998). *Cultivating humanity: A classical defense of reform in liberal education*. Cambridge, MA: Harvard University Press.

Rhoades, G., & Slaughter, S. (2004). *Academic capitalism and the new economy*. Baltimore: Johns Hopkins University Press.

Rooney, S., & Rawlinson, M. (2016). Narrowing participation? Contesting the dominant discourse of employability in contemporary higher education. *Journal of the National Institute for Career Education and Counselling, 1*(36), 20–29.

Shore, C., & Wright, S. (2015). Audit culture revisited: Rankings, ratings, and the reassembling of society. *Current Anthropology, 56*(3), 421–444.

Smith, D. G. (2009). *Diversity's promise for higher education: Making it work* (2nd Edition). Baltimore, MD: Johns Hopkins University Press.

Veiga, A., Magalhães, A., Amaral, A. (2015). The palgrave international handbook of higher education policy and governance. In J. Huisman, H. de Boer, D. Dill, & M. Souto-Otero (Eds.), *From collegial governance to boardism: Reconfiguring governance in higher education* (pp. 398–416). London: Palgrave Macmillan.

Rosemary Deem
Royal Holloway University of London

Heather Eggins
Lucy Cavendish College Cambridge
Staffordshire University and CHEER
Sussex University

PART 1

THE CONTEMPORARY UNIVERSITY: GOVERNANCE AND ORGANISATIONAL FUTURES

SUSAN WRIGHT

2. CAN THE UNIVERSITY BE A LIVEABLE
INSTITUTION IN THE ANTHROPOCENE?

WELCOME TO THE ANTHROPOCENE

On Monday 29 August 2016, the International Geological Congress meeting in Capetown, declared the start of a new geological epoch. The Holocene (defined by glaciers) was over. Its successor, the Anthropocene, is an epoch in which humans are the greatest shapers of the planet. They dated the start of the Anthropocene to 1950. That was when nuclear tests meant radioactive sediments, radionuclides, formed a new stratum on the earth's surface. The great acceleration in mid-20th century capitalism changed the carbon, nitrogen and phosphorous cycles, and saw the increased discarding of metals, concrete and plastic (AWG 2016). Indeed a rival name for the era was the Plasticene, because another geological change in the world is the 288 million tons of plastic produced each year, much of which finds its way into the ocean so that by 2050 plastic will outweigh the fish in the seas (Oceans at MIT, 2014; WEF, 2016, p. 14). One quip was that dating in this era would not be by tree rings but by multinationals' product design manuals. The transition to each new geological epoch also has to be marked by a new fossil record – in this case, chicken bones. Chickens have become the world's most common bird – 60 billion were killed in 2015 – and their bones go into landfills. Between 1945 and 1950 in the U.S, a quick-fattening chicken with bigger bones of a distinctive shape called Arbor Acres was developed and it now dominates the world's genetic stock – half of all other chicken breeds have disappeared (Carrington, 2016). They spread so fast because of the development of factory farming and the liberalisation of trade.

Curiously, the literature most often represents the emergence of the Anthropocene as a switch in the binary relationship between 'humans' and 'nature': nature used to be a passive or supportive backdrop to human action; now human action is ruining nature and endangering the planet. This treats 'humans' as an essentialised species, as if they are all equally implicated, whereas there is a global landscape of inequality in which some people and some countries gain benefits by pursuing these changes and the peripheralised and dispossessed feel the negative effects. As Moore (2016) puts it, the Anthropocene is not the geology of a species, but of a system, capitalism. Indeed the above outline of the World Geological Congress' markers for the new epoch concerns the impacts of the post-Second World War military-industrial complex and the vast expansion of resource extraction and waste, factory farming and global trade. As Moore argues, the epoch really should be called the

R. Deem & H. Eggins (Eds.), The University as a Critical Institution?, 17–37.

Capitalocene. Such a focus on capitalism moves the argument away from how to patch up the damage humans cause to nature with technocratic fixes. Instead, a system approach turns attention to the social, political and economic processes involved, the institutions that people build and the political economy they form.

Even though universities are not the most important institution in the Capitalocene, they are nonetheless implicated in its formation. Since the 1950s, especially in the U.S., they have been bound up with the military-industrial complex and since the 1990s politicians have turned to universities to 'drive' what they call the 'global knowledge economy'. Universities have been reformed to make them focus more narrowly on producing what Slaughter and Rhoades (2004, p. 17) call the two crucial raw materials for this economy – knowledge and high-skilled labour – and to do so at a time when the negative consequences of such a constricted economic focus are finally being identified, named, measured and analysed in the Anthropocene/ Capitalocene. This chapter explores the consequences of universities' becoming entangled with such a predatory system and, using Polanyi's (2001 [1944]) distinction between a 'formal economy' and a 'substantive economy' or 'ecology', asks instead how they can be re-embedded in a wider range of interlaced social, political and economic relations and responsibilities. The situation of academics within this political economy behoves us to question, how can we educate ourselves and our students to be critically reflexive about the 'scene' universities are in? In universities that have been reformed into alignment with the processes generating the Anthro/Capitalocene, how can we use our critical skills to find space to act, so as to develop universities as responsible institutions producing knowledge and citizens with a sense of care for the future not just of humanity but of the globe itself?

UNIVERSITY REFORMS

Since the 1990s, university reforms have been so widespread around the world that they resemble what Morton (2013) calls a Hyperobject. That is, something that is so massively distributed throughout the globe and takes so many different detailed forms, that it is hard to grasp how all its manifestations somehow contribute to a general trend and achieve similar effects. Morton develops this concept in relation to species extinction but it also seems applicable to university reforms and their contribution to what Sassen (2014) calls the 'expulsions' of capitalism. She argues that capitalist systems have developed much narrower interests and sharper edges, beyond which surplus people and unprofitable things are not just 'externalised' and marginalised but expelled and made invisible. How, through a range of different reforms, have universities gradually shifted from a responsibility for being the 'critic and conscience of society' (as framed in New Zealand's legislation) to becoming increasingly implicated in the expulsions of the Capitalocene? The range of ways that universities have been reformed can be illustrated by describing four main approaches: to create 'world class' universities; entrepreneurial universities; universities that are part of a market state; and universities that are drivers of a competition state. The World Bank promoted the first policy, the idea that countries should compete in a so-called global knowledge economy by trying to ensure they had one or more 'World Class Universities' (Salmi, 2009). To achieve this, they should 'pick winners', focus their resources on those universities and engage in 'internationalisation'. The World Bank offered a smorgasbord of methods to achieve this: by distributing public funding on a competitive basis, privatisation of provision, or 'cost sharing' (i.e, charging students' fees). Even countries with state socialism, like Vietnam, found that when they implemented one of these methods, it quickly entailed the others, including pursuing the World Bank's agenda of bringing private and capitalist interests into the state sector (Dang, 2009). In Chile, where Milton Friedman's Chicago Boys created arguably the most privatised education sector in the world with the highest student fees, sustained street protests over many years have led to a change of government and a request to the World Bank to advise them on how to reverse that process (Bekhradnia, 2015). There is no yet a word for how to 're-public-ise' the sector and move out of neoliberal governance, privatisation and the market state.

A second reform route, to create what they call an entrepreneurial university, has been taken by Australia and New Zealand. This means that income generation pervades every aspect of the university. A consultancy report for Australian Universities recommends they should develop new business models for universities, 'streamlining' different income streams (EY, 2012). A report (Barber et al., 2013) staffed and funded by the education publisher and private provider, Pearson, used an older term (first used in Thorne, 1999). They proposed 'unbundling' the activities whose interlacing (and cross-subsidising) has up to now been the distinctive feature of a university. Each activity should be treated as a separate income-generating stream, and organised in such a way as to maximise its own added value. Those that do not make a profit should be closed. Auckland University is perhaps New Zealand's most exemplary 'enterprise university'. In this case income generation and the realisation of intellectual property assets are the most important criteria when setting research priorities. The appointment of staff is based on the enterprise unit's assessment of how much income their research will bring in (rather than academics' assessment of its intellectual quality or the person's contribution to teaching). The conditions of employment have also been changed to reward 'enterprise', with everyone responsible for leadership of the university in that direction (Amsler & Shore, 2015).

The third reform policy is best exemplified in England where successive governments have attempted to turn the university sector into a competitive market for higher education. From the 1980s, reforms have had four main features: university activities were valued in purely economic terms; systems of top-down decision making were introduced, so that, mimicking a corporation, universities could respond to changes in the market; the sector was fragmented according to institutions' 'distinctive missions' so they could compete in different markets; and students were reinscribed as consumers and universities were reframed in terms of the discourses, and to some extent the practices, of commercial enterprises (Wright, 2004). Much of the push for marketization has centred on student fees. In the 1960s, the state paid the fees of each qualified student and provided a means-tested maintenance grant. But from 1976 to 1997, government funding per student was reduced by 40% (Dearing, 1997, p. 267, para 17.16), resulting in a £2 billion annual shortfall in funding for teaching. The Dearing Report argued student numbers should increase to 45% of the 18–19 year cohort to meet the needs of the knowledge economy and graduates should repay 25% of their tuition costs as their personal benefits from higher education were greater than those of industry or society. Instead of following Dearing's plan, the new Labour government first introduced an up-front annual fee for all students of £1125 and then the 2004 Higher Education Bill turned the sector into a market by allowing universities to charge a variable fee based on how they ranked each course in the market. As McGettigan (2013) showed, taxpayers now paid for education twice, first in taxes and then in fees. And the government only squeezed the legislation through Parliament by 'capping' the fees at £3000 for three years. All universities charged the top fee for all courses because of the funding shortage, but the legislation for a higher education market had been put in place. Following another national review (The Browne Report, 2010) the Coalition Government in 2010 raised the cap on annual fees to £9,000, ended government funding of teaching through the block grant (except for STEM subjects), and replaced nearly all student grants with tax-funded student loans. Their argument was that this created a 'level playing field' between public universities and for-profit providers. The result was a spawning of companies offering higher education whose students were eligible for student loans to pay £6000 tuition fees and maintenance costs. Quality checks were not in place to see if the students attended, if the courses were actually taught, and to calculate the completion and drop-out rates. Vast profits were made. For example, St Patrick's International College was too small to register for public-backed loans for students in 2011–2012 but grew within a year to receive £11 million in public-backed funding in 2012–2013 from its 4,000 students. This so-called marketization has generated a system of risk free, state-funded capitalism (Wright, 2008, 2016).

In the fourth policy approach, in Denmark, the elements of the argument for reform were assembled in quite a different way to Chile, Australasia or England. A law in 2003 brought universities under wider public sector reforms to create a 'competition state' in which universities were given a special responsibility to drive Denmark's competitiveness in the Global Knowledge Economy and thence sustain its position as 'one of the richest countries in the world' (Danish Government, 2006). Rather than being directly marketised, privatised or expected to be enterprising themselves, public universities received vastly increased government funding in order for them to produce a faster throughput of qualified knowledge workers and research that could be turned into innovations by industry. The minister's catchphrase for the reform was 'from idea to invoice', and the purpose of increasing public investment was to yield knowledge and high-skilled labour that could be harvested effectively by private-sector knowledge industries. The 2003 law gave universities the status of legal persons, which made them responsible for their own solvency, and meant they could enter into contracts with government and other private and public organisations. The government made them into 'free agents', no longer protected by the state against economic and political interests but responsible for exercising their own agency. Indeed, they were now legally obliged to exchange knowledge with 'surrounding society' whilst protecting their own research freedom and ethics. The law also changed the management of universities, establishing strategic leaders of clearly bounded organisations and units, who had the freedom to manage and to deliver on contracts. Perversely, the government could now steer these 'free agents' much more tightly by setting political aim for the sector, which were translated into performance indicators in 'development contracts' with the strategic leaders, and by tight control of universities' liquidity.

These four examples of university reform illustrate how widespread they have been and also how they differ in terms of how the components have been put together and which aspect of the assemblage has been emphasised and made into the key concept and argument for reform. But if spread and variety are characteristic of a 'hyperobject', another feature of Morton's concept is that the reforms all somehow contribute to general trend and achieve similar effects. Taking this insight, the reforms seem to share two main features that are changing the place of universities in the world and implicate them in wider systemic relationships that were introduced above as the Anthropocene or Capitalocene. First, universities are conceptualised as a new kind of subject in a new context; and, second, this context is treated as an 'economy' in which universities are allocated an instrumental role in the production of knowledge and human capital deemed necessary for successful global competitiveness.

NEW CONTEXT OR FIELD OF HIGHER EDUCATION

The first shared feature of this torrent of reforms is that universities are no longer thought to be in a ring-fenced 'sector' supposedly protected from the dominance of economic and political interests and charged with providing education, research, and public service to the citizenry: they are now a site for value extraction in the Capitalocene. Since the Second World War, especially in the U.S., universities have been deeply engaged with capitalist agriculture and research and development for pharmaceuticals and defence, but now they are positioned amidst a complex array of industries and organisations that connects them to and makes them effective and intelligible within the 'global knowledge economy'. They range from publishers with new business models, to specialists in bibliometrics and data harvesting, organisations producing the university rankings that students use to select their university and other universities and industrial firms use to choose collaboration partners, and also credit ranking agencies whose grades affect the cost of bank loans or finance capital for developing the new buildings and campus services needed to attract 'world class' researchers and students. Whereas universities were meant to service a market, they have in many cases become markets themselves (Robertson & Komljenovic, 2016;

Hartmann, 2008). Companies are specialising in selling software to standardise and manage university administration, staff performance, 'learning platforms' and interfaces with students. Where university functions have been unbundled, a plethora of companies take over not only security, cleaning and catering, but admissions, course delivery, exam marking etc. Some universities have turned all their administration into a service delivery company that then bids to take over the administration of other universities. Internationalisation has spawned new for-profit student recruiters and 'pathway providers' who oil the international trade in fee-paying students, some offering pre-degree or first year courses, often on university campuses. Burgeoning for-profit providers of higher education are establishing colleges throughout the world using a range of business models, often linked to on-line courses, especially MOOCs (Massive Open Online Courses) in which companies developing computing hardware and software, information technology and social media have a major interest. Meanwhile consultancies and audit companies, such as McKinsey, Deloitte and PricewaterhouseCoopers, advise university leaders on how to manage their university's relations with these surrounding interests and ever-changing government policies. They also provide governments and increasingly influential international agencies, such as OECD, World Bank and EU, with ideas for future reforms.

In short, the first common feature of the reform hyperobject is that universities are now located in this vastly expanded field of higher education, surrounded by myriad interests all entitled to make demands on research and education. The university has to become a new kind of subject, responsible for negotiating its relations with these diverse economic, political and social interests in 'surrounding society', and is made responsible for determining its boundaries and maintaining its own values, research freedom and ethics.

THE FIELD OF HIGHER EDUCATION TREATED AS AN ECONOMY

The second common feature of the reform hyperobject that ties the university into the Capitalocene is the way this field of higher education is conceptualised as an economy. This has implications for how universities and their leaders, academics and students can act within this field and the space for manoeuvre they might find. An example of this economy discourse is found in the UK government's white paper, *Success as a Knowledge Economy* (BIS, 2016). The paper starts with a brief mention of the university's role in fostering democracy, culture, criticality and social change, but this discourse is quickly dropped in favour of a dominant focus on 'driving economic growth'. In the white paper emanating from the ministry for business, claims that the 'need for knowledge' is to drive competitiveness and innovation, and the purpose of 'excellent teaching' is to support students' future productivity. The white paper depicts universities in the language of a formal economy. Education and students are turned into commodities, described in terms of markets, competition, price, instrumental outcomes and pursuit of individual interests. It is as if all the university's relations with stakeholders were dislocated from academic and ethical considerations and were market based. This approach abstracts and dislocates a model of the formal economy from the daily life, social relations, values and ethics of academics and students within the university and with surrounding society.

Polanyi's (2001 [1944]) contrast between what he calls two meanings of 'economy' or *oikos*, sheds light on the process of abstraction and dislocation visible not only in the UK's white paper, but in the other examples of reform quoted above. He shows how in the original meaning of *oikos*, as household management economic activities were an integral part of – and relied on – a wide range of social, political, kinship relations and institutions. This he calls a 'substantive' idea of the economy. His historical anthropology showed how in 18th century England, the 'economy' came to be conceptually disembedded from these relations and treated as if it operated according to its own intrinsic logic and was an autonomous sphere. This he called the 'formal' meaning of the economy. Goods, services, labour and land were all ripped from their social context, or alienated, and transacted through price setting in markets. Key to his argument was that land and labour were 'fictitious commodities' that could only be transacted on a market by destroying their social and ecological fabric. This form of capitalism introduced a new notion of scarcity, an assumption that there would be an insufficiency of 'means' to meet everyone's 'ends'. In these transactions, individuals (whether individual organisations or individual people) were conceived of as autonomous, interest-bearing units, exercising rational choice in conditions of scarcity by competing to maximise gains. Polanyi then showed that this economic logic imposed itself back onto other spheres of life from which it had been abstracted. As a result, 'the economy' reshapes its context in its own image.

Whereas this way of thinking was specific to 18th Century England, in neoclassical economics it is presumed to be true for all time and throughout the world. The dangers of disembedding market relations from a wider social and economic milieu are clearly demonstrated by anthropological studies such as Greenwood's (1976) research on Basque farming. In the 1960s, farmers engaged in mixed agriculture and had very complex circuits of exchange. A small component of this mixed economy was the sale of produce to the local garrison town. Farmers therefore always turned some of their yield into commodities for market sale, but treated this as what Polanyi (1963) called a 'port of trade'. That is, they kept these sales contained, only using them to raise the limited cash needed to support the subsistence economy. Their overarching priority was to maintain a sustainable subsistence economy and this is where they placed the highest value. When a younger generation took over the farms, they turned to commodity farming for the market in order to convert their produce into cash for a consumption lifestyle. They found the commercialisation of their farming subjected them to middle class people and they began leaving, preferring to be labourers rather than servants. Their economy also became vulnerable to price fluctuations, but by then the people had dispersed and the knowledge and community relations needed to restore a subsistence mixed economy had gone, with the result that the economy collapsed.

Davydd Greenwood, critical accountant Rebecca Boden and I related this Basque ethnography to recent developments in universities and developed a methodology aiming to distinguish between market and sustainable economic valuations of the work conducted by universities. We tabulated a university's complex circuits of exchange using distinctions between rivalrous and non-rivalrous, and excludable and non-excludable. To this we added the different kinds of exchange involved, using Polanyi's ideas of three major forms of exchange – reciprocity, redistribution and markets – and how each has radically different social consequences. Drawing on further anthropological theory, each mode of exchange (direct versus indirect, specified or not, commensurate or not, and immediate versus delayed or long-term) implies a different kind of relationship and degree of trust (Table 2.1).

Table 2.1. University's multiple circuits of exchange

	Excludable	*Non-excludable*
Rivalrous	*Usual example:*	*Usual example:*
	Private goods e.g. purchased food	Common goods e.g. fish in open sea
	University example:	*University example:*
	Patents	Open innovation systems
	Form of exchange:	*Form of exchange:*
	Market	Reciprocity or redistribution
	Direct, specific (contract) commensurate	Indirect, unspecified, non-commensurate
	Relationship:	*Relationship:*
	Low trust, not sustained	High or intermediate trust
Non-rivalrous	*Usual example:*	*Usual example:*
	Club goods, e.g. cable tv	Public goods, e.g. street lighting
	University example:	*University example:*
	Subscription journals	Public talk
	Form of exchange:	*Form of exchange:*
	Redistributive	Reciprocity
	Direct, access specified but usage not, immediate, commensurate	Indirect, delayed, unspecified, non-commensurate
	Relationship:	*Relationship:*
	Intermediate trust	High trust, long lasting

Source: Adapted from Rebecca Boden, Davydd Greenwood and Susan Wright presentation to 'The Trust University' conference, DPU, Copenhagen, June 2011

Activities which are rivalrous and excludable include research that results in patents, contracts that give the contractor restrictive rights over the results or similar ways that the service of a university is purchased for privileged or exclusive use by certain interests. Here a market form of exchange is based on price. It is also based on presentism, with all values calculated as if they can be stabilised at a particular moment in order to exchange two specified items (fee and service) that are agreed to be commensurate. As mentioned above, Polanyi showed that market exchange is based on the idea that there is a scarcity of means to meet competing ends, and the exchange is between commoditised goods and alienated 'hands', or what is now referred to as 'talent', in price-setting markets. Where each party is trying to get the best out of the deal, trust rests in fulfilment of the terms of the contract, and on its completion, the relationship is concluded.

At the other extreme, activities which are non-rivalrous and non-excludable are open to all and do not diminish with use, so there is no need to compete over scarcity. Many of the ways that universities engage with the public fall into this category and also ways that academics interact with each other and with their students, including public talks or colleagues reading and commenting on each other's drafts to share and develop ideas. Here the relationship is based on reciprocity, where one exchange does not close a deal but, or the contrary, creates a sense of obligation to find some way to make a further exchange. As Mauss (1990 [1925]) put it, gift begets gift, begets gift, begets gift. What is exchanged may not be immediately commensurate; nor is the exchange necessarily direct, as A can give something to B who gives something to C who gives something to A in a circuit of indirect exchange. The parties view their relationships with each other as symmetrical rather than hierarchical even if, in an extensive circuit of indirect exchange, they only vaguely know of each other's identity and presence. This kind of exchange generates high trust and long-lasting relationships.

Exchanges that are non-rivalrous and excludable cover activities where access is through subscription or membership of a club, but where the resource is not diminished by use. A simple example is access to professional journals through subscription (either privately or though membership of a university that has a subscription), and this category can also refer more widely to students' registration giving them access to the resources of the university. If reciprocity denoted exchange between symmetrical groupings, redistribution involves appropriation by a centre and then out of it again to ensure the distribution is sufficiently fair and even to keep the club going. Redistribution requires hierarchical groupings and may be marked by tensions and negotiations, and attempts to resolve them through set procedures and systems of accounting. To hold the groupings together there also needs to be a sense of mutual obligation, which increases with ascent up the hierarchy, to the point that leaders realise that their position depends on acting with care toward those for whom they are responsible and in sustaining rather than tearing the social fabric. Such a social system is characterised by long-term relationships with an intermediate or wary kind of trust.

Activities that are non-excludable but rivalrous refer to common goods and may be based on either reciprocity or redistribution. They are exemplified by fish in the open sea, where supposedly everyone has access but where it is very clear that stocks are not infinitely replenishable. Universities' attempts to create open innovation systems are an equivalent example. Where these activities are successfully organised through reciprocity, the items exchanged can be unspecified and not commensurate and the exchanges can be indirect, between circuits of parties who see themselves as roughly equivalent and in long term relationships of mutual obligation and trust. But where resources are fast depleting and tensions rising, sometimes a redistributive system develops.

Polanyi points out that these four forms of exchange do not just denote personal interrelations, but their different patterns of social integration are 'conditioned by the presence of definite institutional arrangements, such as symmetrical organisations, central points and market systems' (Polanyi, 1957: 251). In universities, and as seen in the example of Basque farming above, these forms of exchange and their associated patterns of integration may be found side by side (Polanyi, 1957: 205). These ideas provide a way of analysing the co-existing circuits of exchange within a university and their interwoven patterns of individual and organisational integration. Universities rely heavily on reciprocities and redistributions as well as markets, but in order to manage the balance between these circuits of exchange, they have to be distinguished. In particular the fundamental difference needs to be clear between reciprocity and redistribution on the one hand and markets on the other, as, although they all redistribute resources, they do so in very different ways and they relate to quite different modes of organisational integration.

Using the analogy of the Basque farmers, for a university to sustain its core values, it would need to maintain its subsistence through a mixed economy with multiple circuits of exchange. To achieve an optimal balance, there would be a small level of activity devoted to rivalrous and excludable research, such as commissioned research or research resulting in patents, but this should be tightly limited as a 'port of trade'; it would be used to support the university's other activities and not allowed to dominate. Slightly more activity would be devoted to excludable and non-rivalrous club goods, such as writing and editing articles in subscription journals. The income from these two categories of work should go towards sustaining the production of common goods, like open access to research, which is important but unfunded, and public goods like contributions to media discussions and public talks, which do not yield sufficient income to cover costs. The overall priority would be to maintain the organisation's subsistence and sustain its core values. Instead, universities' circuits of exchange have gone out of balance, and, private goods are predominating and drawing on the resources of the other activities to maintain their greedy growth.

The important distinction here is not between private and public but between a market-based and a sustainable valuation of the work of universities. As Cantini (2017) shows, differences between ostensibly public versus private institutions cannot be used to make normative judgements about their values and roles in society. In some countries public universities and their state funding have been captured by elites, while some privately funded universities are fulfilling a public purpose by locating and investing in poorer neighbourhoods and providing education for upward social mobility. Rather, it is a question of whether private, excludable, rivalrous goods are allowed to play a dominant and destructive role in the overall political economy of a university and in the field of higher education through separation from their social context, or whether an optimal balance is achieved between the four circuits of exchange. Achieving such a balance, means holding in check the logic of the formal economy, in which the focus is on commodities, comp through etition, markets and price, and all other factors are treated as 'externalities' that either provide unaccrowledged support for the expansion of the market sector, or are 'noise' factors that get in the way. The designation of the Anthropocene, or more accurately, the Capitalocene, highlights the dangerous consequences of the 20th century's externalisation of the environment. If the focus is turned towards the institutions that have been reshaped by the Capitalocene, like universities, the most dangerous move has been turning the public good into an externality. As Jiménez (2006, p. 7) phrases it: the definition of a public good as an externality is 'a residual precipitate of a market transaction' and 'this model works by stabilizing "market" and "society" as distinct arenas of interaction: externalities move from one to the other, hence their separation'. When the language of neoclassical economic capitalism is used to describe the university, it externalises all other relationships and values. More than this, it is used to invade and reorganise the social life of the university in its own 'economic' image. This tries to turn academia into 'fictitious commodities' that can only be transacted on a market by destroying their social and ecological fabric. It repurposes the institution as a driver of a global knowledge economy with the danger that it channels and limits the activities of academics and the aspirations of students. This implicates the university in driving a system that it is responsible for critiquing.

OIKOS AS ECOLOGY

If the university is to have a relationship of responsibility and care towards humanity and the planet, it has to be the 'critic and conscience' of society, rather than the driver of a particular market-driven model of the formal economy. This requires a different way of thinking about the 'scene' or world that universities could inhabit and the relationships that would bring it about. Polanyi (1944) provided an image of such a world when he pointed to the meaning of oikos as a 'substantive' or embedded economy. Using examples from anthropology, he showed that household and social relations, kinship, politics and religion all have economic dimensions: the 'economic' is entangled with all other aspects of living. This links Polanyi's idea of the substantive economy to oikos as the root of 'ecology'. Tsing argues similarly, that whereas the formal economy isolates people and things as resources for investment and exchange, and imbues them 'with alienation, that is, the ability to stand alone, as if the entanglements of living did not matter' (Tsing, 2015a, p. 5), in an ecological approach people conceive of themselves and their institution as actively entangled in worlds made up of interdependencies. This raises the question, what would be the implications of thinking about the university as situated in an ecology, rather than an economy?

As explained above, universities now find themselves in a much more complex world. The idea of the ivory tower was always fictional and universities, especially since the Second World War, have had excludable and rivalrous relations with certain industries that they negotiated through the language of the market. But now the university has to relate to a world made up of many different 'species' of actors, many inspired by economic rationales, price and competition, but others pursuing cultural, democratic and social values. Within the university, relations are not just based on economic considerations and research is not produced by competition and incentives: ideas often emerge through serendipitous conversations and are always refined through debate with academic friends and spread through illicit pdfs of publications as much as through conferences and journals. Teaching encounters, inspiring supervisions and corridor conversations as well as staff meetings spark developments in disciplines and new ideas for teaching. There is a whole social infrastructure of friendships, rivalries, admiration, respect and disagreement behind the generation and dissemination of academic ideas. In Polanyi's terms, this economy of ideas is an 'instituted process' that is tied into many relationships, social institutions and interactions, not only between university people but connected to many different institutions in the higher education field, like editors, rankers, industrial researchers, local authorities, and associations in civil society and local communities. To focus on only the features that 'count' as world class, entrepreneurial, profitable or competitive in a knowledge economy is to externalise, deny, and worse, ruin, the complexity of entanglements and interdependencies that make up a university ecology.

Tsing (2015a) has explored the ruins produced by capitalism's formal economies where only one stand-alone asset mattered, all else was weeds or waste, and where, when exhausted, the disturbed landscape was abandoned. She shows that in such externalised spaces, through an unpredictable interplay of many kinds of beings, which she calls 'interspecies entanglements', a new 'interactive ecology' can emerge in which it is sometimes possible for people to remake 'liveable landscapes'. In her case, she is concerned with the failed industrial forestry policies. For example, after clear cutting the original forests on the U.S. west coast, pine forests were planted amidst the stumps and disturbance, but soon afterwards the market collapsed and the pine forests remained, unharvested. This is one of the ruined spaces of the formal economy; the kind of disturbed and no longer profitable terrain that the Anthropocene externalises and does not recognise. Refugees from the U.S. wars in Laos and Cambodia arrived on the west coast at a time when the state had ceased to invest in immigrants' social and economic integration, and they found in the pine forests a setting where they could recreate a familiar cultural landscape. There, they also found the matsutake mushroom, which only grows in disturbed pine forests. This mushroom is prized in Japan, where it is the highly prestigious gift used to make social relationships, like a present to in-laws over a marriage, or to seal economic deals or heal a rift. But in Japan it had become a rarity. Tsing traces the chain of complex relationships and mutualisms by which the mushrooms collected by forest forages are sold locally to collectors, who sell to exporters who send them to distributors in Japan, who 'place' the mushrooms with well-established clients, so that they end up as prestigious gifts. In their journey, it is only for the brief time it takes to export the mushrooms that are they part of a formal economy, torn from their social context, turned into inventory and transacted as alienated commodities based on price-setting in markets. For the most part, they are embedded with social value in particular life worlds and only need one aspect of commensurality to pass from one social context to another. The result is a supply chain linking varied spaces, but in each the economic value of the mushroom is embedded in other institutions (e.g. community building among refugees and gift giving among Japanese deal makers) so that capitalism extracts value without disturbing the lifeworld. Tsing focuses in particular on how the forest foragers have become part of a 'liveable landscape'. They inhabit the spaces disturbed and ruined by the formal economics of the Anthropocene/Capitalocene; they find ways to circumvent the restrictions on forest use; and recognise that mushrooms, pines, refugees, buyers and forest rangers are all interwoven and transforming each other in what Tsing calls 'necessary mutualisms'. She describes how, in these ever-shifting, unstable mutual relations, each organism disturbs and remakes the worlds around them, shaping the evolution of other organisms to try and make them advantageous for themselves. Sometimes these relations are brutal, hierarchical and predatory; at other times they are synergistic and mutually productive. In this process of continuously coordinating with others, mutualisms are rarely planned and symbiosis occurs 'when unexpected historical conjunctions fall into new coordinations' (Tsing, 2015b, p. 4).

A UNIVERSITY ECOLOGY AND LIVEABLE LANDSCAPE

Universities, especially where they are being 'unbundled', can be the 'forest' or source of several supply chains for capitalist extraction by the multiple interests, described above, who now surround the university. It takes systematic and comprehensive ethnography and a very self-critical, reflexive approach on the part of all the people involved – managers, academics, students – for them to understand the ways in which they are implicated in each other's welfare through their participation in different circuits of exchange and patterns of organisational integration in the university. How are managers, academics and students already contributing to a formal and alienating 'economy'? And, on the contrary how they can develop and sustain a university 'ecology' with a liveable landscape? Levin and Greenwood (2016) have shown how current authoritarian, hierarchical and NeoTaylorist ways of organizing the university are unable to achieve such a change: instead, they see matrix organizations, learning communities and socio-technical systems design, with the participants in the driver's seat and leaders as their coordinators and servants, as the only way forward.

While there is widespread literature referring to the marketization, privatisation and consumerisation of higher education, ethnographic studies are still rare that track in detail the ways universities' activities are the source of capitalist value extraction. In England, Komljenovic (2016) and Komljenovic and Robertson (2016) have traced the multiple ways that a university's administration was interacting with, and contracting functions to, for-profit providers. Wright (2016) has shown how vice chancellors can turn a university into an umbrella or carapace, which enables them to maintain they are working for a public purpose and keep their tax-beneficial charitable status, but under which they not only unbundle higher education into different enterprises and profit streams, but propose a business model of creating what one vice chancellor calls a 'family' of enterprises including further education colleges, Academy schools, technical professional and adult education (Phoenix, 2017). A similar example in the U.S. involves Indiana's major public land-grant university, Purdue University. It has tried to jump into on-line education by purchasing for-profit Kaplan University, and in the process has tied itself into a long term contract to support this huge operation from the failing for-profit sector (Seltzer, 2017). Newfield's (2016) detailed study shows the 'great mistake' over the way public universities in the U.S. have been funded and operated. Fridell (2017) traces similar changes in the political economy of higher education in Canada and drills down to how management consultants, private equity firms and software companies have developed strategies to reduce scholarly costs and turn 'discretionary budgets' into revenue streams for themselves. Some of these studies have derived from reflexive analysis as part of activism in Senate, through an academic union or through an education programme, and they all provide members of the academic community with the information and analytical tools to understand how their universities are being turned into formal economies.

Other studies have begun exploring the possibilities of disrupting alienating supply chains in universities, finding ways of creating liveable landscapes in the spaces ruined and externalised by formal economic calculus by circumventing or sequestering restrictive or dangerous powers, and seeking new, if unpredictable, mutualisms. Three examples will be outlined here. The first way to create the university as a liveable landscape is exemplified by Hansen's (2017) study of the strategies of Danish 'project barons', university professors who are so successful at raising external funding that they run their own research centres, become highly influential in their own institutions and often contribute to shaping national research policy. One plant scientist used metaphors of multispecies symbiosis to explain how he created a liveable landscape for his own centre. He studies plant-insect relationships, and in particular one plant whose leaves make cyanide to poison predators. However, the larvae of the six-spotted burnet moth feed on these plants and they circumvent the plant's defence system by sequestering the poison in their own bodies to protect themselves against predators. The larvae activate a positive response in the plants, so that rather than being a predatory relationship with a parasite logic, this becomes a successful symbiosis. Yet, the scientist points out, like Tsing, that there is no telling what a given species may be capable of, as its capabilities evolve in complex relationships with other species. Hansen saw a parallel between what the scientist had learnt from plant-insect relationships and how he engaged in governance-researcher relationships. Hansen showed that government research policy employed a parasite logic, imagining a unidirectional flow from university knowledge producers to industry innovators. Learning from the plant scientist, this way of extracting without giving weakens the exploited party. University leaders also imagined themselves as steering the university from the top, with their strategies 'trickling down' to shape researchers' actions. Instead, project barons also clearly had power as they are the active researchers with huge networks, big grants, and full professorships, and 'leaders can't move without them'. Hansen then gives an example of how the project baron acted in a toxic policy environment. At one point, the government required all grant applicants to have an industry partner, so the project baron split his lab into a spin-off company. He made an application based on a collaboration between the lab and the company and won the grant. The relationship developed, unexpectedly, into a symbiosis, as they found that the spin off company removed the toxin of repetitive procedures from the lab, and this freed the lab to be more experimental, and more competitive for grants. Using metaphors from plan science, this is a good example of finding spaces and ways to work within the university's new ecology to create a liveable landscape by circumventing restrictions, sequestering toxic powers and turning them to advantage by creating serendipitous synergies. This example does however also have a predatory aspect, as these fairly autonomous project barons draw on resources that sustain the broader basis of the university's activities, so that as Hansen points out members of the lab were celebrating the lab's new grant whilst people from mainstream departments were learning whether they were hit by the university's latest firing round.

A second, more ambitious attempt to entangle universities in liveable landscapes involves engaging in system disturbance and contesting the very basis of a university as an institution of the Capitalcene. Examples of system disturbance are the manifestos and protest movements trying to assert the critical and public purpose of the university. Throughout 2016, Aberdeen University held a series of meetings and seminars to rebuild community, establish trust and reclaim freedom. They produced a manifesto, 'Reclaiming Our University', which has been widely distributed (Reclaiming Our University, 2016). A similar Auckland Declaration arose from the UNIKE project, an EU-funded project to train 14 PhD and Post Docs as future research leaders who not only gained expert knowledge in how universities were being reformed in Europe and the Asia-Pacific Rim, but developed the reflexive abilities to use this knowledge to shape research and higher education institutions. The Declaration elaborated six principles that should underpin the organisation of a public university. These are: Public Good, Social Responsibility, Academic Freedom, Educational Autonomy, University Independence and Humane Workplace. These principles have been accepted at meetings of the Bologna Process, the Council of Europe and Education International and form a coherent basis for developing a university ecology with values and ways of organising internally that enables it to act as a progressive force in society.

A third example of a way to create a liveable landscape is by trying to build a new university based on the Auckland declaration principles. Another outcome of the UNIKE project was the creation of an international group of 37 scholar-activists all concerned to build universities based on mutuality. Using the experience of the very successful and well-established Mondragón university in Spain (Wright, Greenwood, & Boden, 2011), a process of designing a cooperative university in England is underway (Winn & Neary, 2017). Greenwood, Wright and Boden have been working on the design of a 'Trust University' in three senses of that word. First, is the idea of trust as a legal instrument of ownership. The aim is to make it impossible to realise, let alone privatise, the assets of the university by putting their ownership into a non-revocable trust. This is modelled on the experience of the very successful department store, the John Lewis Partnership, whose owner in 1929 separated the legal ownership from beneficial ownership. All employees (our case would include staff and students) are beneficial owners with rights to influence the direction of the business and the distribution of profits, but they cannot sell the business (or in our case the university) and deny its benefits to future generations. To avoid the moral hazard of managers extracting high rent and even (as increasingly in public universities) coming to speak *as* the organisation and even thinking of the institution as 'theirs', the John Lewis Partnership also has strictly fixed salary differentials between managers and rest of the partners. The second meaning of 'trust' is to create a High Trust Organisation based on mutually respectful relations between managers, academics, support workers and students. Greenwood draws on his experience of Scandinavian technical systems design and participatory organisation to develop the principles, values and methods of decision making. The third meaning of trust refers to creating a new social compact to achieve trust between university and surrounding society. Regular use of tried and tested technologies, such as search conferences, involving the university's beneficial owners in dialogue with different categories of people from 'surrounding society' are proposed to identify circuits of exchange and, referring back to the Basque analogy, the work to be done to develop future activities that keep them in optimal balance (Wright & Greenwood, 2017).

CONCLUSION

If universities are not to contribute to the economic and political processes that have brought about the Capitalocene and that are vividly depicted in the markers of nuclear fall-out, plastic waste and industrial agriculture chosen to demarcate the Anthropocene, then a renewal of the public purpose of the university is needed. At the moment, universities are being increasing organised according to the logic of what Polanyi called the formal economy, with their hallmark interlaced activities of research, teaching, public engagement and service unbundled into separate strands of capitalist value extraction. The logic of for-profit activity then dominates and is imposed on all other activities. This attempt to mirror market-thinking inside the university is used to decide what 'counts' and what is accorded value – even if in fact universities are very poor at organising themselves on market principles (Ciancanell, 2008). The result is a narrowing of the purpose of the public university to providing the raw materials for a competitive knowledge economy. This is the way that institutions get implicated in the Capitalocene, focusing on notions of the market and externalising the social and the public.

Rather than thinking of the university as a driver of a 'knowledge economy', using Polanyi's terms, the economy needs re-embedding in the social, political and cultural institutions of which, in an ecological approach, it is a part. If a university is conceptualised as located in a 'liveable landscape', this involves rethinking its relationships in a 'world' of multiple organisations with myriad interests in and demands on the university. If these relationships are thought of as interdependencies and entanglements between companion species, rather than contracts with abstracted balance sheets of benefit and cost, then substantive valuations of these relationships would be based on notions of responsibility, or as Haraway (1991) terms it, 'thinking with care'. This is not a 'longing for a smooth harmonious world'; it involves reflexive analysis 'to acknowledge our own involvements in perpetuating dominant values, rather than retreating into the secure position of an enlightened outsider who knows better' (Puig de la Bellacasa, 2012, pp. 199, 197). It involves leading 'an examined life' and troubling questions about how to act in companion-species webs with complexity, care, and the unsettling obligation of curiosity in order to sustain interdependent worlds (Haraway, 2008, p. 36). Instead of taking post 1945 chicken bones as a fossil marker of the Anthropocene, Haraway refers to the millennia of chicken-human co-existence and treats chickens as a vastly experienced companion species: 'laying hens know more about the alliances it will take to survive and flourish in multispecies, multicultural, multiordered associations than do all the secondary Bushes in Florida and Washington. Follow the chicken and find the world' (Haraway, 2008, p. 274). Such an admonition does not offer a single direction ahead; it involves, as Tsing puts it, finding means for collaborative survival in precarious times without the 'handrails' of the familiar stories of modernization and progress (Tsing, 2015, p. 2).

How then does the university negotiate its relations with the diverse organisations and interests that surround it to turn a 'knowledge economy' into what Tsing calls a liveable landscape? In an ecology conceptualised as an open system with intense interaction between an 'external' environment and the university's 'inner life', how do the members of a university work to achieve and vigilantly maintain a balance between the different circuits of exchange? And how do the staff and students organise themselves to achieve this in what is likely to be a tough and heavily contested process? One starting point is to imagine the principles on which such a liveable landscape would be based. I have drawn on analogies from Basque farming to imagine a sustainable system with balanced circuits of exchange. I have referred to the Auckland Declaration which puts forward an explicit set of principles for discussion, and the work in designing those principles into the organisation of a cooperative or trust university. A second answer is to develop tactics for practical action, aimed at creating new mutualisms. Here analogies were drawn from the mushroom foragers in the U.S. west coast, but as always in such complex ecological relations between fungus, trees, refugees, marketers, and forest rangers, it is not predictable whether successful synergies will result. The project baron drew his own analogies from plant science to explain how he used tactics of circumvention and sequestering to operate in a toxic funding and governance environment. He found spaces and ways to work through new forms of collaboration to create serendipitous synergies and turn the environment to his advantage – although others in the university lost out. The third answer is for academics to educate ourselves and our students to be critically reflexive about the space we are in and how to act. Newfield and Fridell are examples of researchers who have used their positions within universities to analyse current trends undermining the public university and identify ways to act to create alternatives – sometimes with success. How should we, and our institution, act in a Capitalocene – should we continue to be implicated in the reproduction of the Capitalocene/Anthropocene or do we re-think the space that universities are in as an ecology and seek out ways to act with responsibility and care within the university and in interactions with society, in the hope of generating some mutually beneficial synergies and with the ambition of creating a liveable landscape?

ACKNOWLEDGEMENTS

This paper arises from work conducted for the UNIKE project (Universities in the Knowledge Economy) an EU PEOPLE Marie Curie ITN project from 2013 to 2017, project number 317452. Ideas about the dangers of treating the university as a formal economy were developed with Davydd Greenwood and Rebecca Boden and first presented at a conference to develop a blueprint for a 'Trust University', held at DPU, Copenhagen, in June 2011. I thank Davydd Greenwood and Jakob Williams Ørberg for their generous collegial encouragement and for the critical comments and creative suggestions that have helped me to write this paper.

REFERENCES

Amsler, M., & Shore, C. (2015). Responsibilisation and leadership in the neoliberal university: A New Zealand perspective. *Discourse: Studies in the Cultural Politics of Education*, published online. doi: 10.1080/01596306.2015.1104857

AWG. (2016). Media note: Anthropocene Working Group (AWG). University of Leicester, Retrieved 29 August from http://www2.le.ac.uk/offices/press/press-releases/2016/august/media-note-anthropocene-working-group-awg

Barber, M., Donnelly, K., & Rizvi, S. (2013). *An avalanche is coming: Higher education and the revolution ahead*. London: Institute for Public Policy Research. Retrieved 1 April 2017 from http://www.avalancheiscoming.com/

Bekhradnia, B. (2015, January 15). 'Chile steps back from bitter market fruits: South America's neoliberal pioneer is taking higher education out of the market. *Times Higher Education* Retrieved 1 April 2017 from https://www.timeshighereducation.com/comment/opinion/chile-steps-back-from-bitter-market-fruits/2017895.article

BIS. (2016). *Success as a knowledge economy: Teaching excellence, social mobility and student choice* Cm 9258. London: Department for Business, Innovation and Skills. Retrieved 1 April 2017 from https://www.gov.uk/government/uploads/system/uploads/attachment_data/file/523546/bis-16-265-success-as-a-knowledge-economy-web.pdf

Browne Report. (2010). *Securing a sustainable future for higher education: An independent review of higher education funding and student finance*. London: Department for Business, Innovation and Skills. BIS/10/1208. Retrieved 1 April 2017 from https://www.gov.uk/government/uploads/system/uploads/attachment_data/file/422565/bis-10-1208-securing-sustainable-higher-education-browne-report.pdf

Cantini, D. (Ed.). (2017). *Rethinking private higher education: Ethnographic perspectives*. Leiden, the Netherlands: Brill.

Carrington, D. (2016, August 31). How the domestic chicken rose to define the Anthropocene. *The Guardian*. Retrieved from https://www.theguardian.com/environment/2016/aug/31/domestic-chicken-anthropocene-humanity-influenced-epoch

Ciancanelli, P. (2008). The business of teaching and learning: An accounting perspective. *Learning and Teaching: International Journal of Higher Education in the Social Sciences, 1*(1), 155–183.

Dang, Q. A. (2009). Recent higher education reforms in Vietnam: The role of the world bank. *Working Papers on University Reform* (Vol. 13). Copenhagen: Danish School of Education, Aarhus University.

Danish Government. (2006). *Progress, innovation and cohesion: Strategy for Denmark in the global economy – Summary*. Copenhagen: Danish Government. Retrieved from http://www.stm.dk/multimedia/PROGRESS_INNOVATION_AND_COHESION.pdf

Dearing Report. (1997). *Higher education in the learning society: The national committee of inquiry into higher education*. London: Her Majesty's Stationery Office. Retrieved 1 April 2017 from http://www.educationengland.org.uk/documents/dearing1997/dearing1997.html

EY. (2012). *University of the future: A thousand year old industry on the cusp of profound change*. Australia: Ernst & Young. Retrieved 1 April 2017 from http://www.ey.com/Publication/vwLUAssets/University_of_the_future/%24FILE/University_of_the_future_2012.pdf

Fridell, M. (2017, March 24). *Strike for scholarship: Paper given to CHEF seminar*. Copenhagen: Danish School of Education, Aarhus University.

Greenwood, D. (1976). *Unrewarding wealth: The commercialization and collapse of agriculture in a Spanish Basque town*. Cambridge: Cambridge University Press.

Hansen, B. G. (2017). Science/industry collaboration: Bugs, project barons and managing symbiosis. In S. Wright & C. Shore (Eds.), *Death of the public university?* Oxford: Berghahn.

Haraway, D. (1991). Situated knowledges: The science question in feminism and the privilege of partial perspective. In D. Haraway (Ed.), *Simians, cyborgs, and women: The reinvention of nature* (pp. 183–201). New York, NY: Routledge.

Haraway, D. (2008). *When species meet*. Minneapolis, MN: University of Minnesota Press.

Hartmann, E. (2008). The EU as an emerging normative power in the global knowledge-based economy? Recognition regimes for higher education qualifications. In B. Jessop, N. Fairclough, & R Wodak (Eds.), *Education and the knowledge-based economy in Europe* (pp. 33–86). Rotterdam, the Netherlands: Sense Publishers.

Jiménez, A. C. (2006). *Economy and aesthetic of public knowledge*. CRESC Working Paper No. 26. University of Manchester: CRESC. Retrieved 15 March 2017 from http://citeseerx.ist.psu.edu/viewdoc/download?doi=10.1.1.518.9262&rep=rep1&type=pdf

Komljenovic, J. (2016). *Making higher education markets* (PhD thesis). University of Bristol, England.

Komljenovic, J., & Robertson, S. (2016). The dynamics of 'market-making' in higher education, *Journal of Education Policy, 31*(5), 622–636.

Levin, M., & Greenwood, D. J. (2016). *Creating a new public university and reviving democracy Action research in higher education.* Oxford: Berghahn.

Mauss, M. (1990 [1925]). *The gift. The form and reason for exchange in archaic societies.* London: Routledge.

McGettigan, A. (2013). *The great university gamble. Money, markets and the future of higher education.* London: Pluto Press.

Moore, J. W. (Ed.). (2016). *Anthropocene or capitalocene? Nature, history, and the crisis of capitalism.* Oakland, CA: PM Press/Kairos.

Morton, T. (2013). *Hyperobjects: Philosophy and ecology after the end of the world.* Minneapolis, MN: University of Minnesota Press.

Newfield, C. (2016). *The great mistake.* Baltimore: John Hopkins University Press.

Oceans at MIT. (2014). *A quarter million tons of plastic float in our oceans, says Dr. Marcus Eriksen.* Featured Stories 10 December. Retrieved from http://oceans.mit.edu/news/featured-stories/269000-tons-plastic-ocean-now-dr-marcus-eriksen

Phoenix, D. (2017, March 16). Building more bridges. *Times Higher Education, 26.*

Polanyi, K. (1957). The economy as instituted process. In K. Polanyi, C. M. Arensberg, & H. W. Pearson (Eds.). *Trade and market in the early empires: Economies in history and theory.* Glencoe, Illinois: The Free Press.

Polanyi, K. (1963). Ports of trade in early societies. *The Journal of Economic History, 23*(1), 30–45.

Polanyi, K. (2001 [1944]). *The great transformation.* Boston, MA: Beacon Press.

Puig de la B. M. (2012). 'Nothing comes without its world': Thinking with care. *The Sociological Review, 60*(2), 197–216.

Reclaiming Our University. (2016). *Manifesto and archive.* Aberdeen University. Retrieved from https://reclaimingouruniversity.wordpress.com/2016/10/21/the-petition/comment-page-1/#comment-107

Roberson, S., & Komljenovic, J. (2016). Unbundling the university and making higher education markets. In A. Verger, C. Lubienski, & G. Steiner-Khamsi (Eds.), *World yearbook of education 2016: The global education industry* (pp. 211–227). London: Routledge.

Salmi, J. (2009). *The challenge of establishing world-class universities.* Washington, DC: The World Bank.

Sassen, S. (2014). *Expulsions: Brutality and complexity in the global economy.* Cambridge, MA: Harvard University Press.

Seltzer, R. (2017). Purdue's deal for Kaplan U trades a long-term business relationship for low up-front costs while raising worries – especially among faculty groups – about blurred lines between public and private higher ed. *Inside Higher Ed,* 4 May. Accessed on 5 May 2017 at https://www.insidehighered.com/news/2017/05/04/purdues-deal-kaplan-packs-low-front-costs-long-terms-and-boundary-pushing-details#.WQrz0lXUVts.mailto

Slaughter, S., & Rhoades, G. (2004). *Academic capitalism and the new economy: Markets, state, and higher education.* Baltimore: The Johns Hopkins University Press.

Thorne, M. (Ed.). (1999). *Foresight – Universities in the future.* London: Department of Trade and Industry. DTI/Pub 4263/5k/7/98/NP URN 99/982

Tsing, A. L. (2015a). *The mushroom at the end of the world: On the possibility of life in capitalist ruins.* Princeton, NJ: Princeton University Press.

Tsing, A. L. (2015b). *In the midst of disturbance: Symbiosis, coordination, history, landscape.* ASA Firth Lecture 2015, given at the ASA Annual Conference on 'Symbiotic anthropologies'.

WEF. (2016). *The new plastics economy: Rethinking the future of plastics.* Geneva: World Economic Forum and Ellen MacArthur Foundation. Retrieved from http://www3.weforum.org/docs/WEF_The_New_Plastics_Economy.pdf

Winn, J., & Neary, M. (2017). There is an alternative: A report on an action research project to develop a framework for co-operative higher education. *Learning and Teaching: International Journal of Higher Education in the Social Sciences, 10*(1), 87–105.

Wright, S. (2004). Markets, corporations, consumers? New landscapes in higher education. *LATISS Learning and Teaching in the Social Sciences, 1*(2), 71–93.

Wright, S. (2008). Governance as a regime of discipline. In N. Dyck (Ed.), *Exploring regimes of discipline: The dynamics of restraint* (pp. 75–98). Oxford: Berghahn, EASA Series.

Wright, S. (2016). The imaginators of English university reform. In S. Slaughter & B. J. Taylor (Eds.), *Higher education, stratification, and workforce development: Competitive advantage in Europe, the US, and Canada* (pp. 127–150). Dordrecht, the Netherlands: Springer.

Wright, S., & Greenwood, D. (2017). Universities run for, by and with the faculty, students and staff: Alternatives to the neoliberal destruction of higher education. *Learning and Teaching: International Journal of Higher Education in the Social Sciences, 10*(1), 42–65.

Wright, S., Greenwood, D., & Boden, R. (2011). Report on a field visit to Mondragón University: A cooperative experience/experiment. *Learning and Teaching: International Journal of Higher Education in the Social Sciences, 4*(3), 38–56.

Susan Wright
Danish School of Education
Aarhus University

ANTÓNIO MAGALHÃES, AMÉLIA VEIGA AND PEDRO VIDEIRA

3. HARD AND SOFT MANAGERIALISM IN PORTUGUESE HIGHER EDUCATION GOVERNANCE

INTRODUCTION

Since the early 1990s the concept of governance has replaced the modern governing perspectives on policy-making and implementation and has assumed a central position in the public sector of political decision-making. This had impact on the relationship between governance and management, within which the latter has assumed a preponderance over the former, reflecting what has been referred to as managerialism (Magalhães & Santiago, 2012; Deem, 1998). Governance is about setting goals, rules and mechanisms by which the decision-making structures and processes are designed and put in place. Management refers to the implementation of the objectives set out by the governance structures on the basis of established rules and it is concerned with the efficiency, effectiveness and quality of services provided to external and internal stakeholders.

Without denying higher education specificities, the reform of the public sector that has been undertaken in the Western world since the mid-1980s (Pollit & Bouckaert, 2004) is the frame within which higher education reform is taking place. The influence of New Public Management (NPM) in the reform of public systems across Europe is at the core of the on-going governance transformations. In higher education, governance reforms also reflect this influence, namely on the increased technicality of the governance and management instruments and on the enhanced management structures and processes within European higher education institutions (Bleiklie & Kogan, 2007). In spite of NPM dominance, existing research has showed "a mix of signs and symptoms of NPM and NG [Network Governance]" (Paradeise, Reale, Gostellec, & Bleiklie, 2009, p. 245), as well as neo-Weberian (Bleiklie, 2009) and collegial (Ferlie & Andresani, 2009) governance approaches, contributing to introduce nuances in the dominance of managerialism (Magalhães & Santiago, 2012). The relationships between governance and management assume different configurations as NPM is being counterbalanced by other governance narratives and practices (Magalhães, Veiga, Amaral, Sousa, & Ribeiro, 2013).

In this paper, by identifying different nuances between hard and soft managerialism, the assumption of NPM hegemony in the *managerial revolution* (Amaral, Fulton, & Larsen, 2003) is challenged. In the first part, we elaborate on the relationships between governance and (soft and hard) management, taking into consideration governance dimensions such as coordination, goals, values, control mechanisms

R. Deem & H. Eggins (Eds.), The University as a Critical Institution?, 39–53.

and processes. Then, to answer the question, *How do Portuguese governance reforms in higher education reflect different weights of managerialism?* the analysis focuses on the perceptions of higher education professionals as they reflect on the tensions related to the redistribution of the decision-making power influencing the reconfiguration of higher education governance. This analysis is complemented by comparing the perceptions of different groups of respondents according to higher education sector (public and private), subsystem (polytechnic and university) and professional role characteristics (such as the respondents pertaining to the teaching or non-teaching staff, their involvement in decision-making processes and number of years working at the institution) to understand how hard and soft managerialism are being experienced throughout the system.

GOVERNANCE AND (SOFT AND HARD) MANAGEMENT

The concept of governance has assumed a central position in the public sector of decision-making and political coordination (e.g., A. Kjaer, 2010; P. Kjaer, 2010; Osborne, 2010; Rosenau & Czempiel, 1992; Salamon, 2002b) to the detriment of governing. Governing refers to the actions taken by the government to politically steer social systems and corresponds to the way modern states used to regulate and control societies. Governance deals with the coordination of interdependent activities aimed at the pursuit of political goals at the system and/or institutional levels and the rules and mechanisms that frame decision-making structures and processes (Hirsch & Weber, 1999; Meek, 2002). It has to do with the increasing fragmentation of public decision-making and with the degree of interdependence between state and non-state actors. Ultimately, governance is about setting political goals and rule systems, both formal and informal, that drive values and norms affecting actors and constellations of actors' behaviours and attitudes (Hall & Taylor, 1996; A. Kjaer, 2010).

Ideas about enhancing autonomy, improving accountability and developing quality assessment mechanisms have been driving higher education reforms in the last decades. From a regulation perspective, the political assumption is that the more autonomous institutions are, the better they respond to the transformations in their organizational environment, and the more effective and efficient they are as organizations (Amaral & Magalhães, 2001). In the governance structures of higher education institutions (HEIs) this organizational awareness of external transformations is substantiated in the presence of external stakeholders (Amaral & Magalhães, 2001). The attribution of autonomy impinges on institutional governance and management, impacting the relationships between actors, structures and processes. The change from state control to apparently looser contractual relationships does not weaken regulation, as detailed control instruments and procedures have been set up and are, according to Neave (2008), the main driver for the reforms undertaken in the sector. This brings management concerns to the fore.

In the last decades, under the influence of NPM, the narratives on the enhancement of institutional self-regulation have reinterpreted the meaning of institutional autonomy in the field of public policies. In spite of its theoretical fluidity (Boston, 2011), NPM represents the idea that efficiency and effectiveness are to be achieved through management instruments used in the private sector: specifying goals, emphasizing competition for clients, performance measurement and the use of markets as instruments of public policy (Dill, 1997; Meek, 2002). The development of these views and the increased technicality of governance and management instruments have enhanced the managerial structures and processes within European HEIs (Bleiklie & Kogan, 2007).

Governance narratives put together normative/ideological ingredients and technical elements (Ferlie, Musselin, & Andresani, 2009). In each country they "can be linked to specific conceptions and theories regarding the relationship between the state and the society" (Ferlie et al., 2009, p. 13). Governance narratives convene elements from both dominant (e.g., NPM) and resilient/resisting discourses (e.g., NG, Collegial Governance) in their struggle to invest and fix meaning to core concepts of governance and management. The narrative approach allows identifying the field of contestation triggered by the relationship between governance and management. The influence of governance narratives on higher education has been examined (Amaral, Bleiklie, & Musselin, 2008; Amaral et al., 2003; Amaral, Jones, & Karseth, 2002; Gornitzka, Kogan, & Amaral, 2005), along with the influence of European level processes (Amaral, Neave, Musselin, & Maassen, 2009; Veiga & Amaral, 2009).

In Portugal, the 2007 law on the legal status of HEIs (RJIES) was elaborated under NPM's explicit influence (Moreira, 2008). The changes introduced are transforming the Portuguese higher education environment. Institutions were able to opt for a specific identity (public institute or public foundation) and the strategic power of the central governance structure was enhanced to the detriment of traditional collegial power. And although the Portuguese Constitution protects the autonomy of institutions it is completely silent on their self-governance. To this, one can add the growing diversification of governance structures and processes and the increasing diversity of strategies and technologies of hierarchical control (Magalhães & Santiago, 2012). New ways of organizing education and research at the different levels were required, with the shift from traditional academic coordination and control to a more entrepreneurial model and institutional governance pointed out as crucial for that purpose.

The shift from collegial governance to management concepts, structures and methods was expected to enable HEIs to act more strategically and the participation in markets to affect the institutions' capacity to decide about the profile of the academic work they undertake. However, the emphasis on institutional autonomy does not correspond to the retraction of state regulatory power. The transformation of the regulation relationships between the state and institutions has replaced *a priori* control, via funding, by *a posteriori* control based on HEIs output (Neave 2008) inducing the elaboration of instruments based on performance indicators that spread in European higher education policy.

Drivers such as managerialism and the perspectives related to NPM have influenced the changes in higher education governance: the development of 'strong rectorates', the move to appointed rather than elected posts; a reduction in the representation of academic staff, students and administrative staff; stronger managerial roles of rectors, deans and heads of departments, and a private sector style of human resources management (Ferlie et al., 2009). In the Portuguese context, these drivers resulted in an increasing centralisation of power at the institutional top, suppression (or weakening) of the collegial decision-making bodies and the creation of new ones (Magalhães et al., 2013). To this, one must add the strengthening of the presence of external stakeholders in the central decision-making bodies, the adoption of the foundational model, enabling institutions to rule themselves by private law, the use of output-based contracts and the emphasis on accountability, individual responsibility, completion and performance (Magalhães et al., 2013).

Governance reforms have reconfigured the relationships between governance and management which are embedded in mixed developments combining elements of different governance narratives. The extent to which the perceptions of Portuguese higher education professionals reflect these elements were central to understanding different weights of managerialism in higher education governance reforms. These narratives feed and are fed by the perceptions of the professionals about governance and managerial issues as they are the ones who translate the narrative elements into governance and management practices.

GOVERNANCE DIMENSIONS AND THE WEIGHT OF MANAGEMENT

Governance copes with coordination, definition of goals, assumptions on values, and the setting up of control mechanisms and processes. These dimensions have evolved under the influence of governance narratives, including an NPM approach, resulting in harder or softer influence of managerialism, i.e. governance practices stem from the contestation triggered by elements of NPM, New Governance and NG, not to mention Collegial governance narratives.

With regard to coordination, hard influence of management perspectives underlines the NPM hierarchical assumption that 'management must manage', while a softer influence stresses, for instance, elements of New Governance and NG narratives. These elements underline distributed leadership and decision-making based on interpersonal networks rooted in cooperation rationales among actors if "accompanied by horizontal power structures because they are only sustainable if (…) all members benefit from interacting with each other" (Salamon, 2002b, p. 108). NG also emphasizes softer leadership (Paradeise et al., 2013).

The outlining of goals as a governance dimension relies on assumptions about self-governance of HEIs and on their capacity to define and to achieve goals. While hard influence of management induces the tracing of goals oriented by short-medium term objectives and measurable outputs, the soft influence of management promoted by the New Governance perspective relies on the enhancement of collaborative networks centred on building types of relationships directed towards mission oriented goals (Salamon, 2002a, p. 33), i.e., education, research and third mission. In line with this, the NG approach underlines the development of networks designed with the explicit goal of joint problem recognition and joint problem solving (Paradeise et al., 2013).

Assumptions on values of higher education are visible in the interpretation of the changes in the organizational environment and are challenging values associated with collegial governance (Amaral et al., 2003). By promoting the value of competition between individuals and between HEIs, academic values of collegiality are eroded. Hard influence of management has enhanced the development of performance indicators grounded on competition, while softer influence of management stresses collaboration replacing "competition as the defining feature of sectoral relationships" (Salamon, 2002a, p. 14).

With regard to control mechanisms, the hard influence of managerialism is visible in the development of tight control based on efficiency and value for money, inducing a commodification of the organization's activities and emphasising command and control as a preferred management approach. The softer influence promotes negotiation and persuasion on the basis of "incentives for the outcomes they [public managers] desire from actors over whom they have only imperfect control" (Salamon, 2002a, p. 15). In line with NG external control systems take the form of *light touch* systems (Paradeise, Reale, & Gostellec, 2009) evidencing soft influence of managerialism.

The hard influence of management on the dimension of processes enhances hierarchically arrayed management skills. In turn, its softer influence is translated into the enhancement of enablement skills, i.e., those required "to engage partners arrayed horizontally in networks, to bring multiple stakeholders together for a common end in a situation of interdependence" (Salamon, 2002a, p. 16). The softer influence of managerialism brings forward *orchestration skills* in dealing with the fragmentation of decision-making processes.

To sum up, Table 3.1 displays the extremes of the influence of management in each of the dimensions of governance referred to above.

Table 3.1. Influence of management on governance

Governance	Soft influence of management	Hard influence of management
Coordination	Distributed leadership and interpersonal networks (horizontal decision-making)	NPM based *Management must manage* (vertical and hierarchical decision-making)
Goals	Mission oriented goals	Objectives as measurable outputs
Values	Collaboration/cooperation	Performance indicators and competition
Control mechanisms	Negotiation and persuasion (e.g., *Light touch* systems, *Hands off* style)	Command and control (e.g., financial control, efficiency and value for money, and commodification of activities)
Processes	Enablement skills (activation skills, modulation skills and orchestration skills).	Management skills

QUESTIONING THE DATA

The empirical data used in this paper were gathered in the framework of a wider research project on the changes occurring in recent years in Portuguese HEIs. On the basis of an on-line survey, distributed throughout 2014 and 2015 in all higher education institutions, we have selected a set of topics to which respondents were asked to indicate, on a five point Likert scale, the extent to which there was a tendency at their HEI for:

- the most important decisions to be taken by the central management;
- the loss of influence of collegial bodies in decision-making processes;
- the institution to be guided towards the achievement of objectives;
- an increase of administrative workload;
- an increase in the central management's control over the employees;
- an increase in external stakeholders' participation;
- the growth of the support structures for academic (teaching, research and extension) and non-academic activities.

The linkage between these topics and governance dimensions was established, as shown in Table 3.2.

Table 3.2. Working out governance dimensions

Coordination	Goals	Values	Control mechanisms	Processes
The most important decisions to be taken by the central management The loss of influence of collegial bodies in decision-making processes An increase in external stakeholders' participation	The institution to be guided towards the achievement of objectives	The loss of influence of collegial bodies in decision-making processes An increase in external stakeholders' participation	An increase of administrative workload An increase in the central management's control over the employees	The growth of the support structures for academic (teaching, research and extension) and non-academic activities

The answers from a sample of 2060 higher education professionals (1661 from the teaching staff which corresponds roughly to 5% of the population and 399 from members of the non-teaching staff)[1] were analysed.

Governance and management structures and processes of decision-making promoted by the 2007 legal framework and the redistribution of power it triggered underlined the trend towards the loss of collegiality and the emergent centralising governance rationale. This study allowed a deeper understanding of the character and nature of the most relevant changes in the governance of Portuguese HEIs. The analysis of the actors' perceptions shed light on the different weights of managerialism on institutional governance.

By linking governance dimensions to the selected topics of the survey, we assume that the features of the Portuguese higher education system, namely those deriving from both the divide between polytechnics and universities and between public and private institutions can be relevant factors when addressing the influence of managerialism on higher education governance. Public institutions are more rooted in the traditional collegial modes of organization and decision-making than their private counterparts. Furthermore, both historically and by statute universities tend to be comprehensive and more research-oriented (and namely able to offer PhD programmes) whilst polytechnics are generally vocationally-driven institutions. These features were expected to influence the perceptions of higher education professionals as they might perceive differently the changes occurring in the governance of their own institutions. In addition to these institutional characteristics we have selected professional attributes of the respondents that may also be relevant in differentiating their perceptions: (i) being a part of the teaching or non-teaching staff professional groups with traditionally different roles and power in the academia, (ii) the respondents' own role in the decision-making processes at the institution or (iii) the fact that they have or have not been working at their institutions since the implementation of the 2007 law.

The sample's characterization can be found in Table 3.3. Respondents' answers were analysed resorting to statistical techniques. Descriptive statistics were computed to unveil respondents' perceptions of the selected variables. Non-parametric tests (Mann-Whitney and Kruskal-Wallis tests) were run to explore the influence of the selected factors on professionals' perceptions.

THE INFLUENCE OF MANAGERIALISM IN PORTUGUESE HIGHER EDUCATION INSTITUTIONS

As shown in Table 3.4, respondents tended to agree to a high extent that, on the one hand, there is *an increase of administrative workload* in their institutions and, on the other hand, that *the most important decisions* [are] *to be taken by the central management*. These perceptions emphasised the enhancement of control mechanisms and a hierarchical approach to coordination reflecting the harder influence of managerialism on governance.

Perceptions gathering lower mean values are related to *the growth of the support structures for academic (teaching, research and extension) and non-academic activities* and to *an increase in external stakeholders' participation*. These perceptions were not aligned with the harder influence of managerialism on governance processes and values. On the one hand, the growth of the support structures is not perceived as an important feature of governance processes; on the other hand the weight of hard

Table 3.3. Samples' characterization

			N	%
Professional group	Teaching staff		1661	80.6
	Non-teaching staff		399	19.4
		Total	2060	100.0
		Missing	–	–
HE's subsector	Public		1576	79.1
	Private		417	20.9
		Total	1993	100
		Missing	67	–
HE's subsystem	University		1036	52.0
	Polytechnic		957	48.0
		Total	1993	100
		Missing	67	–
Years at the institution	after 2007		555	27.8
	before 2007		1439	72.2
		Total	1994	100
		Missing	66	–
Current role in decision-making	I have no role in the decision-making processes.		907	45.1
	I am consulted in the decision-making processes		798	39.7
	I have influence over the decision-making processes.		249	12.4
	I am responsible for the decision-making.		55	2.7
		Total	2009	100
		Missing	51	

managerialism in coordination and values is not visible in the perceived influence of external stakeholders.

The perceptions on the *increase in the central management's control over the employees*, the institutional focus *towards the achievement of objectives,* and *the loss of influence of collegial bodies in decision-making processes* were 'to some extent' recognized as tendencies in recent years. This might indicate a growing

Table 3.4. HE professionals' perceptions on tendencies in recent years at their institutions

Tendencies of governance dimensions	N	Mean	Median	Mode	S-D
The most important decisions to be taken by the central management.	1816	3.96	4	4	0.828
The loss of influence of collegial bodies in decision-making processes.	1707	3.45	3	4	1.035
The institution to be guided towards the achievement of objectives.	1805	3.61	4	4	0.893
An increase of administrative workload.	1845	4.07	4	5	0.888
An increase in the central management's control over the employees.	1795	3.75	4	4	0.943
An increase in external stakeholders' participation.	1550	2.91	3	3	0.916
The growth of the support structures for academic (teaching, research and extension) and non-academic activities.	1833	2.67	3	3	1.043

influence of the weight of managerialism on governance of control mechanisms and values. However, the analysis of the governance dimension focusing on values (e.g., *An increase in external stakeholders' participation* and *The loss of influence of collegial bodies in decision-making processes*) reflected a softer influence of managerialism.

In sum, the harder influence of managerialism was particularly noticeable in the rise of control mechanisms and on the coordination dimension of governance in which decision-making processes are increasingly hierarchical, concentrated at the central management level and outside the influence of traditional collegial bodies. The weight of managerialism is more pronounced in the perceptions about control mechanisms (e.g., *An increase of administrative workload, An increase in the central management's control over the employees*) and appeared to be more linked to the concentration of power on the central administration, rather than to changes of governance values (e.g., *The loss of influence of collegial bodies in decision-making processes, An increase in external stakeholders' participation*). Nevertheless, the loss of influence of collegial bodies was perceived significantly (3.45) by those surveyed.

COMPARING TYPES OF INSTITUTIONS AND PROFESSIONAL GROUPS

Statistically significant differences between groups of responders were found both at the system level, i.e., between universities and polytechnics, between public and private institutions, and also according to professional groups, namely the respondents pertaining to the teaching or non-teaching staff, their role in decision-making processes and number of years working at the institution (since before or after the implementation of the 2007 law). Data were analysed through Mann-Whitney and Kruskal-Wallis tests for a 0.05 significance level, as shown in Table 3.5, in which the group that perceives to a higher extent the tendency considered is noted (in bold).

Table 3.5. Perceptions of different groups of respondents

Tendencies of governance dimensions	HEI's subsector	HEI's subsystem	Professional group	Years at HEI	Role in D-M
The most important decisions to be taken by the central management.	p=0.826	p=0.352	p=0.352	p=0.162	**p=0.000 (No role)**
The loss of influence of collegial bodies in decision-making processes.	**p=0.000 (Public)**	p=0.922	**p=0.005 (Teaching)**	**p=0.000 (before 2007)**	**p=0.000 (No role)**
The institution to be guided towards the achievement of objectives.	p=0.101	**p=0.000 (University)**	p=0.523	**p=0.001 (after 2007)**	**p=0.007 (Influence)**
An increase of administrative workload.	**p=0.000 (Public)**	p=0.230	**p=0.005 (Teaching)**	**p=0.000 (before 2007)**	p=0.138
An increase in the central management's control over the employees.	**p=0.000 (Public)**	p=0.103	p=0.060	p=0.125	**p=0.000 (No role)**
An increase in external stakeholders' participation.	**p=0.038 (Private)**	p=0.299	**p=0.021 (N-teaching)**	**p=0.000 (after 2007)**	**p=0.000 (Responsible)**
The growth of the support structures for academic (teaching, research and extension) and non-academic activities.	**p=0.000 (Private)**	**p=0.026 (University)**	**p=0.000 (N-teaching)**	**p=0.001 (after 2007)**	**p=0.000 (Responsible)**

As argued above, the growing influence of managerialism was particularly noticeable in the coordination dimension of governance, namely related to the tendency for *The most important decisions to be taken by the central management.* At the system level this was a consensual perception among respondents from both public and private institutions and polytechnics and universities. However, *The loss of influence of collegial bodies in decision-making processes* is significantly more perceived in public institutions where the collegial modes of decision-making traditionally prevailed. In private institutions, collegiality was never as strongly embedded (Magalhães & Santiago, 2012) and, therefore, even if the influence of managerialism might be as strong (or even stronger) than in their public counterparts, the loss of collegiality would not be as intensely felt.

By the same token, and arguably for similar reasons, it is in the public sector that professionals perceive to a higher extent the growth of centralized control mechanisms associated both with *An increase of administrative workload,* and with *An increase in the central management's control over their employees.* Again, these are features reflecting a greater adhesion to a managerialist logic, which are felt in the different types of institutions throughout the system but to which professionals from public institutions respond to in a statistically significant higher degree. In turn, perceptions on the *increase in external stakeholders' participation* are stronger in professionals from the private sector. However, perceptions featuring the values dimension of governance remained relatively low, reflecting a softer influence of managerialism in institutions' governance.

In terms of a growing influence of managerialism on the setting of goals expressed in the tendency for *The institution to be guided towards the achievement of objectives,* it is more highly felt by professionals in universities rather than in polytechnics. In spite of the fact that the growth of support structures was not perceived as a key feature of the governance changes, the analysis shows that respondents from the private sector and from universities are more sensitive to this topic, reflecting a softer influence of managerialism on the processes of governance.

When looking at the governance dimensions, using the lens of the respondents' professional characteristics, to discern a softer or harder influence of managerialism it is worth highlighting that the tendency for *The most important decisions to be taken by the central management* is, perhaps not surprisingly, more highly felt by those who assume that they have no role in decision-making. Additionally, *The loss of influence of collegial bodies in decision-making processes* is significantly perceived to a higher extent by the teaching staff (arguably the professional group traditionally with more power and participation in those collegial bodies), by professionals that have been working at their institutions before 2007 (who probably have a sharper sense of the changes which occurred at the institution since the implementation of RJIES), and, again, by those who feel that they have no role in decision-making processes.

In turn, *The increase in external stakeholders' participation*, a tendency in which we have seen that there seems to be a softer influence of managerialism in Portuguese higher education, is nevertheless, and contrariwise to the previous tendencies, perceived more by the non-teaching staff, by those who have been working at their institutions after 2007 and by those at the very top of the decision-making processes, i.e., those who describe themselves as being '*responsible*' for the decision-making at their institutions. This can also be found when looking at the perceptions of

49

professionals on *The growth of support structures for academic and non-academic activities.* These were, as we recall, the two topics which reflected a softer influence of managerialism in Portuguese HEI's governance.

As for the rise in control mechanisms, another dimension where we could discern a stark influence of managerialism in institutions' governance, *The increase of administrative workload*, while prevalent in all groups under consideration, is again more noticeably perceived by the teaching staff and by those who have been working at their institutions since before the implementation of RJIES. *An increase in the central management's control over the employees* is more highly felt by those who feel they have no role in decision-making. The teaching and non-teaching staff reveal no statistically significant differences concerning this topic, since both perceive it at roughly the same (and high) extent.

As for the tendency for *The institution to be guided towards the achievement of objectives*, related to the definition of goals, we can see that this tendency is most highly perceived by those who arrived at the institution after the implementation of the 2007 law and by those who have influence over the decision-making processes. However, statistical differences emerge between those who have no role in decision-making (and who have a much lower adherence to this proposition) and those who are 'consulted', have 'influence' or are 'responsible' for decision-making.

CONCLUSIONS

The analysis of how the governance reforms of Portuguese HEIs reflect different weights of managerialism corroborate existing research that identified mixed signs of governance narratives in reconfiguring the relationship between governance and management (Magalhães et al., 2013). On the one hand, governance is a contested concept opening the way to diverse interpretations of its meaning contingent on contexts and legitimating different approaches to governance and management. Offe (2009) underlined that 'governance' is a novel form of coordination among actors, which has little to do with the conventional understanding of 'to govern' and which becomes a quasi-substitute for *government* in contexts where an agency with an unambiguous competence to rule does not exist (as in corporate governance or *global* governance).

Narratives such as NPM, New Governance and NG aim to fix the meaning of governance and its relationship with management. This struggle to assign meaning was visible in the different weights of managerialism as reflected in the governance dimensions. The elements of the NPM governance narrative associated with vertical and hierarchical decision-making and command and control were stressed in the coordination and control mechanisms of governance. The growing influence of managerialism was particularly noticeable in these dimensions and was recognised across sectors and types of institutions. This can be explained by the explicit influence of NPM in the 2007 law, which forms the basis of Portuguese higher education governance reform paving the way for a concentration of decision-making power in HEIs' central management bodies.

Notwithstanding, the analysis of governance values showed the tension between the NPM narrative and elements of NG and Collegial Governance in assigning meaning to the redistribution of academic power in decision-making. This shows the mixed influence of governance narratives and practices in the actors' perceptions. Additionally, it contributes to underline the complexity of the governance models to the detriment of a straightforward causality perspective with regard to the influence of managerialism in the governance of HEIs. Actually, the analysis of the actors' perceptions about the different weights of managerialism in the governance dimensions under study illustrates this complexity and substantiates the relationship between hard and soft managerialism.

Furthermore, the loss of collegiality is more strongly perceived by the respondents from public institutions, the teaching staff and those who started working at their institutions before 2007. The perceptions of groups of respondents might reflect the fact that these actors were those more exposed to the changes promoted by the reform and, therefore, reflecting the hard influence of managerialism on the public sector. Apparently, professionals in the universities as well as the teaching staff perceived a higher weight of managerialism in other governance dimensions such as 'goals' and 'control mechanisms', as these institutions and actors were those that have lost power in its redistribution under the NPM-driven reform. By the same token, this issue was particularly visible in the public sector where the increase of control mechanisms was perceived to a higher extent.

The softer influence of managerialism was visible in the perceptions of non-teaching staff, professionals from the private sector, by those who have been working at their institutions since after 2007 and by those at the very top of the decision-making processes. This might indicate that, rather than the influence of other governance narratives, the managerial turn was not as strong as it could be expected under the influence of NPM. However, the perceptions of the increased influence of external stakeholders in the institutions' governance and of the growth of support structures' reflect mixed signs as this increase was not consensual

The analysis of governance dimensions on the basis of the degree of consent/dissent sheds light on the struggle for the fixation of meaning of governance reforms in Portuguese higher education. This study provides relevant insights on system level and institutional management contributing to an increased reflexivity in policy-making and institutional decision-making. This is of importance for the field of higher education studies as it allows for a more complex approach to policy analysis and the reconfiguration of the practices which the policies aim to transform.

The analysis of how individuals as institutional actors appropriate and develop narrative elements to justify and legitimate their decisions and strategies are avenues for further research.

ACKNOWLEDGEMENT

This research was funded by FCT under the project EXCL/IVC-PEC/0789/2012 and the programme UID/CED/00757/2013.

NOTE

[1] In the absence of official statistics about the number of non-teaching staff in Portuguese higher education institutions we are unable to calculate the weight of our sample in the overall population.

REFERENCES

Amaral, A., & Magalhães, A. (2001). On markets, autonomy and regulation the Janus Head revisited. *Higher Education Policy, 14*(1), 7–20.

Amaral, A., Jones, G. A., & Karseth, B. (2002). Governing higher education: Comparing national perspectives. In A. Amaral, G. A. Jones, & B. Karseth (Eds.), *Governing higher education: National perspectives on institutional governance* (pp. 279–298). Dordrecht, the Netherlands: Kluwer Academic Publishers.

Amaral, A., Fulton, O., & Larsen, I. M. (2003). *A managerial revolution?* Dordrecht, the Netherlands: Kluwer Academic Publishers.

Amaral, A., Bleiklie, I., & Musselin, C. (2008). *From governance to identity*. Dordrecht, the Netherlands: Springer.

Amaral, A., Neave, G., Musselin, C., & Maassen, P., (Eds.). (2009). *European integration and the governance of higher education and research*. Dordrecht, the Netherlands: Springer.

Bleiklie, I. (2009). Norway: From tortoise to eager beaver. In C. Paradeise, E. Reale, I. Bleiklie, & E. Ferlie (Eds.), *University governance: Western European comparative perspectives* (pp. 127–152). Dordrecht, the Netherlands: Springer.

Bleiklie, I., & Kogan, M. (2007). Organization and governance of universities. *Higher Education Policy, 20*(4), 477–494.

Boston, J. (2011). Basic NPM ideas and their development. In T. Cristensen & P. Laegreid (Eds.), *The ashgate research companion to new public management* (pp. 17–32). Surrey: Asgate Publishing.

Deem, R. (1998). 'New managerialism' and higher education: The management of performances and cultures in universities in the United Kingdom. *International Studies in Sociology of Education, 8*(1), 47–70. doi:10.1080/0962021980020014

Dill, D. D. (1997). Higher education markets and public policy. *Higher Education Policy, 10*(3–4), 167–185.

Ferlie, E., & Andresani, G. (2009). United Kingdom from Bureau professionalism to new public management. In C. Paradeise, E. Reale, I. Bleiklie, & E. Ferlie (Eds.), *University governance: Western European comparative perspective* (pp. 177–195). Dordrecht, the Netherlands: Springer.

Ferlie, E., Musselin, C., & Andresani, G. (2009). The governance of higher education systems: A public management prespective. In C. Paradeise, E. Reale, I. Bleiklie, & E. Ferlie (Eds.), *University governance: Western European comparative perspective* (pp. 1–19). Dordrecht, the Netherlands: Springer.

Gornitzka, Å., Kogan, M., & Amaral, A., (Eds.). (2005). *Reform and change in higher education: Analysing policy implementation* (P. Maassen Ed. Vol. 8). Dordrecht, the Netherlands: Springer.

Hall, P. A., & Taylor, R. C. R. (1996). Political science and the three new institutionalisms. *Political Studies, 44*(5), 936–957. doi:10.1111/j.1467-9248.1996.tb00343.x

Hirsch, W. Z., & Weber, L. (1999). *Challenges facing higher education at the millennium*. Phoenix, AZ: American Council on Education/Oryx Press.

Kjaer, A. (2010a). *Governance*. Cambridge: Polity.

Kjaer, P. (2010). *Between governing and governance: On the emergence, function and form of Europe's post-national constellation*. Oxford: Hart Publishing.

Magalhães, A., & Amaral, A. (2009). Mapping out discourses on higher education governance. In J. Huisman (Ed.), *International perspectives on the governance of higher education: Alternative frameworks for coordination* (pp. 182–197). London: Routledge.

Magalhães, A., & Santiago, R. (2012). Governance, public management and administration of higher education in Portugal. In G. Neave & A. Amaral (Eds.), *Higher education in Portugal 1974–2009 – A nation, a generation* (pp. 227–248). Dordrecht, the Netherlands: Springer

Magalhães, A., Veiga, A., Amaral, A., Sousa, S., & Ribeiro, F. (2013). Governance of governance in higher education: Practices and lessons drawn from the Portuguese case. *Higher Education Quarterly, 67*(3), 295–311. doi:10.111/hequ12021

Meek, L. (2002). On the road to mediocraty? Governance and management of australian higher education in the market place. In A. Amaral, G. Jones, & B. Karseth (Eds.), *Governing higher education: National perspectives on institutional governance* (pp. 253–260). Kluwer Academic Publishers.

Moreira, V. (2008). O Estatuto legal das instituições de ensino superior. In A. Amaral (Ed.), *Políticas de ensino superior – quatro temas em debate* (pp. 123–139). Lisbon: Conselho Nacional de Educação.

Neave, G. (2008). From guardian to overseer: Trends in institutional autonomy, governance and leadership. In A. Amaral (Ed.), *Políticas de ensino superior – quatro temas em debate* (pp. 45–70). Lisbon: Conselho Nacional de Educação.

Offe, C. (2009). Governance: An "empty signifier"? *Constellations, 16*(4), 550–562. doi:10.1111/j.1467-8675.2009.00570.x

Osborne, S. (2010). *The new public governance: Emerging perspectives on the theory and practice of public governance.* London: Routledge.

Paradeise, C., Reale, E., & Gostellec, G. (2009). A comparative approach to higher education reforms in Western European countries. In C. Paradeise, E. Reale, I. Bleiklie, & E. Ferlie (Eds.), *University governance: Western European comparative perspectives* (pp. 197–225). Dordrecht, the Netherlands: Springer.

Paradeise, C., Reale, E., Gostellec, G., & Bleiklie, I. (2009). Universities steering between stories and history. In C. Paradeise, E. Reale, I. Bleiklie, & E. Ferlie (Eds.), *University governance Western European comparative perspectives* (pp. 227–246). Dordrecht, the Netherlands: Springer.

Pollit, C., & Bouckaert, G. (2004). *Public management reform: A comparative analysis.* Oxford: Oxford University Press.

Rosenau, J., & Czempiel, E. (1992). *Governance without government: Order and change in world politics.* Cambridge: Cambridge University Press.

Salamon, L. (2002a). The new governance and the tools of public action: An introduction. In L. Salamon (Ed.), *The tools of government: A guide to the new governance* (pp. 1–47). Oxford: Oxford University Press.

Salamon, L. (2002b). *The tools of government: A guide to the new governance.* Oxford: Oxford University Press.

Veiga, A., & Amaral, A. (2009). Policy implementation tools and European governance. In A. Amaral, G. Neave, C. Musselin, & P. Maassen (Eds.), *European integration and the governance of higher education and research* (pp. 133–157). Dordrecht, the Netherlands: Springer.

António Magalhães
University of Porto
Centre for Research in Higher Education Policies (CIPES)

Amélia Veiga
Faculty of Psychology and Sciences of Education, University of Porto
and Centre for Research in Higher Education Policies (CIPES)

Pedro Videira
Centre for Research in Higher Education Policies (CIPES)

MYROSLAVA HLADCHENKO, DOMINIK ANTONOWICZ
AND HARRY DE BOER

4. UNDERSTANDING THE CHANGES OF THE HIGHER EDUCATION GOVERNANCE IN POLAND AND UKRAINE

Institutional Analysis

INTRODUCTION

Since the 1980s, the modes of governance of public sectors have undergone substantial changes in most of the Western European countries (e.g. Van Kersbergen & Van Waarden, 2004; de Boer et al., 2010). These public sector wide changes were in many cases inspired and driven by the principles of 'New Public Management' (NPM) that can be viewed as one of the global models of world society (Pollitt, 1990). This shift has also influenced public sector policies in the Central and Eastern European (CEE) countries (Antonowicz & Simonová, 2006; Zgaga et al., 2013). We know that NPM has many faces (Hood, 1991) and that forms, timing and outcomes significantly vary from country to country (Kehm & Lanzendorf, 2006; Paradeise et al., 2009). This also applies to Polish and Ukrainian higher education, where reforms have taken place with the intention of transforming their higher education systems in order to align them more with European higher education systems.

We have chosen Poland and Ukraine as two CEE countries with, at first sight, a common socialistic past but with a different present. Nowadays, Poland is a developed country that became an EU member in 2004, while Ukraine, having undergone two revolutions in 2004 and 2013–2014, is only striving for EU membership and is lagging behind in economic progress.

In this research, we will focus on one specific public sector, namely higher education, and more particularly on changes in higher education governance in these two countries. The key question addressed in this chapter, therefore, is how the models of university governance in Poland and Ukraine have changed since 1990 through the diffusion of the global model of NPM and how differences and similarities in these patterns of change in governance can be explained. To answer these questions, we will use insights from historical and sociological institutionalism. Historical institutionalism, in particular the concept of path dependence, emphasizes 'historical sequences in which contingent events set into motion institutional patterns or event chains' (Mahoney, 2000, p. 507). Sociological institutionalism provides

R. Deem & H. Eggins (Eds.), The University as a Critical Institution?, 55–74.

a useful perspective for exploration of the impact of a world society on shaping the structure and behavior of the nation-states (Meyer, 2010). The combination of these two approaches of neo-institutionalism allows us to explore the institutional phenomenon from different perspectives and can strengthen our understanding of the policy making process in higher education (Dobbins, 2015; Dobbins & Knill, 2009; Nicholson, 1998). Thus, our study aims to address the void in empirical research about policy making in higher education governance applying institutional analysis that is based both on historical and sociological institutionalism.

HISTORICAL AND SOCIOLOGICAL INSTITUTIONALISM

Historical and sociological institutionalism can be considered as complementary approaches, which allow the exploration of institutional development from a variety of perspectives (Nichols, 1998; see also Dobbins, 2015). Historical institutionalism views this development as incremental and path dependent (Krasner, 1989; Steinmo & Thelen, 1992; Pierson, 2000). As historical developments are path dependent, the choices that are made affect future possibilities (Krasner, 1988). The early historical events are viewed as contingent occurrences, which are of primary importance for the final outcome of the sequence. Within the framework of path dependence, two main types of sequences are defined: self-reinforcing and reactive (Mahoney, 2000). In historical institutionalism change is explained by critical junctures that punctuate historical events, creating branching points for the establishment of a new path (Gourevitch, 1986). Change occurs because actors can act strategically within the historically shaped institutional context. Simultaneously, while actors constitute institutions, institutions themselves are also an outcome of agency action. In such processes of institution-moulding or institution-construction, struggles among actors are inbuilt into them, leading to both intended and unintended outcomes (Hay & Wincot, 1998). The abilities of actors to influence institutions are restricted by asymmetric distribution of knowledge about institutions and access to resources (Hay & Wincot, 1998). Mahoney (2000) explains institutional reproduction through a power-based approach, according to which institutions at the same time offer an advantage to one group of actors and disadvantage others, which leads to conflict of interest and promotes incremental change.

Where historical institutionalism is eclectic in nature and combines both calculus and cultural approaches, sociological institutionalism is mainly based on the cultural approach (Hall & Taylor, 1996). World society theory, generated by sociological institutionalism (Meyer et al., 1997) addresses the issue of the impact of global institutions as 'cultural models' or 'models of actorhood' on shaping the behavior, identities and structure of the nation-states, organizations and individuals worldwide (Meyer, 2000, 2010). World society theory considers the nation-state as being culturally embedded and constructed (Meyer, 1999; Meyer et al., 1997; Powell & DiMaggio, 1991) and the culture involved is built on a worldwide basis.

Meyer et al. (1997) assert that if this is the case then the nation-states should be characterized by isomorphism in their policies and structures. DiMaggio and Powell (1983) define three types of isomorphism or so-called mechanisms of diffusion through which institutionalization occurs, namely coercive, normative and mimetic mechanisms. Isomorphic pressures are exercised by transnational organizations, agents of world polity, such as OECD, IMF or the World Bank. New Public Management can be viewed as one of the hegemonic models of world society.

Meyer et al. (1997) link the dynamics of diffusion with countries' embeddedness in world society. Resource-rich nation-states can convincingly adopt policies under exogenous pressure (Meyer et al., 1992), while in impoverished countries enactment of global models can result in decoupling (Meyer, 2010; Ramirez & Rubinson, 1979). Next to decoupling of policies and practices (Boxenbaum & Jonsson, 2008), institutional scholars recently addressed the inconsistencies between practices and outcomes (Bromley & Powell, 2012) when despite coupling policies and practices the intended ends were not achieved because adopted policies were inappropriate (Wijn, 2014) and means became ends in themselves (Grodal & O'Mahony, 2015).

Where historical institutionalism focuses on endogenous sources of institutional changes, sociological institutionalism, in particular world society theory, emphasizes exogenous factors of institutional change. In our view, these approaches are complementary and allow the exploration of institutional changes from different perspectives.

Combining these two approaches, we will explore how both the path dependence and isomorphic pressure of world society imposed through diffusion of the global model of New Public Management affect the modes of governance in higher education in Poland and Ukraine.

THE GOVERNANCE EQUALIZER

In order to determine institutional change – shifts in the modes of governance in higher education in Poland and Ukraine – we used the governance equalizer model (de Boer, Enders, & Schimank, 2007). This governance equalizer distinguishes five dimensions that together configure the governance model of a public sector: state regulation, stakeholder guidance, academic self-governance, managerial-self-governance, and competition (de Boer, Enders, & Schimank, 2007). These five dimensions are:

- State regulation concerns the traditional notion of top-down authority vested in the state. This dimension refers to regulation by directives; the government prescribes in detail behaviors under particular circumstances
- Stakeholder guidance concerns activities that direct universities through goal setting and advice. In public university systems, the government is usually an important stakeholder, but it is certainly not necessarily the only player in the game.

- Academic self-governance concerns the role of professional communities within the university system. This mechanism is institutionalized in collegial decision-making within universities and the peer review-based self-steering of academic communities.
- Managerial self-governance concerns hierarchies within universities as organizations. Here the role of university leadership – rectors or presidents on the top-level, deans on the intermediate level – in internal goal setting, regulation, and decision-making is at stake.
- Competition for resources – money, personnel and prestige, within and between universities.

The governance equalizer model is an analytical tool to 'measure' changes in the governance of higher education systems and 'compare' paths of development in Poland and Ukraine. The New Public Management model can also be interpreted along the dimensions of the governance equalizer. According to our interpretation of an 'idealized' NPM, state regulation should be rather low and the role of academic self-governance should be marginal, while stakeholder guidance, managerial self-governance and competition should score high in New Public Management model (cf. de Boer, Enders, & Schimank, 2007). Our interpretation of the NPM governance equalizer, presented in Figure 4.1, will be used to benchmark the Polish and Ukrainian higher education governance systems.

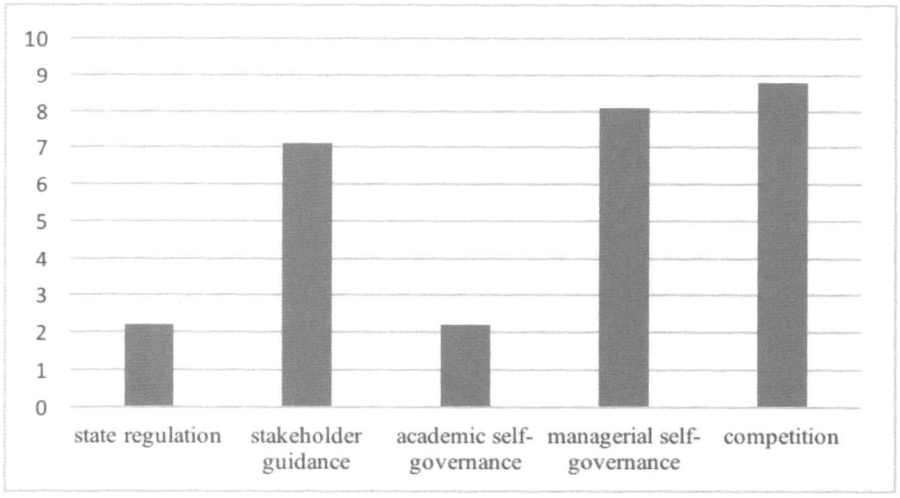

Figure 4.1. NPM-benchmark governance equalizer.
Source: Adapted from de Boer, Enders & Schimank (2007)

In the following section, we present the findings about the changes in higher education governance in Poland and Ukraine. The findings are based on a secondary analysis of legislative and policy documents, white papers and reports as well as scientific journals and reports.

GOVERNANCE OF HIGHER EDUCATION IN COMMUNIST
POLAND AND UKRAINE BEFORE 1990

Poland

Before 1990, the governance of Polish higher education was a mixture of all-embracing state regulation built on the ideological hegemony of communism and the legacy of a Humboldtian tradition (Sadlak, 1995). It provided a typical example of the CEE countries' governance model of higher education with a prevailing role of the state and political interference from the communist party. As Michael Dobbins (2015, p. 20), however, claims, Humboldtian, traditions were somewhat better preserved in Poland than in other CEE countries. Nevertheless, the most significant feature of the governance model refers to the dominant role of *state regulation* (Figure 4.2) in higher education that administrated its issues through an extensive number of detailed regulations and also through the far-reaching institutionalization of communist command structures (Hübner, 1992). All the higher education institutions were under tight bureaucratic control and the state had to approve almost everything: election of the rectors (which at least had to be approved by the ministry), the appointment of professors and the design of teaching curricula. Processes in and organization of universities were prescribed by government imposed regulations.

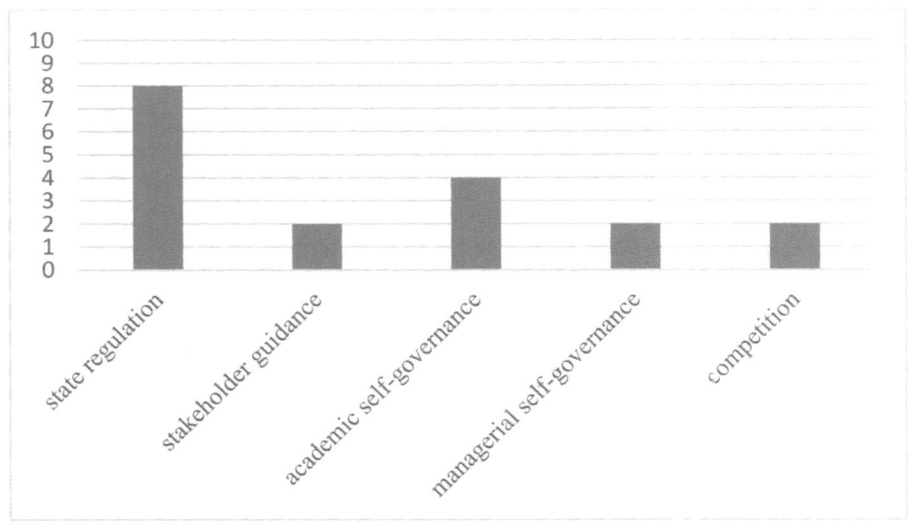

Figure 4.2. Governance equalizer: Poland before 1990

Concerning *stakeholder guidance,* as most CEE countries prior to 1989, Poland was ruled by an authoritarian regime that was characterized by strong centralism. Hence there was no need for any form of intermediary body which could weaken the power accumulated by the government that utterly controlled higher education. However, the communist party (PZPR) can be seen as an external stakeholder and it infiltrated higher education, having power over numerous institutional issues and providing guidelines (or spelling out the demands of the working class) for development of higher education and research (although not always followed by the academic community). By doing so, it wanted to make the university/academic community more responsive to the needs of society and the economy, *'closer to people'* (Szłapczyński, 1968, p. 31). The academic community – socialized to the Humboldtian tradition of the university – however strongly opposed any form of external interference in universities. They perceived these political attempts as a form of curbing the (already limited) institutional autonomy of universities.

Polish universities had been established on the Humboldtian concept of a university which implied a strong sense of *'academic self-governance'* and professional (collegial) control exposed by the professoriate (de Boer & Goedegebuure, 2003). However, in the postwar period, the scope of academic 'self-governance' was rather limited and the state authority (in fact the communist party executive board) drew its boundaries. On the national level, *academic self-governance* was institutionalized as the council of higher education, which was established shortly after World War 2 but only in 1982[1] did it become a democratically elected body. Since 1985, this body was democratically elected, but the government could always refuse to appoint a member due to 'socially important reasons'. The council had limited and mainly symbolic power in terms of the approval of the national plans for research and higher education. It mostly enjoyed rights to express opinions on behalf of the academic community (Waltoś, 2009). On the institutional level, both faculty councils and senates were elected in a democratic way but their role in institutional governance was confined to strictly professional issues. Those who had some administrative authority in higher education institutions (rectors and to lesser extent deans) had to be accepted (formally or informally) by the communist party officials.[2] Thus, the model of higher education governance encompassed only some elements of academic self-governance with limited impact on the functioning of Polish higher education. The scope of academic self-governance was small and symbolic and its boundaries were always defined by the state authority (in fact the communist party) (Antonowicz, 2015).

Overall, prior to 1989 the governance model of higher education did not leave much space for *managerial self-governance.* The role of rectors was strictly limited and constrained by the extensive number of detailed state regulations. Besides administrative roles, rectors acted as *primus inter pares* of the academic community and their role was mainly symbolic. Perhaps their most visible presence was marked during numerous university rituals and ceremonies. Thus, they could only perform administrative tasks following the rules given, as universities were only a part of the state bureaucracy with no space for organizational maneuvering. Consequently, there was also no room for a rectors' organization on the national level, as the authoritarian regime did not want to provide any opportunity for alternative sources of authority in higher education. The communist regime feared that such empowerment of the rectors could possibly lead to a more balanced relation between state and universities. Rectors were, more or less formally, also politically accountable to the government and their nomination had to be approved by the communist party.

The dominance of state regulation and tight control of higher education institutions implied almost no room for *competition*. Institutional competition for funding and personnel did not exist as the state kept control over the mobility of people, even within the country. The authoritarian state and the communist party exercised strong control over the development of higher education and allocation of resources: there was no such thing as 'open competition' prior to 1989.

Ukraine

Ukrainian higher education institutions have a diverse historical and cultural heritage. In 1661 and 1875 universities were established in Lviv and Chenivtsy while the former was under the authority of Rich Pospolyta (Poland) and the latter belonged to the Austro-Hungarian Empire. As for the part of Ukraine that was under the authority of Russian Empire, in 1805, 1834 and 1965 universities were established in Kharkiv, Kyiv and Odessa. As well as educationg students, universities conducted research and were authorized to award degrees of master and doctor. The revolution of 1917 became a critical juncture in the development of Ukraine as an independent nation-state. However, in 1919, Ukraine by force became a part of the Soviet Union, which essentially meant 72 years of political, economic and semi-cultural isolation. The Ukrainian Academy of Sciences that was established in 1918 in a context of nation-building, underwent ideological and organizational restructuring under the Soviets. Regarding higher education institutions, in 1920 all universities were closed and restructured into the higher education institutions which catered to individual areas of industry, e.g. agriculture, as well as teacher training. However, in 1934 higher education institutions established on the basis of the former universities again underwent restructuring and were reopened as universities. A feature of the Soviet model that was established in Ukraine was the division of primarily teaching-oriented higher education institutions from the research institutes of the academy of sciences. In 1984, in Ukraine there were 146 higher education institutions but among them only nine comprehensive universities while others were mono-disciplinary higher education institutions (Bunina, 2013). As Soviet society was built on hierarchies and subordination, which made it easy to be governed, a hierarchy was also established in the system of higher education and science.

During the Soviet period, Ukrainian higher education institutions were operating under strong *state regulation* (Figure 4.3) that was built on even stronger ideological hegemony of communism than in Poland because Ukraine was part of the Soviet Union (Gomilko, Svyrydenko, & Terepyshchyi, 2016).

The system of higher education of the Ukrainian Soviet Social Republic was centrally controlled from Moscow by the Union of the Soviet Social Republics as a supreme state regulator. The system's planning was in the hands of the central authorities of the USSR. These central authorities determined the length of study, the approval of the size of academic staff as well as setting the staff salaries, and the approval of the curricula and educational programs (Council of the Union of the Soviet Social Republics, 1969). Among the powers of the Ukrainian Soviet Socialistic Republic in higher education was the establishment and abolishment of higher education institutions, approval of the educational programs, textbooks and development plans for particular disciplines and research in pedagogical sciences. The educational ministry of the USSR was also responsible for the development of general guidelines about education and research for higher education institutions (Parliament of Ukrainian SSR, 1974).

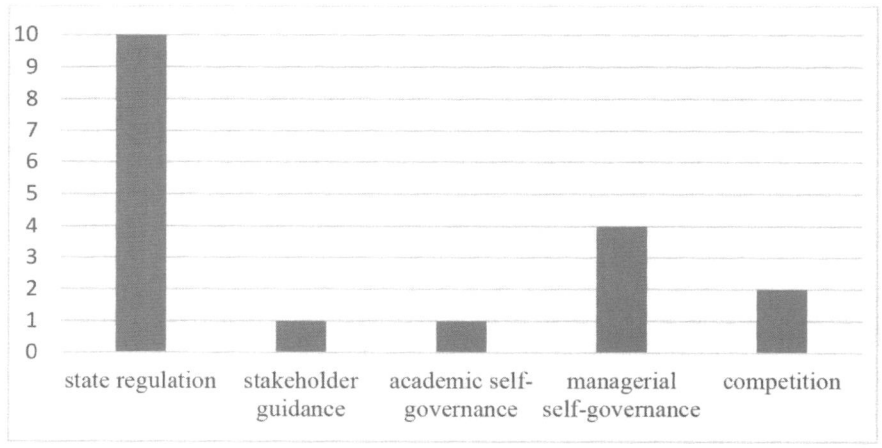

Figure 4.3. Governance equalizer: Ukraine before 1990

Strong state regulation prevented the development of *managerial self-governance* and top-level leadership at the university performed primarily administrative functions. The rector, vice-rectors and chief accountant of higher education institutions were appointed by the education ministry of USSR. According to the law, the rector was appointed from the most qualified academics, having a scientific degree and practical experience (Parliament of Ukrainian SSR, 1974). Powers were allocated at the top of the institutions. It was the rector who headed the Academic Council that consisted primarily of 'administrators' of the university and representatives of the academic staff and student public organizations (Council of the Union of the Soviet Social Republics, 1969). The Academic Council performed primarily an advisory function and this council appointed the deans. The internal governance structure of the higher education institutions, imposed by the central authorities, was clearly hierarchical.

Because of the strong state regulation, *stakeholder guidance* was almost absent and was based on the formal membership of the famous researchers and representatives of industry in the Academic Council (Council of the Union of the Soviet Social Republics, 1969).

The centralized, detailed allocation of resources made *competition* among higher education institutions almost non-existent. The Humboldtian tradition, favoring strong academic self-governance, never was strong in Ukrainian higher education as Soviet society was built on hierarchies and subordination. Hence, Ukrainian higher education under Soviet rule left hardly any space for *academic self-governance*. In this respect, in Soviet times the situation in Ukraine and Poland differed: whereas in Poland academic self-governance was to some extent preserved, it hardly existed in Ukrainian higher education.

GOVERNANCE OF HIGHER EDUCATION IN POLAND AND
UKRAINE FROM 1990 TO 2016

The fall of the communist regime and the Soviet Union became a critical juncture for Poland and Ukraine. However, these two countries took different routes. Having broken rapidly with the past, adhering to a 'shock therapy' way of reforming the economy, Poland became a member of the European Union in 2004. Ukraine opted for a gradual approach to reforming its economy (Langer, 2008) and as a result the country has gone through two revolutions in 2004 and 2013–2014. In order to prevent the continuity of communism, the de-communization and lustration were conducted in Poland but not in Ukraine (Vyatkovych, 2015). Thus, in Ukraine the main actors endowed with power in the Soviet period managed to preserve their powerful positions both in politics and higher education (Kovriga, 2010). Further, the rise of the oligarchy occurred in the country (Marchak, 2016) while the civil society was underdeveloped.

Poland

The period 1990–2015 has been marked by tumultuous and inconsistent changes that revolutionized almost the entire system of higher education governance in Poland (Antonowicz, 2015; Kwiek, 2009; Białecki & Dąbrowa-Szefler, 2009; Duczmal, 2006; Antonowicz, Pinheiro, & Smużewska, 2014). During the entire period (1990–2015) the state remained an important actor in the public realm, and its presence was exercised through multiple detailed *state regulations* (Figure 4.2). The government however did not have adequate capacity to steer the system and it largely withdrew from developing its own agenda (due to lack of resources and political authority). Nevertheless, it attempted to control the expansion of higher education through a growing number of detailed regulations. This resulted in alarming signals about a shrinking quality of education and the de-institutionalization of the university research mission (Kwiek, 2012). The toothless state stripped from its authority (in higher education) largely failed to execute a number of regulations, which had been boldly expressed in reports of the Supreme Audit Office (NIK, 2000). Initially, regulations were focused on financial and administrative issues and, at least in the beginning, avoided direct interference in the core of university performance (research and teaching). With the passage of time, the state however strengthened its steering role through the expanded scope of regulations aimed to make universities more accountable to taxpayers and through setting rules for fair competition (Kwiek, 2014). The major break came with the neoliberal amendments to the law of higher education (2010–2012) when the government attempted to take a dominant role in steering higher education. It separated so-called 'steering from rowing' by re-gaining a steering role and delegating a 'rowing role' to semi-independent funding agencies and intermediary bodies (research) and an accreditation agency (teaching). However, it also still kept a tight bureaucratic control over finance, staff and administrative issues, was little different from the situation prior to the political transformation. Public universities remained relatively closed to any form of external influence (mastering the use of academic freedom to block reforms), although there have been serious developments on the system level. The government implemented the 'steering at a distance' approach (Kickert, 1995), through the establishment of numerous agencies and advisory bodies. Responsibilities for quality assurance were delegated to the Polish Accreditation Committee, funding of basic research was passed on to NCN, funding of applied research to NCBiR. The role of this semi-autonomous organization is gradually increasing. The decentralization of power and *guidance by stakeholders* can be seen as one of the major developments in the model of higher education governance in Poland.

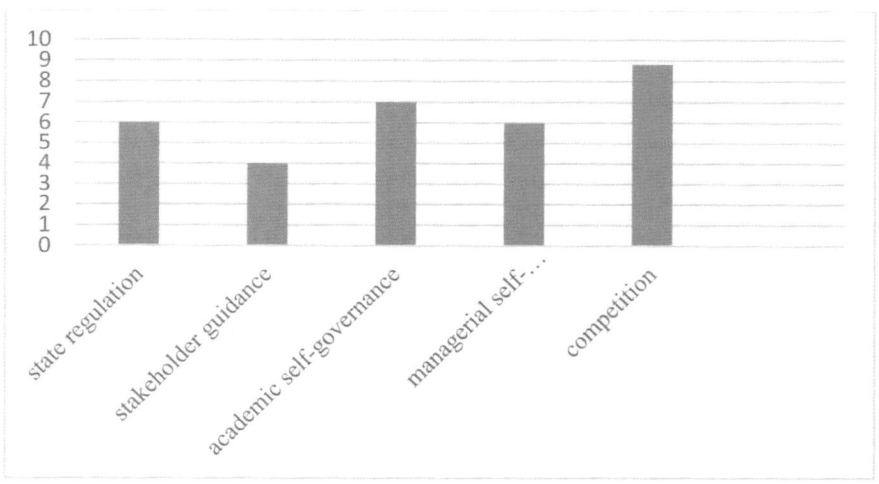

Figure 4.4. Governance equalizer: Poland in 2016

One of the most dynamic changes in higher education governance concerned *academic self-governance*. The fall of the communism in Poland was marked by a re-establishment of a self-governing, democratic mode of governance in public higher education (Scott, 2002). The state – bearing the heritage of a communist past – lost its moral legitimacy to govern higher education, so academic matters were handed over to the academic community, although with critically low resources to be allocated. The state developed 'policy-of-non policy' (Antonowicz, 2012) trying not to interfere in higher education and only keeping basic control over public funding through administrative procedures. The latter extended fundamentally as the state tried to respond to a growing expansion of private higher education by tightening a corset of bureaucratic regulations which – as reported (NIK 2000) – had little impact on a shrinking quality of teaching. But the break of 1989 brought massive empowerment of the academic community and gave a boost to unfettered autonomy (Dobbins, 2015). This lasted until 2010 when the government tried to regain its steering role in higher education. Since then, we can observe attempts to confine self-governance to both the institutional and system level by distributing power to other modes of governance.

The period between 1990 and 2015 can be characterized by a rise and then gradual fall in academic self-governance. Nevertheless Polish universities remain as one of few higher education institutions in Europe with such a broad scope of academic self-governance and an unbelievable strong notion of a university as a self-governing community of scholars (Kwiek, 2015).

Before we elaborate on the role of *university leadership,* one has to bear in mind that before 1989 they were primarily administrators, chosen from the academic community. While, undoubtedly, the role of rectors has changed and to some degree expanded, they still are elected by and accountable to their peers. Their institutional position has been increased and is nowadays stronger than before, but their managerial capacity is still confined by central regulations and collegial bodies. Deans also remain accountable to their peers on the faculty level and quasi-independent from rectors: factors which make governing Polish universities highly complex.

The most significant change concerns the empowerment of rectors on the national policy level. Their organization – Conference of Rectors of Academic Schools (KRASP) – had granted a legal monopoly (in 2005) to represent higher education institutions at the national policy level. This provides an important platform for rectors, in particular those from the most prestigious universities, to voice their interest and influence decision making in higher education.

Finally, one of the hallmarks of the transformation of higher education is the expansion of higher education and the rise of the private sector, which has opened gates to *competition* for resources (staff, students, funding and prestige). Since the early 1990s the role of competition has not only been increasing, but also its nature has been evolving from students' competition for study places to institutional competition for students due to demographic change. In addition, competition has been encouraged by changing the mechanism of resource allocation in research through funding agencies (NCN and NCBiR) as well as by the introduction of institutional research evaluation (KEJN). The research funding for both institutions and individuals is increasingly allocated through competitive mechanisms.

Ukraine

From the Soviet model, the Ukrainian system of higher education and science inherited the division between the primary teaching-oriented higher education institutions and research institutions of the academy of science that persisted after 1991 without teaching obligations (Oleksieynko, 2014; Hladchenko, de Boer, & Westerheijden, 2016; Hladchenko, 2016). After 1991, *state regulation* (Figure 4.5) in Ukrainian higher education has remained rather strong, but in comparison with Soviet times, it has been weakened through the development of the private higher education sector (Parliament of Ukraine, 1991). Licensing, accreditation and awarding of scientific degrees and titles remained among the responsibilities of the state authorities. In 2014, after the Revolution of Dignity (Oleksiyenko, 2016), the ministry of education intended to deregulate higher education steering, hence strengthen university autonomy and delegate a significant part of its responsibilities through establishment of the National Agency of Quality Assurance of Higher Education (NAQAHE) (Parliament of Ukraine, 2015). However, the problems started during the elections of the members of NAQAHE. The representatives from the academies of sciences and Federation of Employees were not elected but appointed by these organizations. Two former officials of the education ministry that were lustrated in 2015 were elected by the rectors of public higher education institutions (Ministry of Education and Sciences of Ukraine, 2015). Further, two representatives of the higher education institutions, were accused of plagiarism (Blahodeteleva-Vovk, 2016). In September 2016, the two lustrated official of the education ministry were substituted by other individuals. However, a further problem arose when these newly elected members of NAQAHE were accused of plagiarism as well (Kvit, 2016). Under all these conditions, the question remains what changes this institution can bring into Ukrainian system of higher education. The establishment of NAHEQA turned into means-ends decoupling, as in the Ukrainian case the institution that should be viewed as a means for the enhancement of the quality of higher education became a goal in itself.

As regards other initiatives aimed to weaken state regulation, the legislation adopted after the Revolution of Dignity declared the strengthening of the financial autonomy of the higher education institutions, a clear indication of the intention to adapt higher education steering and to enhance the institutions' autonomy. In 2015, the government adopted the resolutions that allow higher education institutions to open accounts albeit only in state banks. Before these changes were introduced, the higher education institutions were required to transfer their income to the State Treasury and to follow strict Treasury rules in spending the budget. However, despite the changes in the regulation, the process of opening bank accounts has remained rather complicated and bureaucratic because of the high degree of intrusion of the governmental authorities into this process (Cabinet of Ministers of Ukraine 2015). So, decouplong is caught between the goals declared by the government and means for their achievement. Moreover, public higher education institutions are still restricted in allocating their income. In particular, income from tuition fees can only be spent conditionally: either on salaries to academics or improvement of teaching conditions (but for example not on the establishment of the infrastructure of the science park).

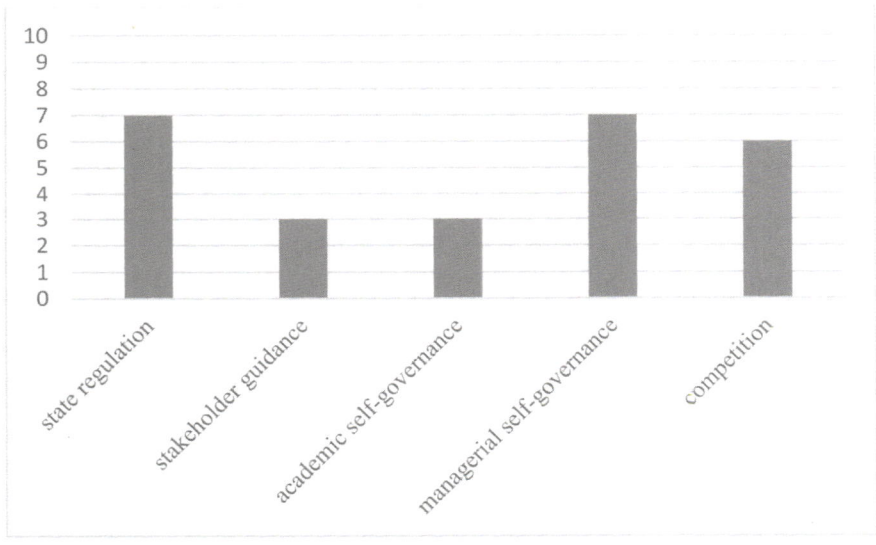

Figure 4.5. Governance equalizer: Ukraine in 2015

As mentioned above, in Soviet times rectors performed primarily administrative functions. In the post-Soviet period rectors managed to strengthen their position, turning from rather passive administrators into active managers in an organizational structure that, inherited from the Soviet model, remained highly hierarchical. The rector is responsible for the development of educational activities, financial management and recruitment of staff and the like. It is compulsory for the rector to have the scientific degree and title. Furthermore, the rector approves the members of an Academic Council. The Academic Council that comprises top- and middle-level managers of the university (vice-rectors and deans), elected members (academics) and student representatives can be regarded as a managerial collegial organ and performs an advisory function (Parliament of Ukraine, 2014). It s the responsibility of the Academic Council to select the deans and heads of the departments who must be then appointed by the rector.

Since 2014, the law prescribes that the same person cannot be in the position of rector for more than two terms (one term is five years). Before 2014, there were no such restrictions, meaning that in some cases rectors had been leading the institution for thirty years (Stadnyi, 2013). Another change concerns the position of the rector vis-a-vis the Academic Council. Prior to 2014, only a rector could be the head of the Academic Council. After 2014 the head of the Academic Council can be elected from members of the Academic Council (Parliament of Ukraine, 2014). For the moment, this turns out to be a change on paper only. In reality, the rector continues to be the head of the Academic Council. Further, according to the legislation, decisions of the Academic Council come into force only if they are based on the rectors' decision.

In order to make management processes of higher education more transparent, since 2014 the rectors have to publish annual reports on the official web site of their higher education institutions. The requirements concerning the content of the report however are not clearly defined.

The Humboldtian tradition was never strong in Ukrainian higher education. After 1991, *academic self-governance* was mainly established through the Conference of Employees, a supreme collegial organ of public self-governance (Cabinet of Ministers of Ukraine, 1996). Academics comprise at least 75 per cent and representatives of the student body at least 15 per cent of the total number of seats of the Conference of Employees (Parliament of Ukraine, 2014). Moreover, the top and middle managers of the university are among the members of the Conference of Employees. The Conference of Employees is chaired by the head of the trade union of a higher education institution. Meanwhile, Ukrainian trade unions can be viewed as the heritage of the Soviet period. They neither are independent from the authorities nor empower their members (Kubicek, 2002). The head of the trade union of the higher education institution looks like an administrative position subordinate to the rector. On behalf of the Conference of Employees, the head of the trade union signs a collective agreement between the employees and the rector of the higher education institution. Before 2014 it was the responsibility of the Conference of Employees to elect the rector, after 2014 academics and students obtained the right to directly participate in the elections of a rector. Nevertheless, academic self-governance remains rather weak and under-developed, because of the decoupling between goals declared in public policy and the means for their achievement.

After 1991, as regards *stakeholder guidance* Supervisory Boards were established in the national universities. The Supervisory Board is expected to perform advisory functions and to execute public control. The state authority appoints the members of the Supervisory Board. Since 2014, it has become compulsory for all higher education institutions to have a Supervisory Board, which consists of the members, external to the institution. However, the influence of these boards on higher education institutions is mainly nominal.

In terms of de-coupling, the establishment of the boards became the goal in itself, and relationships with industry and business remain underdeveloped. The Board of Employees, established at universities since 1991, has heralded the emergence of private higher education institutions and the possibility for public higher education institutions to charge a tuition fee for up to 49% of the admitted students (Parliament of Ukraine, 2002) which has led to an increase in *competition*. In the following years, competition has further increased, not only because of the increased number of higher education institutions (from 146 in 1988 to 353 in 2009, but also because of the constant increase in the number of Ukrainian students that prefer to study abroad (Stadnyi, 2015). The explanation of this tendency is the political and economic crisis in the country. Moreover, the Ukrainian state inherited the funding model from Soviet times. The amount of the funding that the state allocates to the higher education institution depends on the number of whose specialists, training the state orders from the higher education institution. As this approach from the Soviet period was developed in a context of a centrally planned economy, its efficiency is rather dubious under the conditions of a market economy (Oleksiyenko, 2016; Nikolaiev & Dluhopolskyi, 2016). Meanwhile, in 2016 the competition among the higher education institutions increased as because of the allocation of a share of the state funding on the basis of the 'money follows the student' approach (Stadnyi, 2016). Furthermore, in contrast to Poland, in Ukraine the mechanism of competitive allocation of the research funding remains underdeveloped.

DISCUSSION AND CONCLUSIONS

Because of the communist past, in both countries the governance of higher education before 1990 was radically different from what NPM advocates have in mind, except for the rather marginalized role of academics. Under the Soviet regime, most dimensions of the governance equalizer were largely the same in both countries. Some differences in the governance of higher education in Poland and Ukraine before 1990 however have left their imprint on the governance of the two higher education systems today. The Humboldtian tradition and correspondingly academic self-governance was more institutionalized in Poland than in Ukraine. This was not just due to having a different history in higher education governance, but also because of a much stronger influence of the communist ideology in Ukraine compared to Poland. As the result of that, state regulation was (even) stronger in Ukrainian than in Polish higher education, although in Poland state control was severe.

After 1990, we trace changes in all five governance dimensions in both countries, and the changes point in the same directions: (a) less, but still significant state regulation, (b) more stakeholder guidance, (c) more academic self-governance, (d) much more managerial self-governance, and (e) increased levels of competition. In both countries, higher education governance clearly has undergone serious changes in the last 25 years.

We also observe that, with the exception of academic self-governance in Poland, the new governance configurations in the two countries have come closer to what we labeled as the NPM-benchmark. Less state regulation, more stakeholder guidance, stronger managerial self-governance and increased competition match with the

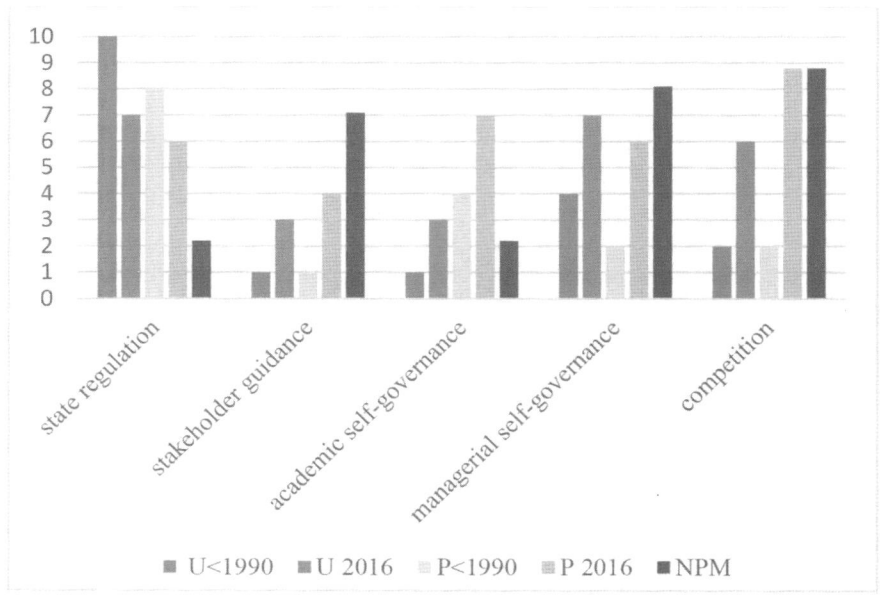

Figure 4.6. Governance equalizer: Ukraine and Poland across time, benchmarked against New Public Management

NPM-ideal. However, perhaps with the exception of managerial self-governance and competition, we cannot speak of higher education systems that are fully governed in a NPM-mode. State regulation remains substantial, stakeholder guidance is limited and academic self-governance, particularly in Poland, is clearly present.

However, managerial self-governance and competition come close to the NPM ideal, which can be seen as a remarkable change in a short period. In both cases academic self-governance has changed as well, to a moderate extent, but in Poland not in the NPM direction. Stakeholder guidance has not reached the NPM level, neither in Poland nor in Ukraine, partially because of the influence of their historical pasts: a strong Humboldtian tradition in Poland while absence of a knowledge-based economy in Ukraine.

It is also clear that, apart from the similarities, the two countries took two different paths. From 1990 to 2016 changes are more intense in Poland than in Ukraine and more in line with NPM (Figure 4.6). Both competition and academic self-governance is stronger in Poland than in Ukraine – as it also was before 1990s. In Ukraine the state still preserves its power and constrains competition despite the gradual diminishing role of state regulation in both countries

The influence of Soviet ideology was stronger in Ukraine than in Poland and this distinction has affected the choices of the actors made during the critical juncture of the 1990s. Having conducted lustration and de-communization and shock reforms, Poland managed to stop the continuity of the communist institutions and actors. The multiplicity of strong European links in Poland have been key drivers for the spread of entrepreneurial modes of higher education governance (Antonowicz, 2015). In this respect, Poland has been more advanced and equipped in implementing the principles of NPM than Ukraine. As for Ukraine, the underdeveloped civil society and the rise of the oligarchy are inconsistent with the global model of NPM. In the Ukrainian case, even after 2014 the majority of public policies are featured by means-ends decoupling what hinders the institutionalization of NPM. The high degree of means-ends decoupling occurs because the nation-state, the same as higher education institutions, are driven by the self-interests of the powerful actors. The more the nation-state aligns with the global models of world society the closer the governance of higher education to the patterns prescribed by NPM.

ACKNOWLEDGEMENTS

Dominik Antonowicz gratefully acknowledges the support of the National Research Council (NCN) through its research grant (UMO-2013/10/M/HS5/00561).

NOTES

[1] Before its members were appointed by the minister.
[2] After the students' protests at universities in 1968 the government decided to stripped the academic community from the right to elect rectors and deans and restored in the early 1980s.

REFERENCES

Antonowicz, D. (2012). External influences and local responses: Changes in polish higher education 1990–2005. In P. Maassen & M. Kwiek (Eds.), *National higher education reforms in a European context: Comparative reflections on Poland and Norway*. Frankfurt am Main: Peter Lang.

Antonowicz, D. (2015). *Między siłą globalnych procesów a lokalną tradycją: Polskie szkolnictwo wyższe w dobie przemian*. Toruń: Wydawnictwo Naukowe Uniwersytetu Mikołaja Kopernika.

Antonowicz, D., & Simonová, N. (2006). Czech and polish higher education–from bureaucracy to market competition. *Sociologický \vcasopis/Czech Sociological Review, 3*, 517–53.

Antonowicz, D., Pinheiro, R., & Smużewska, M. (2014). The changing role of students' representation in Poland: An historical appraisal. *Studies in Higher Education, 39*(3), 470–48.

Białecki, I., & Dąbrowa-Szefler, M. (2009). Polish higher education in transition: Between policy making and autonomy. In D. Palfreyman & T. Tapper (Eds.), *Structuring mass higher education: The role of elite institution*. New York, NY: Routledge.

Blahodeteleva-Vovk, S. (2016). *Plagiarism as a feature of social degradction*. Retrieved from http://gazeta.dt.ua/science/plagiat-yak-oznaka-suspilnoyi-degradaciyi-_.html

Boxenbaum, E., & Jonsson, S. (2008). Isomorphism, diffusion and decoupling. In R. Greenwood, C. Oliver, K. Sahlin, & R. Suddaby (Eds.), *The SAGE handbook of organizational institutionalism*. London, UK: Sage.

Bromley, P., & Powell, W. (2012). From smoke and mirrors to walking the talk: Decoupling in the contemporary world. *The Academy of Management Annals, 6*(1), 483–530.

Bunina, L. (2013). The history of higher education in Ukraine. *Naukovuy Visnyk Donbasu, 3*. Retrieved from http://nbuv.gov.ua/j-pdf/nvd_2013_3_2.pdf

Cabinet of Ministers of Ukraine. (2015). *Resolution on issues of income of state higher education institutions, research institutions and art institutions.* Retrieved from http://zakon0.rada.gov.ua/laws/show/719-2015-%D0%BF

Council of the Union of the Soviet Social Republics. (1969). *On higher education institutions of the union of the soviet social republics.* Retrieved from http://lawrussia.ru/texts/legal_346/doc346a990x441.htm

De Boer, H., & Goedegebuure, L. (2003). New rules of the game? Reflections on governance, management and system change. In J. File & L. Goedegebuure (Eds.), *Real time system-reflections on higher education in the Czech Republic, Hungary, Poland and Slovenia.* Enschede, the Netherlands: CHEPS.

De Boer, H., Enders, J., & Schimank, U. (2007). On the way towards new public management? The governance of university systems in England, the Netherlands, Austria, and Germany. In D. Jans (Ed.), *New forms of governance in research organizations.* the Netherlands: Springer .

De Boer, H., Jongbloed, B., Enders, J., & File, J. (2010). *Progress in higher education reform across Europe: Governance reform.* Enschede, the Netherlands: Center for Higher Education Policy Studies.

DiMaggio, P., & Powell, W. (1983). The iron cage revisited: Institutional isomorphism and collective rationality in organizational fields. *American Sociology Review, 48,* 147–160.

Dobbins, M. (2015). Exploring the governance of Polish public higher education: Balancing restored historical legacies with Europeanization and market pressures. *European Journal of Higher Education, 5*(1), 18–33.

Dobbins, M., & Knill, Ch. (2009). Higher education policies in central and Eastern Europe: Convergence towards a common model? *Governance, 22*(3), 397–430.

Duczmal, W. (2006). *The rise of private higher education in Poland: Policies, markets and strategies.* Enschede, the Netherlands: CHEPS/UT.

Gourevitch, P. (1986). *Politics in hard times.* Ithaca, NY: Cornell University Press.

Hay, C., & Wincott, D. (1998). Structure, agency and historical institutionalism. *Political Studies, 46*(5), 951–957.

DiMaggio, P., & Powell, W. (1983). The iron cage revisited: Institutional isomorphism and collective rationality in organizational fields. *American Sociology Review, 48,* 147–160.

Gomilko, O., Svyrydenko, D., & Terepyshchyi, S. (2016). Hybridity in the higher education of Ukraine: Global logic or local idiosyncrasy? *Philosophy & Cosmology, 17,* 177–199.

Grodal, S., & O'Mahony, S. (2015). *From field consensus to fragmentation: How means-ends decoupling hinders progress on grand challenges.* Retrieved from http://people.bu.edu/grodal/grand_challenge.pdf

Hood, C. (1991). A public management for all seasons? *Public administration, 69*(1), 3–19.

Hladchenko, M. (2016). The organizational identity of Ukrainian universities as claimed through their mission statements. *Tertiary Education and Management, 20*(4), 376–389.

Hladchenko, M., De Boer, H., & Westerheijden, D. (2016). Establishing research universities in Ukrainian higher education: The incomplete journey of a structural reform. *Journal of Higher Education Policy Management, 38*(2), 111–125.

Hübner, P. (1992). Tworzenie ustaw o nauce w latach 1989–1991. *Nauka Polska – Jej Potrzeby, Organizacja I Rozwój* (I/XXVI), 123–153.

Kehm, B. & Lanzendorf, U. (2006). *Reforming university governance: Changing conditions for research in four European countries.* Lemmens.

Kickert, W. (1995). Steering at a distance: A new paradigm of public governance in dutch higher education. *Governance, 8*(1), 135–157.

Kovriga, A. (2001). Urban engagement and local government as new institutions in the new Ukraine. *International Journal of Public Administration, 24*(2), 163–178.

Krasner, D. (1988). Sovereignty: An institutional perspective. *Comparative Political Studies, 21*(1), 66–94.

Kubicek, P. (2002). Civil society, trade unions and post-Soviet democratization: Evidence from Russia and Ukraine. *Europe-Asia Studies, 54*(4), 603–624.

Kvit, S. (2016). *NAQAHE: Expectations and reality.* Retrieved from http://osvita.ua/vnz/52277/

Kwiek, M. (2009). The two decades of privatization in Polish higher education: Cost-sharing, equity, and access. In J. Knight (Eds.), *Financing access and equity in higher education.* Rotterdam/Boston/Taipei: Sense Publishers.

Kwiek, M. (2012). The public/private dynamics in Polish higher education: Demand-absorbing private sector growth and its impilcations. In K. Marek & M. Peter (Eds.), *National higher education reforms in a European context: Comparative reflections on Poland and Norway.* Frankfurt am Main: Peter Lang.

Kwiek, M. (2014). Structural changes in the Polish higher education system (1990–2010): A synthetic view. *European Journal of Higher Education, 4*(3), 266–280.

Kwiek, M. (2015). The unfading power of collegiality? University governance in Poland in a European comparative and quantitative perspective. *International Journal of Educational Development, 43,* 77–89.

Langer, A. (2008). *Big-bang versus gradualism? Towards a framework for understanding institutional change in central and Eastern Europe.* Retrieved from https://www.wiso uni-freiburg.de/dateien/tagungen/reformen/alexander_lenger_big-bang_versus_gradualism.pdf

Mahoney, J. (2000). Path dependence in historical sociology. *Theory and society, 29*(4), 507–548.

Marchak, D. (2016). *With many nulls.* Retrieved from https://birdinflight.com/ru/spets/25/oligopoly/20160824-rise-of-ukrainian-oligarchy.html

Meyer, J. (1999). The changing cultural content of the nation-state: A world society perspective. In G. Steinmetz (Eds.), S*tate/culture: State-formation after the cultural turn.* Ithaca & London: Cornell University Press.

Meyer, J. (2000) Globalization: Sources and effects on national states and societies. *International Sociology, 15*(2), 233–248.

Meyer, J. (2010). World society, institutional theories, and the actor. *Annual Review of Sociology, 36,* 1–20.

Meyer, J., Kamens, D., & Benavot, A., Cha, Y.-K., & Wong, S.-Y. (1992). *School knowledge for the masses: World models and national primary curricular categories in the twentieth century.* London: Falmer Press.

Meyer, J., Boli, J., Thomas, G., & Ramirez, F. (1997). World society and the nation-state. *American Journal of Sociology, 103*(1), 144–181.

Ministry of Education and Sciences of Ukraine. (2015). *Announcement of the ministry of education and sciences of ukraine about elections to the national quality assurance agency.* Retrieved from http://mon.gov.ua/usi-novivni/novini/2015/06/08/zayava-ministerstva-osviti-i-nauki-ukrayiri-z/

Nichols, Ph. (1998). Forgotten linkages – historical institutionalism and sociological institutionalism and analysis of the world trade organization symposium on linkage as phenomenon: An interdisciplinary approach. *University of Pennsylvania Journal of International Law, 19*(2), 461–511.

Nikolaiev, Y., & Dluhopolskyi, O. (2016) Reform of higher education of Ukraine: Implementation of the profile law in 2014–2016. Retrieved from http://www.skeptic.in.ua/wp-content/uploads/HE-shadow-report.pdf

Oleksiyenko, A. (2014). Socio-economic forces and the rise of the world-class research university in the post-soviet higher education space: The case of Ukraine. *European Journal of Higher Education, 4*(3), 249–265.

Oleksiyenko, A. (2016). Higher education reforms and center-periphery dilemmas: Ukrainian universities between neo-Soviet and neo-liberal contestations. In J. Zajda & V. Rust (Eds.), *Globalisation and higher education reforms* (pp. 133–148). Springer International Publishing.

Paradeise, C., Reale, E., Bleiklie, I., & Ferlie, E. (2009). *University governance.* the Netherlands: Springer .

Parliament of Ukraine. (2002). *Law on higher education.* Retrieved from http://zakon5.rada.gov ua/laws/show/2984-14

Parliament of Ukraine. (2014). *Law on Higher Education.* Retrieved from http://zakon5.rada.gov.ua/laws/show/1556-18

Parliament of Ukrainian SSR. (1974). *Law of Ukrainian soviet social republic on public education.* Retrieved from http: //search.ligazakon.ua/l_doc2.nsf/link1/T742778.html

Pierson, P. (2000). Increasing returns, path dependence and the study of politics. *American Political Science Review, 94*(2), 251–267.

Pollitt, C. (1990). *Managerialism and the public services: The Anglo-American experience.* Cambridge, MA : Basil Blackwell.

Polonska-Vasylenko, N. (1955). *The Ukrainian academy of sciences.* Part I. München

Powell, W., & DiMaggio, P. (1991). *The new institutionalism in organizational analysis.* Chicago: University of Chicago Press.

Ramirez, F., & Rubinson, R. (1979). Creating members: The political incorporation and expansion of public education. In J. Meyer & M. Hannan (Eds.), *National development and the world system.* Chicago: University of Chicago Press.

Sadlak, J. (1995). In search of the 'post-communist' university – the background and scenario of the transformation of higher education in Central and Eastern Europe. In K. Hufner (Eds.), *Higher education reform processes in central and eastern Europe.* Peter Lang: Frankfurt am Main.

Stadnyi, Ye. (2013). *Why do the rectors support the law of the deputies from the party of regions.* Retrieved from http://osvita.ua/vnz/reform/35036/

Stadnyi, Ye. (2015). *Ukrainian students in foreign higher education institutions.* Retrieved from http://www.cedos.org.ua/uk/osvita/kilkist-studentiv-ukraintsiv-za-kordonom

Stadnyi, Ye. (2016). Conceptual model of the state funding of the higher education institutions according to their performance. Retrieved from https://www.cedos.org.ua/uk/osvita/kontseptualna-model-derzhavnoho-finansuvannia-vnz-za-rezultatamy-diialnosti

Steinmo, S., & Thelen, K. (1992). *Structuring politics: Historical institutionalism in comparative analysis.* Cambridge University Press.

Szłapczyński, K. (1968). *Zarząd szkołą wyższą w Polsce Ludowej.* Warszawa: PWN.

van Kersbergen, K., & Waarden, F. (2004). Governance as a bridge between disciplines: Crossdisciplinary inspiration regarding shifts in governance and problems of governability, accountability and legitimacy. *European journal of political research, 43*(2), 143–171.

Waltoś, S. (2009). Korzenie współczesnego szkolnictwa wyższego – ściezki tradycji. In *Szkolnictwo wyższe w Polsce. Ustrój -Prawo – Organizacja,.* Rzeszów: Wydawnictwo WSIiZ.

Wijen, F. (2014). Means versus ends in opaque institutional fields: Trading off compliance and achievement in sustainability standard adoption. *Academy of Management Review, 39*(3), 302–323.

Zgaga, P., Klemenčič, M., Komljenovič, J., Miklavič, K., Repac, I., & Jakačić, V. (2013). *Higher education in the western Balkans: Reforms, developments, trend: [key findings from field research].* Ljubljana: Faculty of Education, Centre for Educational Policy Studies.

Myroslava Hladchenko
Center for Higher Education Policy Studies
University of Twente
and
Faculty of Humanities and Pedagogy
National University of Life and Environmental Sciences of Ukraine

Dominik Antonowicz
Institute of Sociology
Nicolaus Copernicus University in Toruń

Harry de Boer
Center for Higher Education Policy Studies
University of Twente

SINA WESTA

5. WHAT DOES ACADEMIC FREEDOM MEAN FOR ACADEMICS?

A Case Study of the University of Bologna and the National University of Singapore

INTRODUCTION

The aspiration towards academic freedom is not new for the academic community. From the Middle Ages on, universities struggled against the influence of local communities to pursue teaching and learning for the sake of knowledge (Zonta, 2002). At that time they were backed up by the two strongest powers, the Pope and the Emperor. These central authorities understood universities as institutions capable of securing the ideological support and the intellectual framework to maintain the unity of the Christian world and the Holy Roman Empire. In turn they gave universities the privilege of experiencing academic freedom and university autonomy with respect to the local authorities (Rüegg, 2002). Even so, universities were protected by the Pope and the Emperor to guard a certain ideology their history was also a story of emancipation from the Church (Zonta, 2002). The struggle for academic freedom continued throughout the history of universities and today academic freedom is still a major concern in many countries.

This freedom is considered especially important as the introduction of new management regimes reshaped the understanding of university autonomy. Such autonomy under new public management regimes is not anymore a right of the academic community as a self-governing body but has been turned into a right for university managers (Erikkilä & Piironen, 2014). Whereas university autonomy was traditionally perceived as condition for academic freedom (Anderson & Johnson, 1998), many scholars argue today that it might even endanger academic freedom (Zgaga et al., 2015; Erikkilä & Piironen, 2014; Zgaga, 2012).

There is still no coherent definition of academic freedom and the concept is understood differently in different countries. In Denmark, for example, academic freedom only covers freedom in research and not in teaching (Danish Government, 2011). Slovenia focuses on the term university autonomy which emphasises collegial self-governance but includes the freedom in teaching and learning as well as in research in its Higher Education Act (Legislative and Legal Service, 2013). In the United States academic freedom is closely linked to tenure after a certain probation period (AAUP, 1970[1925]). These are just some examples, to illustrate the fact

R. Deem & H. Eggins (Eds.), The University as a Critical Institution?, 75–92.

that the understanding of academic freedom varies from context to context. The understanding and meaning also varies according to the individual situation of each person as academic freedom is a relational concept and dependent on time and place.

Despite these varied views on academic freedom, it is seen as having an important value and a condition for following truth, for securing "long term perspectives in favour of short-term fashions" (Hamilton, 2000, p. 212), for serving society as a whole and for the personal development of individuals (Rüegg, 2011). Academic freedom is a burning topic not only in Europe and the US but also in many other parts of the world. Zha (2012), for example, discusses the appropriateness of this value, rooted in the history of European universities, for higher education in China. Bruneau (2015) describes threats to academic freedom in Canada, and Yamamoto (2015) shows how academic freedom is present in Japanese policies.

Due to the plurality of definitions and understandings of academic freedom in scholarly discussions as well as policies, this chapter aims at depicting contemporary understandings and meanings of academic freedom from the perspective of academics in different cultural contexts. It also shows the extent to which policies frame the understanding of this complex concept. The ultimate goal of this chapter is to provide a framework that facilitates a more pluralistic and deeper discussion on the topic from a grass-roots perspective.

RESEARCH METHODOLOGY

In order to achieve the aim of depicting the meaning of academic freedom in a pluralistic way this chapter draws on two case studies from culturally different places, namely the University of Bologna (Italy) and the National University of Singapore (Singapore).

The University of Bologna as one of the oldest universities founded in 1088 is a good example of exploring what academic freedom means in the European context as it is strongly linked to academic values. It even initiated the drafting of the Magna Charta Universitatum, one of the first strategic papers that engages with academic values and especially with academic freedom (Magna Charter Observatory, 2016[1988]). Moreover, Italy was one of the countries which signed up to the adoption of the Bologna Process (Moscati, 2009; Luzzato & Moscati, 2007) and hence can be seen as a good example for a 'European University System' in a contemporary sense.

As academic freedom is often assumed to be a European value due to its roots in the history of European universities it seems worthwhile to consider its meaning also in a non-European context. In contrast to the European view on academic freedom the National University of Singapore serves as a good second case. It is a rather new university founded in 1905 as a medical school in Malaysia during its colonial time under Britain. In the course of its history the medical school transformed into the University of Malaya which was renamed in University of Singapore in 1962 with the independence of Singapore. In 1980, the university was re-established under the name National University of Singapore (NUS) as a result of merging the University of Singapore and the Nanyang University (NUS, 2016a). The idea to merge these two universities derived from the perceived need of the Singaporean government to have a single strong national university in the country (Mukherjee & Wong, 2011; Kim, 2001). Thus, NUS has its roots within the British higher education system but transformed itself towards the Confucian higher education zone under the People's Action Party which involves a strong emphasis on state control and the aim of world-leadership (Marginson, 2011). In other words, Singapore's higher education is influenced by the European idea of the university but it developed in a different direction after independence. NUS also hosted the Association of Pacific-Rim Universities during the period in which this study was conducted. Hence, it can be seen as a place that is concerned with, and involved in, university developments in this region.

To gain a deeper insight into the meaning of academic freedom in both countries, this chapter considers national polices and recent reforms that frame higher education in each country. Furthermore, it evaluates how the national policies are reflected at an institutional level depicted by mission and vision statements, strategic plans of the universities and the university websites. The national and institutional documents serve as the context in which academics experience academic freedom at an individual level. Special emphasis is given to the individual perspective of academics on academic freedom at the micro level as individual experiences of academic freedom are rarely researched in a qualitative way. Focusing on academics' individual experiences of academic freedom and their understanding of the concept makes it possible to depict diverse meanings of academic freedom that are related to the daily work of academics.

In order to gain an insight into these diverse meanings of academic freedom from different perspectives this study draws on semi-structured, in depth interviews with 11 academics from the University of Bologna and 7 from the National University of Singapore (see Tables 5.1 and 5.2 for more details) which were conducted in the wider framework of my PhD thesis and the UNIKE (Universities in the Knowledge Economy) project. Each interview lasted for around one hour and covered topics related to academic freedom, teaching and research as well as to the personnel career and history of the participants. This chapter focuses on the parts of the interviews that are directly related to the understanding of academic freedom and hence covers only a part of the full interviews.

As the main aim of this study is to gain a diverse insight into academic freedom the sample of participants includes academics from different disciplines, at different career stages and includes both genders. This is important as these factors might influence the view on academic freedom and hence including these different groups in the interviews makes it more likely that different versions of academic freedom will be put forward. In other words, the object of this research lies on capturing diversity instead of a narrowly-focussed opinion.

Thematic analysis is used to analyse the interviews and documents as it offers the possibility to identify patterns in the data and hence to remain open for new emerging aspects that might be connected to academic freedom (Braun & Clark, 2006). This is an effective way of opening up new emerging themes in the data and hence providing a framework for discovering the diversity of meanings of academic freedom.

Table 5.1. Interview participants national university of Singapore

Participant code	Gender	Discipline	Position
S 1	Male	Natural Science	Adjunct Lecturer
S 2	Male	Medicine	Professor, leadership position
S 3	Male	Humanities	Professor; leadership position
S 4	Female	Arts and Social Science	Professor, leadership position
S 5	Male	Arts and Social Science	Professor
S 6	Male	Engineering	Lecturer
S 7	Female	Medicine	Lecturer

Table 5.2. Interview participants university of Bologna

Participant code	Gender	Discipline	Position
I 1	Male	Statistics	Full professor; leadership position
I 2	Male	Medicine	Researcher
I 3	Female	Law	Full professor; leadership position
I 4	Female	Law	Junior Researcher
I 5	Male	Astronomy	Full professor; leadership position
I 6	Female	Bio-Technology	Full professor; leadership position
I 7	Male	Statistics	Full professor
I 8	Male	Mathematics	Full professor; leadership position
I 9	Male	Sociology	Researcher
I 10	Female	Political Science	Full professor
I 11	Male	Psychology	Full professor

THE CONTEXT: ACADEMIC FREEDOM IN ITALY AND SINGAPORE

Academic Freedom Is Not Only a Constitutional Right in Italy

Academic Freedom in Italy is first of all a constitutional right. Article 3 of the Italian constitution guarantees universities the "freedom of art and science and the teaching thereof" and states that "[h]igher education institutions, universities and academics, have the right to establish their own regulations within the limits laid down by the law" (Senato della Repubblica, 1948). Hence, the constitution gives universities the autonomy to make their own regulations and gives individual teachers the freedom to engage in research and teaching. Despite, this theoretical right of academic freedom and university autonomy that is laid down in the constitution, Italy only adopted university autonomy in practice after the 1990s. Before this time the Italian University system was, in reality, highly centralised and based on a strong bureaucracy (Moscati, 2009; Luzzato & Moscati, 2007).

Despite the discrepancies between policy and practice it is still important to consider the legal regulations when thinking about academic freedom as they define the context in which universities exist. Hence, at this point, a closer look will be taken at the most recent higher education reforms in Italy. As the most recent higher education laws have not yet been translated into English, academic literature that evaluates the reforms will be quoted instead of analysing the policy texts themselves.

A new comprehensive reform (Law 240/2010, or 'Gelmini Reform') was implemented in Italy in 2010. This reform changed the whole institutional governance structures and the internal organisation of Italian universities (Donina, Meoli, & Palerari, 2015). Officially the Riforma Gelmini aimed at increasing university autonomy which includes more direct responsibility for finances, teaching and research. Despite this official aim the reform had several other characteristics that influence Italian higher education. These include serious funding cuts, the reduction in the number of university staff who could be re-appointed and the possibility of privatizing institutions (Donina, Meoli, & Palerari, 2015; Moscati, 2012).

With regard to the internal structure of universities, the reform meant in practice the reduction of the number of faculties to a maximum of twelve per university which led to the merging of smaller units into bigger faculties. This feature aimed at avoiding useless faculties that would not benefit the employment market. The appointment of young researchers was also an object of change; permanent contracts for emerging researchers would be replaced by short term contracts. Only after six years and two short term contracts is there now the possibility of obtaining a permanent position as associate professor. Despite this draw-back the reform aimed at increasing the salaries for young researchers to ease the entrance into an academic career (Donina, Meoli, & Palerari, 2015; Moscati, 2012).

In addition to these structural changes, the reform also changed the financing modalities of universities and the payment of academics. It introduced the concept that universities should be financed by the state depending on their ability to conform with high quality criteria. The idea of quality-dependent pay for academics was also part of the reform but never implemented (Donina, Meoli, & Palerari, 2015). The performance and quality measurements of universities that should have effects on the financial support include student opinions and student evaluations of professors. The national agency ANVUR, an independent juridical personality, was made responsible for the evaluation of higher education and research. Its judgement is based on the alliance with externally set guidelines (EHEA, 2007). Next to external quality assurance, a code of ethics should prevent conflicts concerning the appointment of new staff and within the administration. This code of ethic should be drafted by each university independently (DIH, 2014).

Overall, the Gelmini Reform suggests that universities now have more autonomy in financial and material terms. Nevertheless, they are less free in deciding on their internal structure and on the appointment of young academics. Moreover, universities are increasingly dependent on external evaluation which might also hinder academic freedom. Despite the first impression, many authors claim that the reform did not lead to more university autonomy and a reduction of academic freedom as professors still have a great amount of autonomy and freedom (Donina, Meoli, & Palerari, 2015; Ballarino & Perotti, 2012; Moscati, 2012). The decision making process at Italian universities is still largely based on internal consensus rather than on steering at a distance (Donina, Meoli, & Palerari, 2015). Hence, Italy provides a good framework for exercising academic freedom at least on a practical level.

Academic Freedom: Unknown Words in Singapore's Higher Education Policies

In contrast to the Italian situation, Singapore does not even know the words "academic freedom" or individual rights of academics in its official documents and policies including the Singapore Management University Act Chapter 302A (The Law Revision Commission, 2014), the Education Act Chapter 87 (The Law Revision Commission, 1987), and the National University of Singapore (Corporatisation) Act Chapter 204A (The Law Revision Commission, 2006). This is not obvious from the beginning on as Singapore's higher education was strongly tied to the British higher education systems due to its colonial past, the fact that at the beginning most academics and leaders were still educated in Britain and Singapore's aspiration to offer degrees that were recognised there (Kim, 2001). After independence, Singapore changed its higher education system from the British-American one that stands for a general liberal education for all towards the German-Swiss model that aims at a technical or vocational education for most students (ibid.).

With the aim of economic growth but a lack of resources, the People's Action Party understood that higher education, R&D and innovation were the only chance for economic success of the country (Wong, Ho, & Singh, 2007). Thus, reforms were put into place in order to nationally manage universities with the explanation that universities and academics "lack the will to tackle economic strategies" (Kim, 2001, p. 170). Today, Singapore can look back on a long history of informal bans of certain topics connected to religion, local corruption, governmental policies and politics (Mukherjhee & Wong, 2011; Altbach, 2001). These informal bans were exercised through penalties for raising sensitive issues in the classroom and the fact that funding often depends on "appropriate academic and political behaviour on the part of the faculty" (Altbach, 2001, p. 213). Thus, it will be of particular interest to see how academics working in Singapore experience their situation concerning academic freedom.

Nevertheless, the Constitution of the Republic of Singapore (The Law Revision Commission, 1999) includes a section called fundamental liberties that refer to the liberty of the person, the prohibition of slavery and forced labour, the protection against retrospective criminal laws and repeated trials, equal protection to the prohibition of banishment and freedom of movement, the freedom of speech, assembly and association, the freedom of religion, and rights in respect to education. Taking a closer look at the part of the constitution that is most relevant for academic freedom it becomes clear that the right of free speech, assembly and association only applies to citizens of Singapore and is restricted in many other ways. The Constitution states:

14. [...]

(a) every citizen of Singapore has the right to freedom of speech and expression;

(b) all citizens of Singapore have the right to assemble peaceably and without arms; and

(c) all citizens of Singapore have the right to form associations.

(2) Parliament may by law impose

[...] such restrictions as it considers necessary or expedient in the interest of the security of Singapore or any part thereof, friendly relations with other countries, public order or morality and restrictions designed to protect the privileges of Parliament or to provide against contempt of court, defamation or incitement to any offence; [...]. (The Law Revision Commission 1999:Art. 14)

In short, freedom of speech, assembly and association can be restricted for several reason which do not only include security matters but also matters of morality. The law clearly states that privileges of the parliament need to be protected in any case against these freedoms of Singaporean citizens.

The part of the Constitution that engages with rights in respect to education deals only with the aspect of non-discrimination of students and is not directly related to academic freedom as it states that

16.—(1) Without prejudice to the generality of Article 2, there shall be no discrimination against any citizen of Singapore on the grounds only of religion, race, descent or place of birth. (The Law Revision Commission, 1999:Art 16)

Overall, freedoms are part of the Singaporean Constitution but they are restricted not only for security reasons but also for public order and morality. Hence, it is a risk to apply these freedoms as the law includes a big area for manoeuvring and punishing free speech or the right for association and assembly. Compared to the Italian case it becomes evident that academic freedom is not as easy to implement in Singapore.

The policy background goes in line with Wong, Ho and Singh (2007) who emphasis that

[A]cademic faculty members are effectively state employees, and university administrators are usually government appointees, tasked to carry out government policies. As such, they tend to have much less autonomy than public universities in Europe, let alone the private universities in the United States (p. 942)

In other words, universities and academics in Singapore are mainly seen as supporters of the government and the success of the country.

Even if academic freedom is not part of any legislation in Singapore there is still one document applicable to Singapore that protects academic freedom in research and teaching as well as university autonomy. As Singapore has been a member state of UNESCO since 2007, it should be aligned to UNESCO's recommendation concerning the Status of Higher Education Teaching Personnel (1997). (Italy had already became a member of UNESCO in 1948.) This recommendation acknowledges academic freedom as it states

> that the right to education, teaching and research can only be fully enjoyed in an atmosphere of academic freedom and autonomy for institutions of higher education and that the open communication of findings, hypotheses and opinions lies at the very heart of higher education and provides the strongest guarantee of the accuracy and objectivity of scholarship and research. (UNESCO, 1997, p. 1)

Overall, freedoms of any kind are highly restricted in Singapore. Nevertheless, they exist and there is even a basis on which academics could claim academic freedom in Singapore. In the next part, I will take a closer look at the status of academic freedom on an institutional level at the University of Bologna and the National University of Singapore.

THE CONTEXT: ACADEMIC FREEDOM AT AN INSTITUTIONAL LEVEL

The University of Bologna

The main document from the University of Bologna that depicts the official mission, vision and values of the universities is the strategic plan for the years 2013–2015. This document reflects the struggle of the universities to balance their traditional values such as academic freedom and university autonomy with the demands of society and the government. The university describes itself as

> [P]roud of its heritage and its records; strong in its autonomy and the wealth of its knowledge; aware of its scientific and educational vocation and high social and moral responsibilities, the alma Mater aims to be a natural environment for the innovation of knowledge, the recognition of merit and the full education of its citizens. (Alma Mater Studiorium, 2013, p. 17)

Next to adapting to this traditional role the University of Bologna is aware of new challenges due to unstable times and the new Riforma Gelmini described in the previous section. Concerning the new reform the strategic plan depicts problems due to the

> continuing reduction of the grants from the national government [that] make[s] it impossible to ensure the quality levels and sustainability of research and teaching activities in the medium term. (ibid.:25)

Concerning the general situation in Italy the strategic plan expresses concerns about the local employment structure that is based on multiple small businesses that cannot afford to employ the qualified staff educated at the university (Luzzato & Moscati, 2007). Problems for the employment of university graduates are also based on economic crises and the suspension of recruitment in the public sector. Despite these challenges the University of Bologna is still attached to traditional values as it states that the university has to

> Strive in all institutional areas to affirm the principles of university autonomy in order to reduce the centralist and bureaucratic interventions limiting the potential of the research and teaching programmes planning; the Alma Mater is determined to define its strategies following its historical tradition as a wide-ranging University and in its distinctive multi-campus nature, but it is also aware that it must face a highly unstable situation. (ibid.:5)

Overall, the strategic plan of the University of Bologna that is based on the mission and vision of the university strongly promotes university autonomy. However it is also eager to adapt to challenges and to modernize itself for the benefit of students, academics and society.

Academic freedom itself is not mentioned in the whole document but there is an emphasis on the importance of the academic community that is described as a

> responsible community of students, teaching, administrative and technical staff, the Alma Mater working to ensure that everyone, and in particular young people, can grow by experiencing the uniqueness of culture with rigour and passion, in a multitude of disciplinary and scientific languages. (ibid.:17)

Another part of the document could be interpreted in form of academic freedom as it states that the university is

> an institution open to both internal and external dialogue, pursues its goals in conformity with the values of autonomy, respect for diversity and social responsibility. (ibid.:19)

Autonomy here could be interpreted as autonomy for the individual but it is not clear from the strategic plan if autonomy refers only to the institution or also to its individual members. Hence, the status of academic freedom is not clear taking the strategic plan as a measurement. Nevertheless, the university website includes a link to the Magna Charta Observatory and the hence the Magna Charta Universitatum which can be seen as a clear sign that the University of Bologna supports academic freedom.

The National University of Singapore

In the case of the National University of Singapore, the brochure "NUS at a Glance" 2016/2017 represents nicely how the university presents itself. The mission and vision of NUS are stated in very short words.

Vision

A leading global university centred in Asia, influencing the future

Mission

To transform the way people think and do things through education, research and service. (NUS, 2016a)

This statement already shows that the focus of the National University of Singapore is on world leadership and excellence in teaching, research and service. The brochure also describes how this aim is achieved and mentions in this respect the equipping of students with life skills and not only knowledge from textbooks, the employment of world leading professors, interdisciplinary and high level research, entrepreneurial education offers, partnerships with other leading universities and research organisations and global networks, artistic and cultural events and courses, and the community work that creates a value for society. This list provides a wide range of activities and promotes the idea that students can gain much more than just a higher education degree at this university.

In line with state regulations and laws of Singapore the whole document and other sources of the university such as the Status and Regulations of the National University of Singapore (2016b) do not mention academic freedom or rights of students and academic staff. Hence, academic freedom is neither a talked about issue in Singapore nor in the National University of Singapore.

Without having a real framework of academic freedom it will be even more interesting to depict what academics working in this environment think about academic freedom. Do they think that it is even worth considering a European value such as academic freedom and, if so, do they have it, and what does it mean for them? The next section will engage exactly with such questions and will depict how academic freedom is described by academics from the University of Bologna and the National University of Singapore.

ACADEMICS' PERSPECTIVE ON ACADEMIC FREEDOM

The analysis of the interviews with academics from the University of Bologna as well as from the National University of Singapore raised five major topics in relation to academic freedom. These five topics will be discussed in the following sections by answering the following questions: (1) What is academic freedom?; (2) Why is academic freedom important and, if not, why not?; (3) What are necessary restriction to academic freedom?; (4) Do you enjoy academic freedom?; and (5) What are the restrictions to academic freedom that you experience as problematic in your work and what do you really need to support your academic career?

As already shown above, academic freedom is not an easy concept to talk about in Singapore; hence the interviews from Italy provided much more detailed answers to questions one and two. On the other hand, participants from Singapore could much better describe their needs for advancing in their academic career and research.

This might be also connected to the focus on world class research and education within the National University of Singapore. In the next part some examples from the interviews will be given in order to answer the five questions posed. A more comprehensive picture of both cases will be given in the conclusion.

What Is Academic Freedom?

In the interviews many academic were able to describe several aspects of academic freedom but there was also some confusion between the concept of academic freedom and universities autonomy. The former refers to the freedom of the individual, whereas the latter refers to the autonomy of the institution. The descriptions of academic freedom included the idea of teaching on the one hand and of research on the other hand. Nevertheless not all academics could think about issues of academic freedom in teaching.

Academic freedom in teaching and research is related to the freedom of expressing opposing ideas. This might be challenged by other academics due their perception that

> … there are schools of thought which are rather strict in promoting only their way of thinking and banning the opposite or even alternative ways of thinking … That can also interfere with the freedom of teaching. But it s more a freedom of interpreting, so I can see that publishing in journals … you can see these fights, which are fights against different interpretations and schools of people who made their career out of some particular interpretation . . (I7)

The freedom in research is described in much greater detail than freedom in teaching in the interviews and it includes aspects such as the freedom to choose one's own research topics and to independently judge which research is important:

> A researcher in my opinion should be granted to be free to work on subjects that he or she thinks are important. (I5)

> … academic freedom means … the freedom to do research and to have appropriate tools for it. It means that you can work in a team and decide on a topic that is important to advance your discipline. (S3)

Freedom for some academic also means the freedom from governing bodies:

> I would think that academic freedom is about freedom from the governing power. (I9)

As well as that

> … by academic freedom we understand that an academic just because of his position should be free to think and write and publish and produce the kind of knowledge he believes is important. (I2)

Overall, academics came up with various meanings of academic freedom that overlap, but not all academics think spontaneously about all these different aspects. Academic freedom in both cases referred to the freedom of expression, the freedom to choose own research topics and methods as well as to freedom in teaching within the university structures. One point that becomes clear when looking at descriptions of academic freedom is that there is not one prevalent definition of academic freedom within the academic community but that there is a feeling about the concept that is present not only for academics from the University of Bologna but also from the National University of Singapore.

Why Is Academic Freedom Important and, If Not, Why Not?

The academics who had a concrete idea about the meaning of academic freedom also had some suggestions why he thought that academic freedom is an important value in academia. One reason can be readily extracted from one of the descriptions of academic freedom. According to the statement that academic freedom should allow opposing ideas it is in turn important for having various research traditions and a diverse set of ideas on hand. Other academics state that academic freedom is necessary to

> ... develop the ideas that you find consisting and motivating. (I7)

> ... have some space to create in the in the world of ideas. (I10)

Academic freedom is also important to guarantee necessary time for thinking and research as one participant from Singapore points out.

> Sometimes you need a series of discoveries before it leads to something big; ... research is like that! You don't know where it is going to lead. (S2)

The idea that academics are professionals in their field and who know best how to proceed in research is also an explanation mentioned in favour of academic freedom.

> ... of course, you need some freedom because you know your field best and you talk to practitioners about their needs ... so you're responsible that your research has some impact, I mean not immediately but in the long-term. (S4)

Academic freedom is not only necessary for research but also for teaching.

> ... and so the faculty is free to innovate and use different kinds of pedagogy that would encourage discussion ... and sort of debate .... (S6)

Overall, academic freedom is perceived in both cases as an important aspect for academic work as it provides a framework in which research, innovation and high-level teaching can take place. Despite the different policy backgrounds academic freedom seems to be important for academics in both cases whereas a judgement about the necessary degree of freedom in academic work cannot be made based on the interview data from this study.

What Are Necessary Restrictions to Academic Freedom?

In addition to the fact that academics consider academic freedom to be important they also see the obligations that are connected to academic freedom. Hence, the freedom in designing and conducting teaching needs to be

> … integrated into an organised setting. (I10)

in order to guarantee well organised and harmonised study programmes for students. Furthermore, the issue of peer control was raised.

> … of course you need a sort of peer pressure, because I cannot say, okay, I am an astronomer, I have academic freedom and now I start to do astrology (I9).

Some academics even think that academia does not deserve academic freedom anymore as

> I think that if we were, we the academics today, were really challenged by society we couldn't resist the challenge and we should surrender a part of our academic freedom. (I9)

This participant strongly believes that most academics are not fulfilling their role and responsibility towards their students and society. Thus, he states that some academics are afraid that

> … they would lose a part of their freedom in the sense of … in the end of not doing their work, not freedom in the sense of being free to do their work, to conduct their work as they deem better. (I9)

The responsibility for society and students is emphasised by many academics and one participant form Singapore frames it like this.

> Having freedom does not mean to stop communicating with your environment … you need to be aware of their needs and you have to contribute to society … (S4)

Summarising, it can be stated that the interview participants saw a strong connection between academic freedom and a responsibility towards students and society. Nevertheless, there remains the view that not all academics embrace this responsibility.

Do You Enjoy Academic Freedom?

Overall, the academics I talked to in Italy thought that they have academic freedom in their work but some experienced the costs for the freedom to do things differently.

> If you don't ask for power then you have a very large autonomy you can do almost everything you want. Within the laws, of course, but you are very free to do anything you want. But then ... you don't have to ask for resources or funds or money or power within the organization et cetera. But ... if you are willing to leave all this aside you are really free in Italy. (I9)

Young academics especially claimed that the possibility of exercising academic freedom depends on their own experience.

> ... the amount of freedom that you have ... I think is directly ... linked ... to your experience. (I4)

This connection between freedom and experience was not seen as problematic but rather as a natural process of becoming an established researcher and teacher. Especially the freedom in research was considered to be granted but embedded in a funding game.

> You can select ... on the basis of your ... professional ... competence....the topic, or the research question that you feel is most important in your field at the moment. In this respect, you are free, of course ... if you ask for funding ... there are selection processes ... so you are free to apply for it [the funding] with your topic ... then of course you are compared with other topics ... so it might happen that your topic is considered to be less important than other topics, that's all part of the game. (I10)

Not only academics in Italy thought that they have freedom as also interviewees from Singapore identified areas in which they experienced a certain degree of freedom. One academic described for example the process of designing course programmes and stated that

> Obviously you have to follow the general structure ... but I do know that you have freedom to structure it and of course, someone has to approve it when you come up with a plan. (S1)

Another one mentioned that

> Faculty members are free to innovate, to use different pedagogies to encourage discussion, debates and so on ... (S4)

This is also related to the attitude of students that has changed during the last five to ten years in Singapore:

> And you should see these young students ... so they are fearless they now say whatever they want ... (S3)

The comparison between Singapore and other Asian countries also led to the conclusion that Singapore is not that restrictive and

> More than any other country probably Singapore has handled its ...
> authoritarianism better than most, so there are certain topics that are banned
> In particular you cannot say anything personal about ... but its lower than in
> China ... so the limitations are much more restricted. (S5)

Hence academics in both cultures experience freedom even though to a different
degree. It becomes clear from the interviews that Singapore is moving steadily in the
direction of more openness for criticism and some academic even state that

> ... at least I know exactly what I can talk and what I cannot talk about. (S5)

On the other hand, academics is Singapore are aware that

> The government has scared a lot of people out but it's by no means heading to
> disaster. (S3)

*What Are the Restrictions to Academic Freedom That You Experience as Problematic
in Your Work and What Do You Really Need to Support Your Academic Career?*

The problem of funding has already been mentioned in the previous parts and in
fact funding is an issue for academics. In this respect academics from Singapore see
themselves in a very good position as they have a very supportive environment in
this respect.

> ... so I have been in the right place at the right time because in Europe and in
> the US funding has been cut so badly that now even if you have a very good
> grant proposal it is almost impossible to get the money ... and that meant that
> you could do so much more [here] because without the money you cannot do
> anything ... even if [you have] got great ideas. I have been given everything
> that I needed because in the US you would be much more stressed to produce
> more ... and you know in Europe finding research funding is very tough. (S2)

This participant mentions in this quote the problem of publication stress and the
European focus on the production of publications which is also reflected in interviews
with academics from the University of Bologna.

> ... exceptional weight that is now put on the number of papers that you write,
> how many students you have. Of course some check is useful but you cannot
> classify people just saying one of you published ten papers the other published
> nine papers ... (I5)

This participant continued by explaining that bigger research collaborations can
easily produce hundreds of papers but that more theoretical focused individuals
cannot do so. This lies in the nature of the research they are doing, for example, a
theoretical researcher needs fewer resources but more time than a more practical
orientated researcher. According to some interviewees this has also effects on the

research areas that are chosen by young researchers because they have to publish in order to get promoted. Therefore, they usually tend to choose more practical topics and the theoretical and basic research is in danger of not getting new talents. Overall, this point is again connected to funding as the problem does not only lie in the act of counting publications but on making a choice against less productive academics.

CONCLUSION

This chapter showed that academic freedom is not equally adopted in all countries and that the degree of freedom varies according to the legal framework in which academics work. Nevertheless, even if academic freedom is not guaranteed as in the case of Singapore, academics still find some spaces where they can exercise freedom in their daily work. Academic freedom does not only vary between countries but also between the career stage of academics as the younger ones still have to learn and need to be fully integrated in the academic community in order to gain the same amount of freedom that their supervisors enjoy.

Academic freedom has two sides from the point of view of the interviewees in this study. On the one hand, it needs to be given to provide a productive and creative atmosphere. On the other hand, it needs to be based on a responsible attitude towards students and society. Hence, peer review and competition for funding are considered valuable to secure the integrity of academics. Despite, the idea that academic freedom and social responsibility are two sides of the same coin not all academics perceived this as having been adopted in the whole academic body.

The definition of academic freedom and its perception have been shown to vary between different persons. This also depends on the point of reference in which academics compare their own situation with others.

Overall, money was seen as a significant aspect of successful research. Hence academics from Singapore thought that they have many benefits working in their country due to generous funding. Most of them did not want to work anywhere else. In other words, academic freedom is not the only and most important issue when it comes to high quality research. Due to a good infra-structure and generous funding the National University of Singapore manages to employ leading researchers and provides an atmosphere in which academics feel that they are in a good place. In which way academic freedom and funding are weighted is probably highly dependent on the research topic and own preferences. Nevertheless, a certain degree of freedom seems to be important for academics in both contexts in order to fulfil their duty as academics.

Overall, this study gave an insight into the ideas, experiences and significance of academic freedom in two culturally different contexts. Due to the small sample size and the selection of only two universities, clearly it cannot provide definite answers to the questions raised. Nevertheless it is hoped that it will provide a good starting point for further investigations into the ideas about academic freedom from an international perspective.

ACKNOWLEDGEMENT

This work was supported by the European Commission FP7 People programme: Marie Curie Initial Training Network UNIKE (Universities in Knowledge Economies) under [Grant Agreement number 317452].

REFERENCES

AAUP (American Association of University Professors). (1970[1925]). *1940 statement of principles of academic freedom and tenure with 1970 interpretative comments.*

Alma Mater Studiorium. (2013). *Strategic plan 2013–2015.* Retrieved 20 Mai 2016 from http://www.unibo.it/en/university/who-we-are/strategic-plan

Altbach, P. G. (2001). Academic freedom: International realties and challenges. *Higher Education, 41,* 205–219.

Anderson, D., & Johnson, R. (1998). *University autonomy in 20 countries.* Commonwealth Department of Education, Training and Young Affaires. Retrieved 20 Mai 2016 from http://www.magna-charta.org/resources/files/University_autonomy_in_20_countries.pdf

Ballarino, G., & Perotti, L. (2012). The bologna process in Italy. *European Journal of Education, 47*(3), 348–363.

Braun, V., & Clark, V. (2006). Using thematic analysis in psychology. *Qualitative Research in Psychology,* (3), 77–101.

Bruneau. (2015). Five defences of academic freedom in North American higher education. In P. Zgaga, U. Teichler, H. G. Schuetz, & A. Wolter (Eds.), *Higher education reform: Looking back – looking forward.* Frankfurt: Peter Lang.

Danish Government. (2011, June 22). *Danish government 2011* (Vol. 695). Retrieved 12 July 2016 from http://ufm.dk/en/legislation/prevailing-laws-and-regulations/education/files_the-danish-university-act.pdf

DIH (Deutsches Italienisches Hochschulzentrum). (2014). *Riforma Gelmini: Die Italienische Bildungsreform.* Retrieved 25 November 2014 from http://www.deutschitalienischeshochschulzentrum.org/page.asp?pag=1675

Donina, D., Meoli, M., & Palerari, S. (2015). Higher education reform in Italy: Tightening regulation instead of steering at a distance. *Higher Education Policy, 28*(2), 215–234.

EHEA (European Higher Education Area). (2007). *Bologna process national reports 2005–2007 Italy.*

Erkkilä, T., & Piironen, O. (2014). Shifting fundaments of European higher education governance: Competition, ranking, autonomy and accountability. *Comparative Higher Education, 50*(2), 177–191.

Hamilton, S. (2000). University autonomy and external dependencies. In G. Neaves (Ed.), *The universities' responsibilities to society: International perspectives.* Amsterdam, Lausanne, New York, Oxford, Shannon, Singapore, Tokyo: Pergamon.

Kim, T. (2001). *Forming the academic profession in East Asia: A comparative analysis.* New York, NY, London: Routledge.

Legislative and Legal Service. (2013). *Higher education act unofficial consolidates text (ZViS-NPB10).*

Luzzato, G., & Moscati, R. (2007). University reform in Italy: Fears, expectations and contradictions. In A. Gornitzka, M. Kogan, & A. Amaral (Eds.), *Reform and change in higher education: Analysing policy implementation.* Dordrecht, the Netherland: Springer.

Magna Charta Observatory. (2016[1988]). *The magna charta universitatum.* Retrieved 02 August 2016 from http://www.magna-charta.org/magna-charta-universitatum/the-magna-charta-1/the-magna-charta

Marginson, S. (2011). Higher education in East Asia and Singapore: Rise of the confucian model. *Higher Education, 61*(5), 587–611.

Moscati, R. (2009). The implementation of the bologna process in Italy. In A. Amaral, G. Neave, C. Musselin, & P. Maassen (Eds.), *European integration and the governance of higher education and research.* Dordrecht, Heidelberg, London, New York: Springer.

Moscati, R. (2012). University governance in changing European systems of higher education. In A. Curaj, P. Scott, L. Valsceanu, & L. Wilson (Eds.), *European higher education at the crossroads: Between the bologna process and national reforms.* Part 1. Dordrecht, Heidelberg, New York, London: Springer.

Mukherjee, H., & Wong, P. K. (2011). The national university of Singapore and the university of Malaya: Common roots and different paths. In P. G. Altbach & J. Salmi (Eds.), *The road to academic excellence: The making of world-class research universities.* Washington, DC: The International Bank for Reconstruction and Development/The World Bank.

NUS (National University of Singapore). (2016a). *NUS at a Glance 2016/2017.* Retrieved 15 August 2016 from http://www.nus.edu.sg/images/resources/content/about/glance-en.pdf

NUS (National University of Singapore). (2016b). *Statutes and regulations of the national university of Singapore.* Retrieved 15 August 2016 from http://www.nus.edu.sg/registrar/info/statutes/ NUSStatutesRegulations-Full.pdf

Rüegg, W. (2002). The Europe of universities: Their tradition, function of bridging across Europe, liberal modernization. In N. Sanz & S. Bergan (Eds.) *The heritage of European universities.* Strasbourg: Council of Europe Publishing.

Rüegg, W. (2011). *A history of the university in Europe: Universities since 1945* (Vol. 4). Cambridge, New York, Melbourne, Cape Town, Singapore, Sao Paulo, Delhi, Dubai, Tokyo, Mexico City: Cambridge University Press.

Senato della Repubblica. (1948). *Constitution of the Italian republic.* Parliamentary Information Archives and Publication Office of the Senate Service for Official Reports and Communication.

The Law Revision Commission. (1987). *Education act chapter 87.*

The Law Revision Commission. (1999). *Constitution of the republic of Singapore.*

The Law Revision Commission. (2006). *National university of Singapore (Corporatisation) act chapter 204A.*

The Law Revision Commission. (2014). *Singapore management university act chapter 302A.*

UNESCO. (1997). *Recommendation concerning the status of higher-education teaching personnel.* Retrieved 15 December 2016 from http://portal.unesco.org/en/ev.php-URL_ID=13144&URL_ DO=DO_TOPIC&URL_SECTION=201.html

Wong, P.-K., Ho, Y.-P., & Singh, A. (2007). Towards an "Entrepreneurial University" model to support knowledge-based economic development: The case of the national university of Singapore. *World Development, 35*(6), 941–958.

Yamamoto, S. (2015). Higher education reform: Why did it start and has it ended? In P. Zgaga, U. Teichler, H. G. Schuetze, & A. Wolter (Eds.), *Higher education reform: Looking back – looking forward.* Frankfurt: Peter Lang.

Zgaga, P. (2012). Reconsidering university autonomy and governance: From academic freedom to institutional autonomy. In H. G. Schütz, W. A. Bruneau, & G. Grosjean (Eds.), *University governance and reform: Policy, fads, and experience in national perspective.* New York, NY: Palgrave Macmillan.

Zgaga, P., Teichler, U., Schuetze, H. G., & Wolter, A. (2015). Introduction: Reforming higher education for a changing world. In P. Zgaga, U. Teichler, H. G. Schuetz, & A. Wolter (Eds.), *Higher education reform: Looking back – looking forward.* Frankfurt: Peter Lang.

Zha, Q. (2012). Intellectuals, academic freedom, and autonomy: In university governance and reform. In H. G. Schütz, W. A. Bruneau, & G. Grosjean (Eds.), *University governance and reform: Policy, fads, and experience in national perspective.* New York, NY: Palgrave Macmillan.

Zonta, C. A. (2002). The history of European universities: Overview and background. In N. Sanz & S. Bergan (Eds.), *The heritage of European universities.* Strasbourg: Council of Europe Publishing.

Sina Westa
Faculty of Education
University of Ljubljana

PART 2

WIDENING PARTICIPATION, CURRICULAR INNOVATION, RESEARCH POLICY

VIKKI BOLIVER, STEPHEN GORARD AND NADIA SIDDIQUI

6. HOW CAN WE WIDEN PARTICIPATION IN HIGHER EDUCATION? THE PROMISE OF CONTEXTUALISED ADMISSIONS

INTRODUCTION

Widening participation in higher education has been on the UK policy agenda for more than fifty years. Yet, despite some progress across the UK higher education sector overall (DfE, 2016), students from less socioeconomically advantaged backgrounds remain severely under-represented among entrants to the UK's most academically selective universities. In 2014/2015, those from state schools, lower social class backgrounds, and low HE participation neighbourhoods, made up just 78%, 23% and 7.6% of entrants to Russell Group universities, compared to 93%, 37% and around 20% of all young people nationally (Boliver, 2015). Similarly, those eligible for free school meals at age 15 made up just 4.6% of entrants to the UK's top-third most selective universities in 2012/2013 compared to their wider population proportion of 13% (DBIS, 2015). The figures are particularly poor at universities which routinely place in the top ten of university league tables, including Oxford, Cambridge, Bristol and Durham. The Russell Group of universities has claimed that "real progress has been made over the last few years" in relation to widening participation at its 24 member institutions (Russell Group, 2015, p. 5). However, the statistical reality is that little has changed in the last ten years (Boliver, 2015, Crawford et al., 2016). Widening access to higher education, and in particular to the UK's most selective institutions, remains a persistent problem.

For decades, one of two main strategies for widening participation in higher education has involved efforts within the secondary and further education sectors to improve the pre-university academic attainment of pupils from disadvantaged backgrounds. This work is important because the evidence is clear that disparities in levels of pre-university academic achievement mean that young people from disadvantaged backgrounds are substantially under-represented in the pool of young people eligible for admission to university by age 18 (Chowdry et al., 2013). The second main strategy has involved outreach work by higher education providers to encourage young people from disadvantaged backgrounds to aspire to university, to choose upper secondary education pathways that are most likely to make them competitive applicants for admission, and ultimately to apply for admission when the time comes. The evidence in relation to this second set of barriers to widening

R. Deem & H. Eggins (Eds.), The University as a Critical Institution?, 95–109.

participation is less clear cut than the first. Research has shown that many young people, including those from disadvantaged backgrounds, express a desire to go to university (Kintrea, St Clair, & Houston, 2011), indicating that limited aspirations play only a small role in the uneven social composition of university entrants (Bowes et al., 2015). Indeed, after taking differences in school achievement into account, young people from disadvantaged backgrounds are roughly just as likely as their more privileged counterparts to apply to university, including highly selective institutions. Young people from disadvantaged backgrounds *are* less likely than their advantaged peers to study A-levels – considered the 'gold standard' for university entry – and to choose the most highly regarded A-level subjects – labelled 'facilitating subjects' by the Russell Group (Russell Group, 2016). However, it is not obvious why highly selective universities favour A-levels over other qualification routes, nor why some A-level subjects are deemed 'better' than others given that the vast majority of degree courses have few or no formal A-level subject prerequisites (Dilnot & Boliver, forthcoming).

What is notable about the part highly selective universities have seen fit to play in widening participation is that the focus has overwhelmingly been on efforts to raise aspirations that are in fact already high (Anders & Micklewright, 2015). There has been little if any reflection on the part of highly selective universities as to whether A-level qualifications generally and in 'facilitating subjects' in particular should be regarded as unequivocally the best forms of preparation for study at degree level. Moreover, persistent social disparities in pre-university achievement levels have been bracketed off by highly selective universities, at least to some extent, as something that is not their problem to deal with (Russell Group, 2015). And yet, highly selective universities could address both of these real barriers to widening participation by radically reconsidering their admissions policies. Indeed, of all the things which influence widening participation that are within the direct control of highly selective universities, their own admissions policies occupy the top spot.

This paper focuses on how highly selective universities could – and for reasons of social justice should – fundamentally alter their approach to admissions in order to make a major contribution to widening access. We argue that highly selective universities can and should set academic entry requirements with due regard to the fact that social group differences in pre-university achievement levels are wide, seemingly intractable, and a reflection of social inequalities that impact on learning opportunities and outcomes rather than necessarily a reflection of innate ability or true potential. We suggest that universities could substantially lower entry requirements for disadvantaged students without fear of setting students up to fail, especially if ambitious contextualised admissions policies are accompanied by equally ambitious programmes of academic support for students throughout their higher education careers.

CONTEXTUALISED ADMISSIONS

A contextualised approach to university admissions rests on acceptance of the principle articulated in the Schwartz Report that "equal examination grades do not necessarily represent equal potential" (Schwartz, 2004, pp. 5, 6) and that "it is fair and appropriate to consider contextual factors as well as formal educational achievement, given the variation in learners' opportunities and circumstances" (see also Universities UK, 2003). It involves taking into account information about the socioeconomic and/or educational circumstances of applicants when deciding whom to admit, in recognition of the fact that "the school attainment of disadvantaged learners often does not reflect their full potential" (CoWA, 2016, p. 10). A contextualised approach to university admissions challenges the assumptions of the prevailing 'meritocratic' approach in which pre-university attainment is treated as an objective indicator of academic ability, and the focus is on ensuring 'formal equality of opportunity' by requiring all to meet the same criteria for admission. A problem here is that some analyses of university admissions data suggest that highly selective universities fall short of achieving 'formal equality of opportunity'. Applicants to highly selective universities are less likely to be offered places if they are from state schools (Boliver, 2013; Noden, Shiner, & Modood, 2014), lower social class backgrounds (Zimdars, Sullivan, & Heath, 2009; Boliver, 2013; Noden, Shiner, & Modood, 2014) or areas with low rates of participation in higher education (Boliver, 2015; UCAS, 2016), even when they have the same grades at A-level as their more advantaged peers.

Contextualised admissions, in contrast to formal equality of opportunity for equal prior attainment, emphasise the need to consider pre-university achievement in light of the socioeconomic and/or educational context of the applicant in order to identify academic *potential*. This represents a shift from a concern with 'formal equality of opportunity' to a concern with 'fair equality of opportunity' (Rawls, 1999 [1971]). As the Scottish Government's Commission on Widening Access puts it, currently "the applicant pool is being unnecessarily, and unfairly, limited by an over reliance on school attainment as the primary measure of academic ability" (CoWA, 2016, p. 36).

Contextualised admissions was pioneered by Scottish universities, most notably the University of Edinburgh, in the 1990s, and has been advocated widely in recent years (Panel on Fair Access to the Professions, 2009; DBIS, 2011, 2014; Cabinet Office, 2011; Social Mobility Commission, 2012, 2013, 2014; SPA, 2014; CoWA, 2016; Universities Scotland, 2016). Currently more than half of all UK universities use contextual data to inform admissions decisions in some way (SPA, 2015). Most often contextual data is used to inform which applicants to shortlist, invite to interview, prioritise for admission conditional on meeting standard academic entry requirements, or accept at confirmation in cases where standard entry requirements have not quite been met (Moore, Mountford-Zimdars, & Wiggans, 2013). In contrast, a variant of contextualised admissions which involves reducing academic entry requirements for disadvantaged students is rarely used. A very small number universities reduce academic entry requirements by one or two grades for specified applicants from disadvantaged backgrounds (e.g. Bristol University) and fewer still reduce academic entry requirements by as much as four grades (e.g. Edinburgh and Glasgow universities). However, given the large and persistent socioeconomic gap in school achievement levels, it is precisely this rarely-used variant of contextualised admissions that may be needed to substantially widen participation. This also means considering a wider set of indicators for HE admissions rather than just selecting students based on their school attainment records.

An important criticism of such contextualised admissions policies which involve reducing academic entry requirements for disadvantaged students is that they could set students up to fail. However, this critique assumes that current university entry requirements have been set with a clear appraisal of what is needed to succeed at degree level, an assumption which is at odds with the substantial increase in university entry requirements during the past decade. Between 2006 and 2015 the UCAS point score of the average university entrant rose from 320 to 360, equivalent to a shift from ABB to AAA (Figure 6.1). Although these UCAS point scores relate to the sum total of entrants' academic qualifications, not just those included in entry requirements, they evidence indirectly the extent to which universities have been asking more and more of prospective entrants over time. It is not the case that these rising UCAS point scores are (solely) due to A-level grade inflation. During the same period, average A-level performance improved by just 10 UCAS points (equivalent to an increase of one half of one grade in a single A-level). This small increase was caused entirely by the introduction of the A* grade in 2010; about half of all grades awarded that would have been an A are now A*, which attracts an extra 20 UCAS points (Wikipedia, 2015).

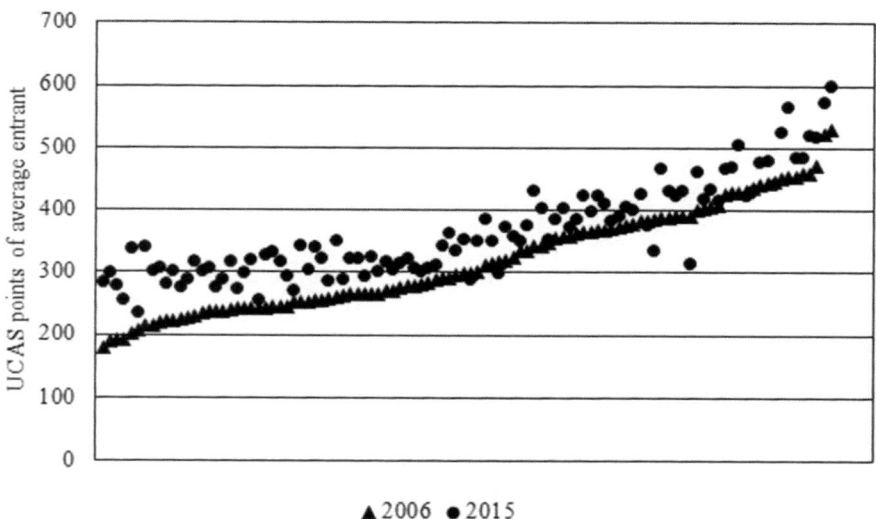

Figure 6.1. Average UCAS points of entrants to UK universities in 2006 and 2015. Source: Complete University Guide, N=104 HEIs

What has *not* been driving this increase is a concern that entry requirements needed to be higher to ensure that entrants are capable of studying at degree level. On the contrary, as CoWA notes, "in many cases, [university] entry requirements have risen well beyond what is required to succeed in degree level study" (CoWA, 2016, p. 10). Rather, a key driver of this inflation of entry requirements has been the rise in the number of university applications in the context of a relatively fixed number of university places; highly selective universities have sought to bring applicant demand down to more manageable proportions by raising the bar for admission (CoWA, 2016). A further driver has been the fact that the average UCAS point scores of entrants is included in the calculations underpinning university league tables, providing prestige-chasing universities with an incentive to set academic entry requirements as high as possible (and an apparent disincentive to lower them for disadvantaged applicants). Universities are likely to be concerned that reducing entry requirements for disadvantaged applicants will adversely affect their league table ranking. However, as entry requirements typically contribute just 10% to league table calculations, in reality any shift in rankings is likely to be small. Moreover, if all universities reduced entry requirements to a similar degree, their relative standing in league tables would not change.

The case for lowering entry requirements for disadvantaged students is often supported by reference to evidence that such students can perform better at degree level than their more advantaged peers who entered with the same grades at A-level. Students from state schools have been found to outperform comparably qualified students from private schools at St Andrew's University (Lasselle, McDougall-Bagnall, & Smith, 2014), Oxford University (Ogg, Zimdars, & Heath, 2009; but cf. Sumnal, 2015 in relation to Cambridge), Bristol University (Hoare & Johnston, 2011) and in UK universities as a whole (HEFCE, 2014; Crawford, 2014a). Students whose own secondary educational achievements are higher than the average for their school have also been shown to outperform comparably qualified students once at university (HEFCE, 2014).

On the other hand, studies employing individual-level indicators of contextual disadvantage such as free school meal status, or neighbourhood-level indicators of contextual disadvantage such as local higher education participation rate or neighbourhood deprivation level, have found that contextually disadvantaged students perform less well at degree level than more advantaged students with the same levels of prior attainment (Crawford et al., 2016; Croxford et al., 2014; Crawford, 2014b; HEFCE, 2014). The findings of these studies indicate that, although disadvantaged students' pre-university achievement levels do not always do justice to their true potential, we cannot assume that their true potential will simply be unleashed once they enter university. Such students may well continue to perform at a level below their true potential at university if they continue to experience socioeconomic disadvantage, and/or if their academic knowledge and skills continue to lag behind those of their more advantaged peers. This has two important implications. First, it implies that lower entry requirements for contextually disadvantaged students cannot be deemed justified or unjustified simply on the basis of evidence regarding the degree level performances of such students relative to their comparably qualified but more advantaged peers. Secondly, it will be important that universities consider not only their admissions policies but also the kinds of support they provide to help students realise their potential once at university. For some, if not all, universities this may require a radical change to existing pedagogical assumptions and practices, perhaps particularly in higher tariff institutions where students have traditionally been expected to do well at university as a matter of course.

Recently the Scottish Government Commission on Widening Access (CoWA) made an unprecedented call for universities be required to set substantially lower entry requirements for applicants from disadvantaged backgrounds:

> By 2019 all universities should set access thresholds for all degree programmes against which learners from the most deprived backgrounds should be assessed. These access thresholds should be separate to standard entrance requirements and set as ambitiously as possible, at a level which accurately reflects the minimum academic standard and subject knowledge necessary to successfully complete a degree programme. (CoWA, 2016, p. 15)

CoWA does not go into any detail as to how "access thresholds" should be determined. As such, there is work to be done to identify what counts as "the minimum academic standard and subject knowledge necessary to successfully complete a degree programme." Identification of a "minimum academic standard" requires looking at how different levels of achievement in different types of pre-university qualifications are associated with academic achievement at degree level. Similarly, identifying what constitutes necessary "subject knowledge" will require looking at how subjects studied prior to university entry as well as levels of achievement in those subjects relates to degree success in particular disciplines.

What it means to "successfully complete a degree programme" also needs to be thought through. At one pole, successful completion could be taken to mean making it through to the end of a degree programme and ultimately obtaining a degree qualification, regardless of what the final degree classification is, and perhaps also regardless of how long it takes. At the other pole, it might mean completing a degree programme (on time) and ultimately achieving what is sometimes termed a "good degree", that is a first or upper second class honours degree qualification. It will be important to examine both of these outcomes – completion and attainment – as part of the processes of deciding whether to focus concern on one or the other or both.

Whether "success" is defined in terms of completion or level of attainment, because of its categorical nature it is also necessary to determine what counts as a desirable (or at least an acceptable) probability of a successful outcome. This probability of success might be set at a conservatively high level – for example, an access threshold might be set at a level associated with a probability of success at least as good as that of the average student. However, if access thresholds are to be ambitiously set, it is likely that the probability of success will need to be significantly lower than the average, and could conceivably be as low as 50%. A case could be made for a probability of success that is lower still, but from an ethics point of view an even chance of success might be considered the minimum that is acceptable. It is not obvious what would constitute a desirable or acceptable minimum probability of success and detailed conceptual and empirical work is needed to guide this decision.

It will be important to consider the trade-off between the positive impact of lower entry requirements on widening access on the one hand and any negative effects on student completion and achievement rates on the other. Lowering entry requirements too much could lead to some of the widening access gains made at the point of admission being lost by the point of graduation, which would be not only partially self-defeating, but also personally damaging for those students who had been 'set up to fail', and damaging to the reputation of institutions. The empirical component of this paper explores which levels of pre-university attainment are associated with average and 'evens' (50%) rates of degree success, with a view to determining how low entry requirements for disadvantaged students could be set.

DATA, INDICATORS, AND METHODS OF ANALYSIS

The statistical analysis presented in this paper draws on individual-level longitudinal data provided by the Higher Education Statistics Agency (HESA) on the attainment in higher education of those who completed full-time degree programmes in UK higher education institutions in 2011/2012. The HESA data includes information about university students' qualification type and grades on entry, and enables us to identify what final degree classification they achieved upon graduation. In addition, the HESA dataset contains several contextual variables, including individual-level measures relating to type of school previously attended, parental educational level, and social class background, as well as a neighbourhood-level measure of the young higher education participation rate associated with the student's home postcode (POLAR). Individual-level contextual indicators relate directly to the circumstances of individuals and their immediate families or households. Neighbourhood-level indicators, in contrast, relate only indirectly to the circumstances of individuals, but could be used to infer something about individual circumstances, or about the wider socioeconomic and educational context in which individuals are located. The suitability of these and other potential indicators of contextual disadvantage, in theory and in practice, have yet to be rigorously and systematically examined, but it is helpful to summarise here some of the key matters of concern in relation to validity, reliability, completeness and availability (for a fuller elaboration of the issues, see Gorard et al., 2017).

First and foremost, it is important that any indicator of contextual disadvantage is valid; that it captures with a high degree of accuracy the concept it is intended to capture – in this case socioeconomic or educational disadvantage that is likely to have impacted negatively on achievement at school. The validity of an indicator is compromised if it yields a significant number of false positives; that is, if a significant number of individuals are identified as contextually disadvantaged when they are not. An example of a contextual indicator with low validity in this respect might be the use of a simple distinction between individuals educated in state and private schools, since many state educated pupils are not socioeconomically or educationally disadvantaged. Similarly, having parents who are not university graduates does not necessarily imply disadvantage, nor does living in an area of low HE participation for individuals who are not themselves typical of others living in the same locale. The validity of an indicator is also compromised if it yields a significant number of false negatives; that is, if a significant number of individuals are identified as not contextually disadvantaged when they are. An example might be the use of low parental social class as an indicator of contextual disadvantage given that those with parents in social classes just above the cut-off point for classification as disadvantaged are likely to be experiencing very similar circumstances.

It is also crucial that any indicator of contextual disadvantage has high reliability; that it captures with a high degree of consistency the concept it is intended to capture. The reliability of an indicator is diminished if yields inconsistent results across different individuals or on different occasions for an individual whose circumstances have not changed. The reliability of an indicator may vary depending on the source of information – for example, self-reported information (such as parental education and parental social class) is likely to be less reliable than information that has been administratively verified, due to misreporting, whether intentional or unintentional.

The usefulness of contextual indicators may also be compromised by problems of missing data arising from non-response to requests for self-reported status; for example a university applicant may leave the 'parental higher education' field blank. Missing data may also compromise neighbourhood-level indicators of contextual disadvantage for the same reason although this may not be immediately apparent. For example, although all postcodes are assigned values on neighbourhood-level measures of disadvantage, the underlying individual-level data is likely to be subject to a degree of non-response.

Finally, potential indicators of contextual disadvantage can only be used to inform admissions decisions if they are available at the point of admissions decision-making. A range of contextual indicators are currently available to universities via UCAS, and UCAS is currently looking at improving its service to universities in this regard. Some universities supplement the contextual data provided by UCAS with administrative pupil and school data and with additional neighbourhood-level metrics available from government and commercial sources. There are, however, some potentially useful contextual indicators that are not currently available at the point of admissions decision-making. For example, universities do not have access to family income data for applicants, but this could be made available in theory by HMRC and/or the Student Loans Company.

To determine how well graduates from disadvantaged groups perform at degree level in both absolute and relative terms at given levels of pre-university attainment, we use a series of binary logistic regression models to estimate the probabilities of achieving a first or upper second class degree (a "good degree" for short), rather than a lower second class, third class or pass degree. We compare outcomes for graduates from advantaged and disadvantaged social groups with the same best three A-level grades on entry. We focus on students who graduated between 2008 and 2010 from Russell Group universities – 24 of the most academically selective and socially elite higher education institutions in the UK. We restrict our analysis to who entered university aged 21 or younger with 3 or more A-levels. All models control statistically for higher education institution attended and degree subject area studied, so as to remove the effects of these influences on degree classifications. The analysis presented below provides a picture for Russell Group universities as a whole; in due course further analysis will explore possible variations in the overall pattern by individual institution and degree subject area where sub-sample sizes permit.

RESULTS

Figure 6.2 presents the predicted probabilities of achieving a "good degree" for private school entrants (more advantaged group) and those from state schools (less advantaged group) with A-level grades on entry ranging from a low of CCC to a high of AAA. Below CCC there are too few cases in the data to draw reliable conclusions. For the cohort in our data, AAA was, at the time, the highest possible achievement in three A-levels, as A* grades had yet to be introduced. Vertical lines have been added to the figure to indicate the achievement in three A-levels associated with Russell Group average success rates (85% in this data) and 'evens' success rates (i.e. 50% or above). In terms of relative degree performance, state school students were more likely to achieve a "good degree" than comparably qualified entrants from private schools high HE participation areas, except at the two extremes of the A-level grades distribution. Considering success rates in absolute terms, students from state schools could be admitted with grades somewhere between AAB and ABB or above at A-level and have a probability of success at least as good as the average Russell Group student. For an evens chance of success, entry requirements for such students could be set as low as CCC.

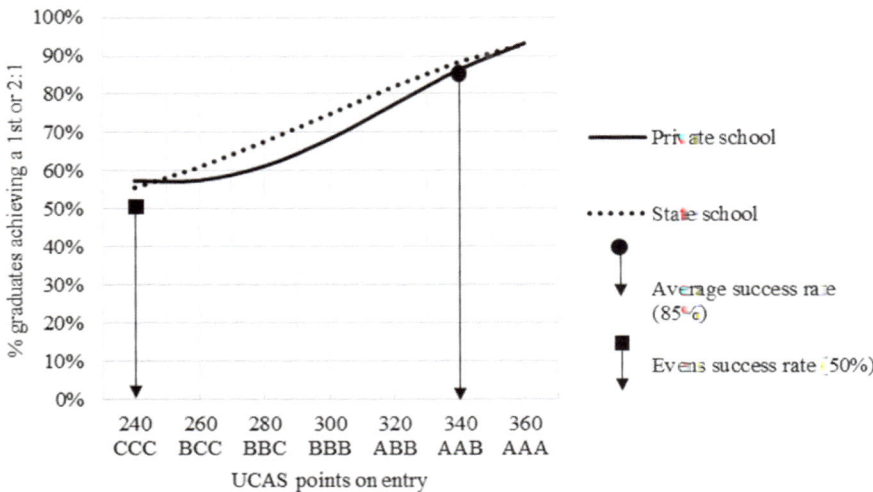

Figure 6.2. Predicted probabilities of achieving a "good degree" for graduates from private schools and state-maintained schools

Figure 6.3 presents the predicted probabilities of achieving a "good degree" for entrants with graduate parents (more advantaged group) and non-graduate parents (less advantaged group). In terms of relative degree performance, students whose parents were not higher education graduates were no more and no less likely to achieve a "good degree", with the exception of those entering with CCC at A-level where success rates were slightly lower for those with non-graduate parents. In terms of absolute success rates, students with non-graduate parents could be admitted with AAB or above at A-level and have a probability of success at least as good as the average Russell Group student. For an even chance of success, entry requirements for students with non-graduate parents could be set as low as CCC.

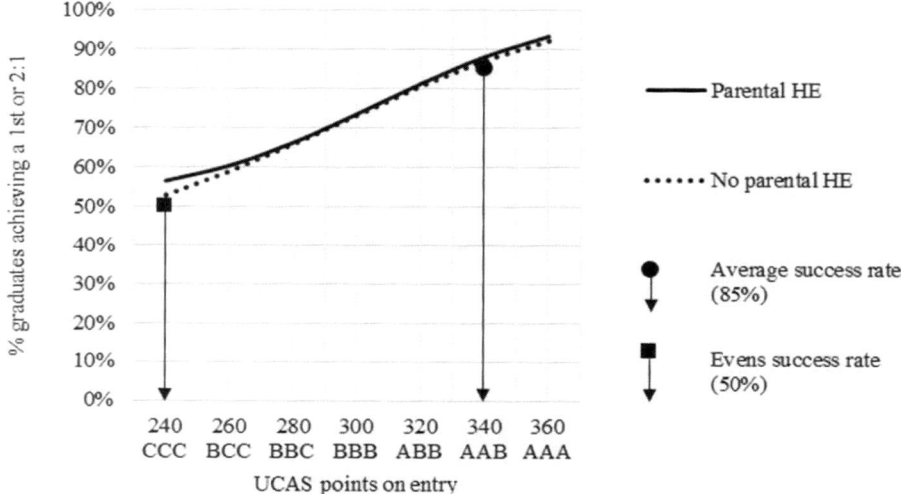

Figure 6.3. Predicted probabilities of achieving a "good degree" for graduates with and without graduate parents

Figure 6.4 presents the predicted probabilities of achieving a "good degree" for entrants with parents in social class I (more advantaged group) and social classes VI and VII (less advantaged groups). In relative terms, students from lower social class backgrounds were less likely to achieve a "good degree" than students from the highest social class, by around 5 percentage points across the A-level grades scale. In terms of absolute success rates, students from lower social class backgrounds could be admitted with grades midway between AAB and AAA or above at A-level and have a probability of success at least as good as the average Russell Group student. For an evens chance of success, entry requirements for students from lower social class backgrounds could be set at BCC.

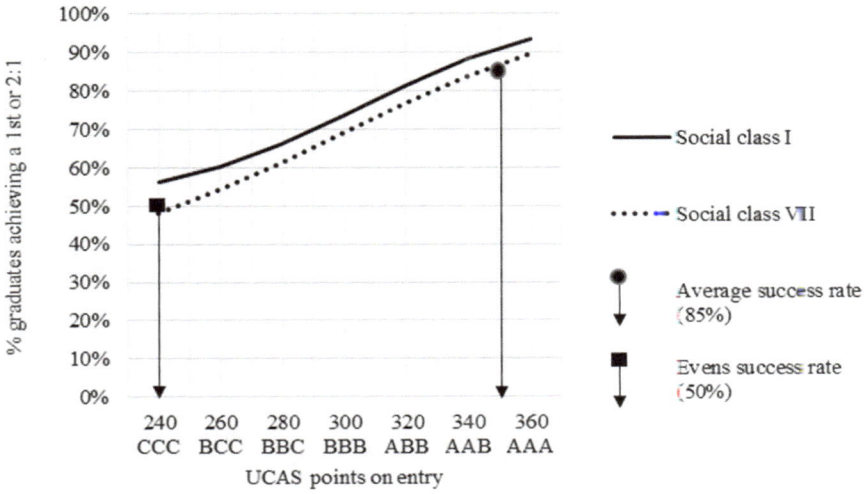

Figure 6.4. Predicted probabilities of achieving a "good degree" for graduates from social class I and social class VII backgrounds

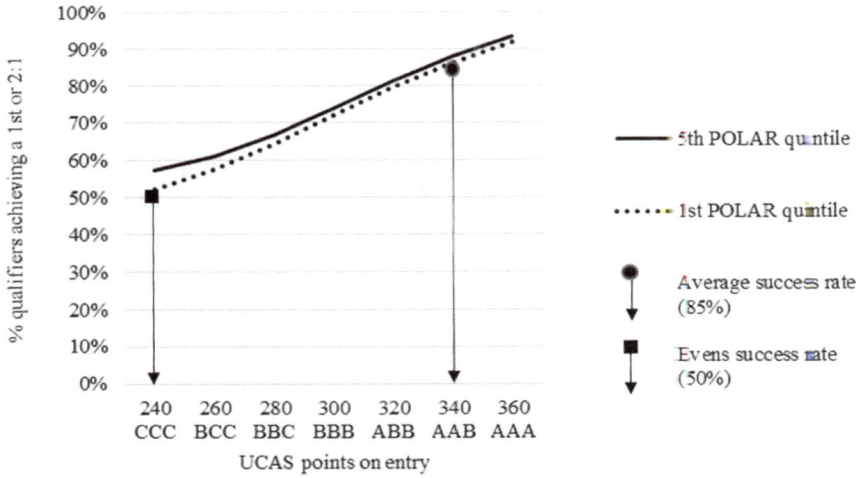

Figure 6.5. Predicted probabilities of achieving a "good degree" for graduates from the highest (5th) and lowest (1st) POLAR quintiles

Finally, Figure 6.5 presents the predicted probabilities of achieving a "good degree" for entrants from neighbourhoods in the 5th quintile when ranked according to the young HE participation rate (more advantaged group) and those

105

from neighbourhoods in the 1st and 2nd quintiles (less advantaged groups). In terms of relative degree performance, students from low HE participation neighbourhoods were no more and no less likely to achieve a "good degree" than those from high HE participation areas, provided they entered with BBB or above at A-level. However, a growing disparity emerges as A-level grades decline from BBB to CCC. Considering success rates in absolute terms, students from low HE participation neighbourhoods could be admitted with AAB or above at A-level and have a probability of success at least as good as the average Russell Group student. For an evens chance of success, entry requirements for such students could be set as low as CCC.

DISCUSSION AND CONCLUSIONS

What the findings presented above demonstrate is that highly selective universities could admit students from socioeconomically disadvantaged backgrounds with AAB or better at A-level without fear that they would, as a group, perform worse than the average student. Moreover, they could move to entry requirements of BBC or CCC for students from disadvantaged backgrounds safe in the knowledge that such students would be more likely to succeed than to fail. If an 'evens' success rate seems too risky – whether for the student or for the institution – then BBB at A-level could be chosen as the threshold instead. BBB at A-level is considerably lower than the advertised entry requirements of most courses at most Russell Group universities, but with associated rates of success in higher education of 70%, it is clearly good enough.

It is important to stress, that the evidence used here to identify a lower entry requirement threshold for disadvantaged students has been gathered in a context where universities do little to support disadvantaged students to achieve their full potential. Often it is assumed that admitted students will do well as a matter of course, with those who struggle academically often deemed personally culpable. Such an approach is clearly at odds with an acknowledgement of the fact that socioeconomically disadvantaged students' pre-university attainments do not do justice to their true potential. If anything we should expect to see disadvantaged students outperform more advantaged peers with the same pre-university attainment once at university. The fact that we typically don't see this indicates that universities are failing to deliver fully, as educators, to support students to achieve their true potential. Clearly, contextualised admissions policies cannot be solely about entry requirements; what is also needed is a radical shift in the pedagogical practices of universities. We will know that this has been achieved when we begin to see disadvantaged students who have entered higher education with qualifications that do not do justice to their true potential do better at degree level than ostensibly comparably qualified entrants from more advantaged backgrounds.

In closing, it is useful to consider how much traction could be gained with regard to widening access to highly selective universities as a result of implementing contextualised admissions policies which substantially reduce entry requirements for disadvantaged students. Figure 6.6 illustrates the distributions of 'best three A-level grades' on entry to university among 2010/2011 graduates from advantaged and disadvantaged backgrounds as measured by the indicators discussed earlier in this chapter: school type, parental education, social class background, and POLAR quintile. What becomes clear is that, if highly selective universities chose to restrict eligibility for admission to only those with AAB+ at A-level, some 53 percent of individuals from private schools would be eligible, as would 35 percent of those with graduate parents, 38 percent of those from social class I, and 37 percent of those from neighbourhoods with the highest rates of participation in higher education. In contrast, only 26 percent of individuals from state schools and just 22 percent of individuals with non-graduate parents would be eligible for admission, with eligibility rates much lower still for those from social class VII (7 percent) and neighbourhoods with the lowest HE participation rates (18 percent). Keeping entry requirements at AAB+ for advantaged applicants, but setting them at BBC+ for disadvantaged applicants, would go a long way towards evening things up.

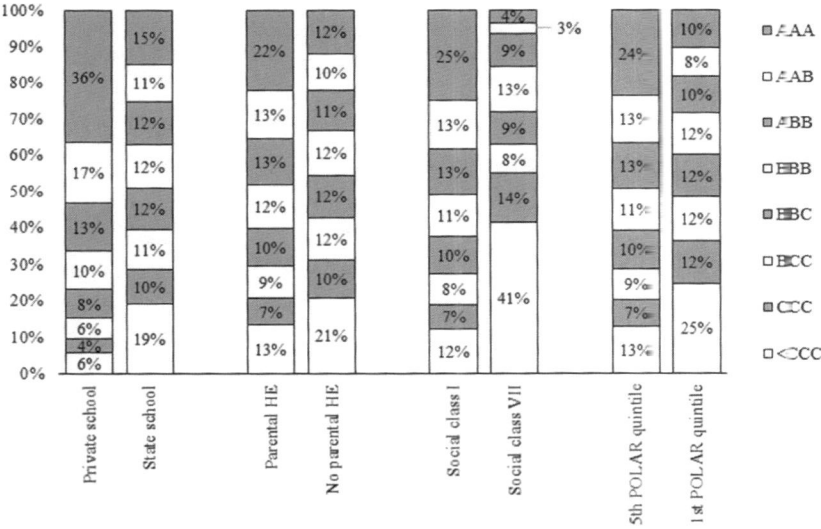

Figure 6.6. Best three A-levels obtained by students graduating with university degrees in 2010/2011, by social group

In sum, ambitious contextualised admissions policies which reduce entry requirements for disadvantaged students, and which support disadvantaged students to realise their full potential, represent the most promising means of significantly widening participation in higher education generally, and at highly selective universities in particular.

107

REFERENCES

Anders, J., & Micklewright, J. (2015). Teenagers' expectations of applying to university: How do they change? *Education Sciences, 5*(4), 281–305.

Boliver, V. (2013). How fair is access to more prestigious UK universities? *British Journal of Sociology, 64*(2), 344–364.

Boliver, V. (2015). Lies, damned lies, and statistics on widening access to Russell Group universities. *Radical Statistics, 113*, 29–38.

Bowes, L., Evans, J., Nathwani, T., Birkin, G., Boyd, A., Holmes, C., & Jones, S. (2015). Understanding progression into higher education for disadvantaged and under-represented groups. *Department for Business, Innovation and Skills.* Retrieved from https://www.gov.uk/government/uploads/system/uploads/attachment_data/file/474269/BIS-15-462-understanding-progression-into-higher-education-final.pdf

Cabinet Office. (2011). *Opening doors, breaking down barriers: A strategy for social mobility.* London: HMSO.

Chowdry, H., Crawford, C., Dearden, L., Goodman, A., & Vignoles, A. (2013). Widening participation in higher education: Analysis using linked administrative data. *Journal of the Royal Statistical Society: Series A (Statistics in Society), 176*(2), 431–457.

Complete University Guide. Retrieved from http://www.thecompleteuniversityguide.co.uk/

CoWA. (2016). *A blueprint for fairness: The final report of the commission on widening.* Access. Scottish Government.

Crawford, C. (2014a). *Socio-economic differences in university outcomes in the UK: Drop-out, degree completion and degree class.* London: Institute for Fiscal Studies.

Crawford, C. (2014b). *The link between secondary school characteristics and university participation and outcomes.* http://www.ifs.org.uk/publications/7235

Croxford, L., Docherty, G., Gaukroger, R., & Hood, K. (2014). Widening participation at the university of edinburgh: Contextual admissions, retention, and degree outcomes. *Scottish Affairs, 23*(2), 192–216.

Crawford, C., Dearden, L., Micklewright, J., & Vignoles, A. (2016). *Family background and university success: Differences in higher education access and outcomes in England.* Oxford: Oxford University Press.

DBIS. (2011). *Students at the heart of the system.* London: Department for Business, Innovation and Skills.

DBIS. (2014). *National strategy for access and student success. BIS 14/516.* London: Department for Business, Innovation and Skills.

DBIS. (2015). *Free school meals: Pupil progression to higher education.* London: Department for Business, Innovation and Skills. Retrieved from https://www.gov.uk/government/statistics/free-school-meals-pupil-progression-to-higher-education

DfE. (2016). *Widening participation in higher education, England, 2013/14 age cohort. SFR32/2016.* London: Department for Education. Retrieved 3 August 2016 from https://www.gov.uk/government/uploads/system/uploads/attachment_data/file/543126/SFR37-2016_-_WPHE2016_01.08.2016.pdf

Dilnot, C., & Boliver, V. (forthcoming) Admission to medicine and law at Russell Group universities: The impact of A-level subject choice). In A. Hayton & J. Stevenson (Eds.), *Widening participation in higher education: Towards a reflexive approach to research and evaluation.* Trentham.

Gorard, S., Boliver, V., Siddiqui, N., Banerjee, P., & Morris, R. (2017). *Which are the most suitable contextual indicators for use in widening participation to HE?* Education Working Paper Series, Working Paper 1, ISBN978-0-907552-12-3, http://dro.dur.ac.uk/20937/

HEFCE. (2014). *Differences in degree outcomes: Key findings.* Bristol: HEFCE.

Kintrea, K., St Clair, R., & Houston, M. (2011). *The influence of parents, places and poverty on educational attitudes and aspirations.* Joseph Rowntree Foundation.

Lasselle, L., McDougall-Bagnall, J., & Smith, I. (2013). School grades, school context and university degree performance: Evidence from an elite Scottish institution. *Oxford Review of Education, 40*, 293–331.

Moore, M.-Z., & Wiggans. (2013). *Contextualised admissions: Examining the evidence.* Cheltenham: SPA.

Noden, P., Shiner, M., & Modood, T. (2014). University offer rates for candidates from different ethnic categories. *Oxford Review of Education, 40*(3), 349–369.

Ogg, T., Zimdars, A., & Heath, A. (2009). Schooling effects on degree performance: A comparison of the predictive validity of aptitude testing and secondary school grades at Oxford University. *British Educational Research Journal, 35*(5), 781–807.

Panel on Fair Access to the Professions. (2009). *Unleashing aspiration: The final report of the fair access to the professions*. London: Cabinet Office.

Rawls, J. (1999[1971]). *A theory of justice*. Oxford: Oxford University Press.

Russell Group. (2015). *Opening doors: Understanding and overcoming barriers to university access*. Russell Group. Retrieved from http://russellgroup.ac.uk/policy/publications/opening-doorsunderstanding-and-overcoming-the-barriers-to-university-access/

Russell Group. (2016). *Informed choices: A Russell group guide to making decisions about post-16 education* (5th edition). London: Russell Group.

Schwartz, S. (2004). *Fair admissions to higher education: Recommendations for good practice*. London: HMSO.

Social Mobility and Child Poverty Commission. (2012). *University challenge: How higher education can advance social mobility*. London: HMSO.

Social Mobility and Child Poverty Commission. (2013). *Higher education: The fair access challenge*. London: HMSO.

Social Mobility and Child Poverty Commission. (2014). *State of the nation: 2014 report*. London: HMSO.

Sumnall, C. (2015). *ANOVA on A*s at A-level and tripos performance*. http://www.admin.cam.ac.uk/offices/admissions/research/docs/Astar_Alevel_Tripos.pdf

Supporting Professionalism in Admissions. (2014). *Contextualised admissions – issues and considerations for HE providers introducing and implementing contextualised admissions*. Cheltenham: SPA.

Supporting Professionalism in Admissions. (2014). *SPA's use of contextualised admissions survey report 2015 (with HEDIIP)*. Cheltenham: SPA.

UCAS. (2016). *UCAS undergraduate reports by sex, area background, and ethnic group*. Cheltenham: UCAS. Retrieved from https://www.ucas.com/corporate/news-and-key-documents/news/ucas-publishes-first-equality-reports-individual-universities

Universities Scotland. (2016). *Futures not backgrounds, Edinburgh: Universities Scotland*. Retrieved from http://www.universities-scotland.ac.uk/wp-content/uploads/2016/09/10537-%E2%80%A2-Futures-Not-Backgrounds-web.pdf

Universities UK. (2003). *Fair enough? Wider access to university by identifying potential to success*. London: Universities UK.

Wikipedia. (2015). Joint council for qualifications. Retrieved from https://en.wikipedia.org/wiki/Grade_inflation#UK_ALevel_classifications_from_June_1989_to_2015

Zimdars A, Sullivan A, & Heath, A. (2009). Elite higher education admissions in the arts and sciences: Is cultural capital the key? *Sociology, 43*(4), 648–666.

Vikki Boliver
School of Applied Social Sciences
Durham University

Stephen Gorard
School of Education
Durham University

Nadia Siddiqui
School of Education and Applied Social Sciences
Durham University

DANIEL KONTOWSKI AND DAVID KRETZ

7. LIBERAL EDUCATION UNDER FINANCIAL PRESSURE

The Case of Private German Universities

INTRODUCTION

This article discusses the question of how financial pressure influenced the liberal education mission of private, German liberal education institutions.

European universities are predominantly offering disciplinary and professional study paths. Germany, the largest higher education system in Europe, is the paradigm case. It has developed strong disciplinary traditions (often said to be following the Humboldtian model), comprehensive state control and up now very recently limited international orientation. Yet across Europe, there has also begun a quiet small (re-)emergence of more general education oriented undergraduate curricula over the last three decades. Rooted in ancient and medieval traditions of "artes liberales", and their modern reinterpretation as "liberal (arts) education" (Kimball, 1995; Rochblatt, 2003), more than 70 interdisciplinary programs operate currently in diverse curricular and organizational settings (Godwin & Altbach, 2016; van der Wende, 2011) [1]

These European liberal education initiatives often possess a range of features that make them welcome additions to higher education landscapes. Small size and flexibility often make such institutions ideal incubators for educational experimentation (Grant & Riesman, 1978), and they can be a valuable seed of diversification of higher education systems (Huisman & Vught, 2009). The general non-vocational mission shows a healthy distance from the neo-liberal marketization of higher learning, and potentially moves towards an alternative to the structured higher education system that tends to reproduce social injustices (Nussbaum, 1998, 2012). Social integration of academic learning with campus-based communities promotes the self-organization of students and the democratization of university bureaucracies in terms of curriculum and pedagogy, the egalitarian nature of learning as evidenced in the weakening of the student-teacher dichotomy and disciplinary boundaries, and through small-scale, discussion-based seminars with an interdisciplinary integrated curricula all provide a healthy balance to dominant models.

But those few privates who choose the path of liberal arts are still more fragile than their public counterparts.[2] With little to no state-funding, nor tax-enhanced cultures of private philanthropy, many innovative private institutions across Europe often had to rely on tuition, thus risking elitist exclusivity, or else went bankrupt

R. Deem & H. Eggins (Eds.), The University as a Critical Institution?, 111–133.

after a short time. Though in Germany as in Europe they seem to be on the rise, they also still struggle a lot with averse financial conditions and academic cultures.

This paper analyses three German cases in detail asking how private, German liberal education (GPLE) initiatives can sustain their liberal education mission under increased financial pressure. The focus on the understudied case of Germany assures the comparability of cases, while also promising insight that generalizes well to other higher education systems characterized by:

- primarily public funding and tuition free system,
- lack of private philanthropy culture,
- focus on disciplinary or professional training, and
- widespread perception of academic inferiority of private institutions.

Germany may be the least likely case for development of private liberal education; therefore this niche analysis of attempts to disrupt a homogenous system of higher education offers condensed pictures of the struggles that can be observed elsewhere.

RESEARCH APPROACH

Study Design & Sample

Unlike most European liberal education initiatives (notably Dutch and British), GPLEs do not use the liberal arts label and therefore they can easily be overlooked by researchers describing the rise of liberal arts in Europe. We defined our object as currently operating higher education institutions offering undergraduate programs with the following characteristics drawing on (Godwin, 2013) (first three, adapted) and the specifics of our German sample:

- curricula with distribution requirements in at least two different areas of knowledge, and
- some general education protocol (academic courses required from all students at the institution), with
- elements of engaging, small-scale pedagogies;
- displaying non-entirely professional aim of education,
- established and primarily accredited as German institutions (rather than as an international branch campus).[3]

Our sample is described in Table 7.1.

The study hopes to highlight educational ideals bearing complex relation to liberal education features. UWH, ZU and BCB underwent (sometimes mediatized) crises in 2008, 2014 and 2013 respectively. Unlike Humboldt-Viadrina School of Governance, all three survived. BLS did not have a crisis.[4] JUB is in the process of a restructuring and declined interviews. Therefore we decided to focus on UWH, ZU and BCB as they seemed to be the most comparable.

Table 7.1. Basic institutional figures of five German liberal education initiatives: Bard College Berlin (BCB), Bucerius Law School (BLS), Jacobs University Bremen (JUB), University Witten-Herdecke (WH), Zeppelin University (ZU). All numbers refer to 2016 values.

Name	Est.	Location	Main language of instruction	Sticker tuition p.a.	Students (approx.)	Research & teaching staff (approx.)	Number of programmes
BCB	1999	Berlin	English	17,325€	150	46	BA: 2
BLS	2000	Hamburg	German	12,000€	650	150	LLB 1 LLM: 1
JUB	2001	Bremen	English	20,000€	1200	270	BA: 15 Master: 10
UWH	1982	Witten	German	4368€ – 6510€	2300	520	BA: 5 Master: 8
ZU	2003	Friedrichshafen	German	7800€ – 9200€	1200	270	BA: 4 Master: 4 Exec Master: 6

The study offers a close-up analysis of three GPLEs to identify the resiliency-increasing features and strategies, both on the curricular and the institutional level, that best allow them to realize their liberal education features even under adverse financial circumstances.

Methodology

As institutional crises are rarely described externally, the exploratory study was primarily based on semi-structured, qualitative interviews with key members of GPLEs studied, including senior administration, faculty members, and students, and including people formerly associated with the institutions. Each of those institutions have been approached by one of the investigators with an invitation for participating in the study and naming their representative, and independently some of the key sources have been identified through snowball sampling and approached directly.

The interviews have been conducted in English or German (then subsequently translated by the interviewer), recorded and transcribed verbatim. Participants were anonymized and confirmed in writing their informed consent. 10 interviews with members of the all five GPLEs have been executed, each lasting between 45 and 120 minutes. The interviews took place in 2015 and 2016, partially face-to-face and sometimes using Skype. All transcripts have been authorized by the respondents; all quotes come from the interviews conducted during the study.

Additional sources include official websites of the institutions that contained mission statements and curricular documents and accreditation reports.[5] Relevant literature has been consulted to harness basic data about the programmes, curricula, press releases and marketing materials. Media accounts were included, though treated with caution. Due to the word limit, references have been kept to absolute minimum; unfortunately, this is not the case with acronyms and last names of founders.

The topic guide for the interviews included a question about the nature and duration of the affiliation of the interviewee with his or her institution, questions about the extent and duration of financial pressure, questions about the institutional and curricular state before, during, and after increased financial pressure (where applicable), a meta-question about the topic guide, and a question about further potential interviewees.

One author (Kretz) is an alumnus of one of the institutions studied (BCB).

Variables and Hypotheses

Designing the study, we expected some centrally organised "new beginning" after a financial crisis (including hiring freezes and restructuring), complemented by intensive fundraising (given that those institutions do not attract big research money). In terms of curricula, more cost-effective solutions might have to been introduced to reduce costs, but their impact on offering liberal education was hard to predict. Major research projects are typically funded with grant money and therefore could be quite independent from institutional crises; but "going for grants" might be a survival strategy for a struggling institution. In the short term, with a diverse sample, we expected no clear trends, with the exception of a research faculty outflow. The most significant changes we expected to see were in tuition and other costs and admissions policies, as they are easy to change and bring short term solutions to the crisis.

Curricular and institutional dimensions of GPLE were conceptualized and operationalised. In the first category, we looked at the numbers and character of offered degree granting programmes, size and format of classes, core curriculum and distribution requirements, undergraduate research and student-organised classes. In the latter category, we reviewed admissions numbers and procedures, the diversity of applicants and students, tuition and related study costs, forms of institutional external partnerships, research, faculty and infrastructure. In both cases, the impact of the crisis, strategies of the leadership, as well as innovative and unique features, were given special attention.

OVERVIEW OF INSTITUTIONS AND THEIR DYNAMICS

The Big Picture

All three institutions followed a similar general pattern. Their founding impulse was a desire to offer a better alternative to existing university education, through pioneering general education that defies strict disciplinary boundaries (which was sometimes cast as a return to the university how it used to be and should be).

Brought to life by charismatic, spirited leaders, they enjoyed both the blessings and shortcomings of such a leadership model: financial and leadership crises went hand in hand. Power vacuums and intransparencies were often a result of lacking legal statutes normally regulating institutional operations. High dependency on leadership also affected fundraising strategies, which often focused on a single person with good connections or a single source.

Immediately into a financial crisis, all institutions had initial cut backs/freezes, in terms of staff, faculty, or programmes, but all also chose to grow and quickly recovered. In retrospective, they restructured rather than shrunk.* Infrastructure has been found to be the bottleneck for further growth in all cases (especially hard to finance during the economic recession). In the aftermath, all institutions are led by new generation of leaders.

Universität Witten/Herdecke

UWH is the first state-accredited private university in Germany. The founding intention in 1982 was to offer degrees in medicine, and then economics, with a strong liberal education component – one day each week solely devoted to *Studium Fundamentale* (StuFu). The main campus is located in Witten; the double name derives from Herdecke hospital nearby. The university attracts students from all over (former) Western Germany. Instruction is in German. There are about 2400 students, 500 professors and some 100 PhD students are affiliated with the place. The university does not have a residential component.

The initial dream was to operate with neither public money nor tuition fees. Currently, UWH distinguishes itself by offering a solid alternative to public "universities on four dimensions": access (admissions procedures alternative to *Abitur*), pedagogy (problem-based learning), curricula (*Studium Fundamentale* and heterodox medicine[7] and economics classes) and financing (UCV) the studies.

Liberal Arts Features

In StuFu students pick a course each semester from a broad offer of courses. Economy students can pick for example acting classes as part of their studies, mixing with students from across the university. Reserving one separate day for this gives them a temporary break from their daily professional pursuits and allows for reflection on their programs. Organizationally, StuFu was first offered by an institute, which developed a faculty (2002).

Initially, StuFu ran as a distribution requirement for courses from different disciplines. A recent revamp of the curriculum sorted courses according to the competences they develop: artistic, reflexive and communicative. Another aim was for students to learn different languages and argumentation by different disciplines. Though not without controversies, the programme remains a cornerstone of UWH.

Developing from StuFu, a full degree in *Kulturreflexion* (Reflection on Culture, KR) was introduced in 2002, already in the BA/MA format. KR bridges theory of culture and culture management and prides itself in its interdisciplinary, individualist approach. The highly elective curriculum of KR has been successfully accredited and second iteration of KR ditched the language of soft skills for more traditional phrasing. Since 2009 the unusual academic faculty is called jointly Fakultät Für Kulturreflexion – Studium Fundamentale.

There was a strong culture of doing extra things "extra" at UWH, a tradition of engagement and participation. While there was no common university pedagogical policy, the idea that "you get the study experience you deserve" was central, and professors are more responsive to student interests than forcing them to learn predefined content, especially in the social sciences. Students are expected to develop as human beings, not just specialists, and master a critical approach; since 1990s a combination of deep and broad knowledge and skills is often referred to as a T-shaped professional. Examples of alternative character of studies at UWH include project based learning in medical sciences and courses in heterodox economy. The aim was both to question existing believes, developing judgement, and consciously, reflexively reassembling a student worldview.

Crisis and Stabilization

As a private university in Germany, UWH had received national attention after some time, thanks to attractive and effective research programmes. Konrad Schily, its founder and president (1982–1999, 2002–2004), is credited with securing the (regulatory and financial) support of the state of North Rhine-Westphalia during the first crisis in early 1994, as well as attracting some people of influence (like a Deutsche Bank CEO or the Bertelsmann founder) and big companies (Krupp) to donate to UWH.[8] The institution had no statute (*Grundordnung*) and Schily gathered a lot of competences. Schily wanted a university without departments, convinced that cutting edge research does not spring from just one discipline. This has proven impossible (Berndt, 1999).

After Schily stepped down, the new leadership attempted to overtake his personal fundraising connections, but with little success. Schily returned in 2002.

In 2008, four years after his second retirement, things got even worse. 'There had always been no money', as the saying went, but now UWH was really at a breaking point. The threat of withdrawal of *Land* financial support, and subsequent similar declarations by some major donors, coinciding with both the opening of an expensive new medical faculty building, and the global financial crisis, pushed UWH to the brink of closure.

Students protested in front of *Land* parliament to save the university. Ultimately, UWH survived thanks, on the one hand, to 1.3m euros raised by an Alumni Initiative from just over 1000 alumni they had back then, but most importantly, a rescue fund provided by Software AG Stiftung, and financial guarantees from Community Hospital Herdecke.[9] The institution started operating on a different financial model, expanded its degree portfolio, and started planning expansion. UWH, alongside its professional and research profile, has largely remained dedicated to liberal education.

Overview of Changes

Curriculum and pedagogy. The original pedagogical impulse for UWH was problem-based pedagogy in medical education that starts with the patient (a problem) and learns through problem-solving, rather than first acquiring a body of knowledge that is then deductively applied. It values the practitioner before researcher. This went against the dominant trends in public faculties of medicine (which referred to UWH a "fallen child"), but recently gathered more followers.[10]

A biomedical degree has been scrapped for financial reasons, but the core curriculum has not been affected as the desire for holistically educated practitioners was sustained. This constituted a bridge over classical vocational-liberal education distinction; the founders of UWH believed that professional education in aims requires holistic, multidimensional curricular and pedagogical tools, not a single-minded transmission of bodies of knowledge into students' heads.[11]

Professional programmes with fixed cohort size retained previous student-faculty ratio, but the average class size in economics and StuFu slightly increased.

KR still runs only in a seminar format, and lectures in other degrees remain quite small. Tandem seminars, co-taught by professors often from different departments, are still offered. However, since the crisis co-teaching professors are paid only 50% for these classes.

Students can still ask for lectures and courses in the areas of their interests, and are often consulted with regards to the curriculum. Only students in the economics degree pushed for more "school-like" pedagogy and "internationalization" – understood as going English and being less heterodox. This seems to be a departure from original fear that mainstream economics is "amoral."

The institution was conceived as an open space for teachers, where they could teach and research without pressure. German Council of Science and Humanities (Wissenschaftsrat, WR) recommendations might succeed in limiting this approach.

Costs and aid.   Until 1994 UWH was not allowed by the state to charge tuition. But the annual *Land* contributions of up to 4 million DM covering the difference between income and expenses were later started on a condition of introducing tuition, which UWH calls 'student contributions'.

UWH charges for a degree, not for semester, thereby not punishing students for taking longer to graduate. While the initial ideal was for all students to pay the same tuition (so that money would not drive degree choice), soon tuition rates have been unbundled, with medicine and dental medicine almost twice as expensive as other programmes. The basic rate doubled during the first decade after introduction in 1995, and then stalled at around 30.000 euros for a full degree.

WH does not offer institutional aid. The only options available are externally funded scholarships and emergency loans from a solidarity fund. However, since the introduction of tuition in 1995, a Student Association (SG) was established to offer an income-share agreement called UGV (*Umgekehrter Generationenvertrag, inverse generational contract*).

UGV is an income-share agreement through which students do not pay tuition fees while they study but rather pay a percentage of their income for several years afterwards once their income exceeds a certain amount. "Through the UGV people can study independently of their backgrounds and independently also from future career wishes." Because of big data sets, UWH is able to determine future income of the students depending on a degree, and price the upfront value of a degree accordingly. UGV rates and duration remain common. The system is quite flexible: students owe money for 20 years, of which they repay during 10; if their payments exceed 200% of upfront tuition, they are resolved from further duty. One participant summarised that UGV is therefore "basically speculation on your future income".

It might be argued that instead of a customer model, it is more similar to a "grateful alumni" model. While it should not be forgotten that this gratefulness is prescribed in a contract, in case of UWH, one should remember that UGV alumni were willing to even pay "extra" in donations when the university got into financial trouble.

Over time, UGV rates have increased from 8% for 8 years to 13% over 10 years and 12% for 12 years now. The SG's profit margin is 20%, from which they finance operational costs and build capital used for loans; they also encourage former students to invest in SG. It is now the biggest funder of studies in Germany. Chancen AG, a spin-off company of UWH, is now offering UGV to students at other private universities, and UGV is offered at Zeppelin University (below) and at Bucerius Law School.[12]

Several sources suggested a fair level of socio-economic diversity of UWH students, but we were unable to receive numbers to verify the claim.

Student body. To avoid a popular allegation of non-existing admissions standards, UWH developed a multi-step admissions procedure, which involved a letter of intent, handwritten full-text CV, and a personal assessment of candidates in small groups invited for an application day. The process was resource and time extensive, it included teams of faculty members and current students having to reach unanimous decision on each of 6 candidates. Recently medicine switched to assessing bigger groups of 50 applicants for one full admissions weekend.[13]

During the crisis, winter enrolment had been added. Study places at fixed programmes (professional) had been slightly increased, while psychology programmes (state-supported) experienced growth.

Currently students at UWH come from all over Germany, with one English degree (PPE MA) being offered. The minority of international students, mostly in this program, remains difficult to integrate into university life since all events are in German. Right into the crisis, most jobs in the international office had been made redundant, but restored a few years later. International experience for students is not necessarily strongly encouraged: resistance to blanket internationalization might be related to the idea of staying heterogeneous and enabled strong alumni pride (which supported philanthropic acts that saved the university in 2008).

Research.   While research was present from the very beginning, UWH primarily focused on teaching. WR recommended improving research outcomes, especially in medicine. It is the only university to offer PhDs in nursing sciences in Germany.

The KR faculty, with just four professor positions, had 1 million budget to run StuFu courses for 2000 students. Due to WR recommendation, the number of chairs recently increased to increase research productivity.

Management and institutional relations.   The crisis was deep but short. UWH adopted a different financial model (for example offering shares in UWH foundation), expanded its internal regulations, but did not significantly alter its structure and foci. Immediately in the crisis 30 administrative positions had been cut, and restored over the span of few years. UWH continues to receive public funds from several sources, and have currently annual budget of ca. 36 m euros.

The university remained conservative, and somewhat uncoordinated, in terms of branding and marketing. For example, branding Witten as a "university city" or rebranding the university website were accomplished with the help of some external donations, not on an institutional budget.

Zeppelin University

ZU was established in 2003 in Friedrichshafen in the Bodensee region, by three UWH alumni (Stefan Jensen as a president, Katja Volker and Tim Goebel as senior administrators). As one respondent put it: "In the last analysis, ZU is a UWH spin-off".

Named after Count Zeppelin, the Zeppelin Foundation (*Zeppelin Stiftung*, ZS) managing his estate remains the biggest donor to the University. ZS is operated by city authorities, redirects income from two sister companies, it is solely devoted to culture and science. Despite close ties to the city, ZU is a private institution using "privately gained money (…) designated for the public good"

Jansen, a businessman and management scholar, served until 2014, developing a Civil Society Centre, and establishing a research profile in the social sciences. Dirk Baecker, an accomplished researcher from the tradition of systems theory and supervisor of Jansen's PhD at UWH, joined the newly founded university, creating the "axis Bielefeld-Friedrichshafen" in German Luhmannian social sciences. Important research topics (for both UWH and ZU) are family businesses and digitalization.

119

During the first years the university had over 1000 applicants for just around 100 places.

Already in 2007–2008, ZU build a second campus in Konstanz. ZU is highly selective and teaches almost exclusively in German. While there is a small dormitory mostly used by international students, the majority of ca. 1300 ZU students live independently in the city.

Liberal Arts Features

ZU sees interdisciplinarity as a necessity in times of global challenges: its motto is "Bridging Business, Culture, and Politics".[14] It claims to be following the "Humboldtian Bildungsideal", with holistic/general education along a research profile and all levels of degree programmes. "We are not a business school and do not want to become one. We are a university and want to keep a university level".

The curriculum contains a "Zeppelin Year" designed for general education, that includes a set of 5 courses focusing on developing skills, methods, and conducting individual research. Zeppelin Year forms a core requirement for all students regardless of which of four interdisciplinary BA degrees they attend. Students choose from a variety of ZY courses, to which one afternoon each week is solely devoted. A significant part of curricula is elective. The final 'Humboldt' year requires students to conduct a full small-scale research project affiliated with a research group at ZU.

ZU calls itself also *"Präsenzuniversität"*, with smaller classes and more interactive pedagogies, distancing itself from online learning. Finally, the small academic community at ZU constitutes a space for a plethora of extracurricular and even curricular activities. The latter includes "StudentStudies" – courses proposed and organised by students, academically approved by faculty, in one case co-financed by alumni.

Crisis and Stabilization

ZU generally operates on the financial model of "Drittelfinanzierung": one third comes from tuition fees, one third from the Zeppelin Foundation, one third from donations and external cooperations (including research funded by public sources).

In 2014 the President of the Board (former CEO of Telekom) retired, and the whole founding team decided they will step down the next year. Already during the search for a new president, the chancellor was fired without notice, and soon news broke that Jansen and some faculty received remarkable provisions without awareness of the donors. Trust relations with the city and the donors were damaged, and members of the Zeppelin family attempted to redirect the funds to aviation research, which was denied by courts.

The leadership crisis went hand in hand with a financial crisis: ZU accumulated 4 million in debt due to lavish spending for state-of-the-art facilities at a new campus but also, for example, travel costs for senior management. Around that time, and just a month before the start of the academic year, ZU was almost bankrupt.

Finally, there was a crisis in organisational culture. The place that, according to students, always felt creative, extraordinary, and grassroots managed, turned out not to be transparent in its decision making processes. There was a widespread perception among engaged students that while they "were working for the university, for the ideas" other people were working "for their own pockets."

All three dimensions of the crisis were especially ill-received in the region, Swabia, known for its high esteem of fiscal conservatism. Already looked at with curiosity but also some suspicion, because of its status as a private and, in its own terms, "undisciplined" university, ZU started to appear as an alien element (*Fremdkörper*).

A newly appointed acting president and interim chancellor stabilised the situation and put forth long-deserved transparency of finances of the institution, both externally and internally, as well as some immediate cutbacks. Initial fears of closure were put behind with the repayment of debt by Zeppelin Company, restoring the trust of sponsors and increased applications due to the media attention proved that 'there is no such thing as bad press'.

The academic year 15–16 started with a new management and a sense of relief. Jansen left in 2016 and his research centre was subsequently closed. Some administration members left but gaps were quickly filled. On the whole, it is more appropriate to speak of a restructuring and a generational change, rather than a shrinking.

Although the institution survived, it did so at the cost of raising student numbers in some classes, putting a hiring stop for faculty and administrative positions, the selling of a Berlin satellite campus. A creative solution was cross-subsidizing existing programmes with stronger liberal education components through some of the newly established executive education degrees.

Overview of the Changes

Curriculum and pedagogy. The new management reviewed executive education programmes, discontinuing those that were running in red and developing the profitable ones (some have been tailor made for big companies).

Politics, Administration, and International Affairs (PAIR) and Culture, Communication, and Management (CCM), as well as Sociology, Politics, and Economics (SPE) degrees seem less tuition-paying students; they are effectively cross-subsidized by Corporate Management and Economics (CME) and executive programmes. PAIR is also not very popular among traditional college age students as the degree consists primarily of administration.

Under the interim management, faculty members successfully pushed for an increase in the number of credits per course to 6. This change reduced the number of courses taught by each professor, but also the total number of courses from which students were able to choose.[15] While professors believed they are over-worked, the financial necessity of that remains unclear, and some students considered it a blow to ZU's curriculum.

121

Mandatory classes remained capped at 35–40 students, and electives (which form the largest part of the curricula) are even smaller. Statistics classes enrollment was raised to 60–70 students as they were thought to demand more passive skill acquisition.[16]

Costs and aid. Tuition increases of about 1000 more euros over 8 semesters were mostly adjusting for the inflation since 2005.

Similar to UWH, ZU students either pay tuition in cash, take a low-interest loan from a local bank, or recently also apply for UGV from a spin-off UWH student company called Bildungsfond. Alongside programmes offered by external foundations,[17] 48 tuition waivers are offered by ZU at both BA and MA levels

During the first five years, ZU attracted primarily students with a strong financial wherewithal, in line with a stereotype of private HE in Germany and some stereotypes influencing negative self-selection. More recently economic diversity increased, getting closer to the shared feeling that ZU "wanted to be different from the public universities, but also from the really rich ones" and a hint that truly nonconventional students ZU was looking to attract might have unconventional backgrounds. Respondents unanimously suggested that growing economic diversity can be credited to the media exposure that raised the awareness in social spheres that might not usually know about ZU. Other dimensions of student diversity did not change significantly.

Student body. Applicant numbers were relatively high just before the crisis due to *Doppelabitur*[18] and abolishment of military duty, yet the class admitted in the fall of 2015 was even 150 students larger. The institution does not plan to grow beyond the total of 1400 students due to limited infrastructure.

Research. Institutional funds for research, used by chairs to attend conferences etc., were further trimmed. Without adequate funding, attracting top performing researchers might become more difficult. But so far, ZU did not experienced faculty outflow from ZU, despite proposals from competitors.

Maintaining curricular liberal arts features require sources exceeding the amount collected through tuition. In ZU case, apart from private contributions, executive education became a fourth pillar in *Drittelfinanzierung*.

Management and institutional relations. The new management was able to restore the trust of existing donors, losing the support of just one company, and taking a proactive stance towards attracting new ones, contrary to the previous administration's sometimes polarizing style.

A moratorium on all commissions received by professors and administrative staff has been established, and they and leadership were persuaded to renounce on certain, past contractual rights to such commissions. In an effort to rationalize expenses, a Berlin campus (est. 2011) has been closed, with ZU renting rooms from partner institutions according to its modest needs. A hiring stop for administration already had been in effect between 2014 and 2016.

ZU tries to attract alumni for lifelong learning programmes, teaching gigs, attendance at search committees, and alumni meetups, yet as a young institution, it only started developing such long-term strategies.

EUROPEAN COLLEGE OF LIBERAL ARTS – BARD COLLEGE BERLIN

Bard College Berlin was founded in 1999 under the name of European College of Liberal Arts by Stefan Gutzeit, later joined by Jan Werner-Müller and Erika Kiss. One of the inspirations was Stanford University and the American liberal arts model, in which they saw the true heir to Humboldt's vision. They hoped to reanimate what they saw as an ossified German higher education landscape. Supported by a group of German foundations and a range of well-known international intellectuals, they held a first summer school in 2000 and in 2002/03 offered a first one-year programme with 7 professors and 49 students.

In 2003 it became clear that the original support would not allow the college to grow to become the "Harvard of Germany". The Christian A. Johnson Endeavour Foundation (CAJEF) from New York,[19] bought the institution and re-founded it as a gGmbH (non-profit Limited) in 2002. The initial founders left. From then onwards Thomas Norgaard and Peter Hajnal ran the institution academically, initially with Richard H. Shriver as provost and general manager, later replaced by Laurent Boetsch, both experienced educators from the US.

The initial founding generation had envisioned to grow the place to a few thousand students, to be about equally dedicated to research and teaching, and to give space to natural and social sciences as well as the humanities. The new administration, on the other hand, decided from the outset to keep the place deliberately small to preserve its character as an intimate learning community, as evidenced by seminars run in professors' offices. The aim was to offer a personalized learning experience, and focus almost exclusively on teaching, rather than research. Since 2002, according to official corporate history, ECLA was "emphasizing interdisciplinary studies and permitting no academic departments".

Admission was need-blind and name-blind and most students were on full scholarships. Soon, a second one-year programme was introduced.

Liberal Arts Features

In 2009, the college started to offer its first full four-year B.A. programme in Value Studies – a new approach to liberal arts that combined some aspects of traditional Great Books degrees with problem-based approaches and was built on the central idea of creating a sustained and common reflection on pre-disciplinary value questions – what, how, and why do we value? – through small-scale, discussion-based seminars and a focused engagement with core texts and artworks (Norgaard & Hajnal, 2014). In 2010 they achieved state recognition as *Universität*, which was crucial for obtaining student visas for international students. The recognition as university came with the condition that it starts offering graduate programmes in the future.[20]

Crisis and Stabilization

Generous support from CAJEF (4m euro annually) lasted until 2011, when Bard College,[21] from Annandale, NY, took ownership of the college and financial responsibility for its expenses. Senior administration was replaced, and two years later, the name was changed to Bard College Berlin.

Bard College does not have an endowment, instead covering its expenses through a steady inflow of donations. The financial situation at BCB became very tight. It had to incrementally learn how to operate under new realities, rather than overcome a temporary crisis. Five years into the process, it seems that most of the adaptation and financial rebalancing of the institution is now done.

Overview of Changes

Curriculum and pedagogy. The Value Studies approach initially entailed an extensive common core component, which took up almost 60% of the degree at one point and involved a lot of co-teaching, which is obviously expensive. After the takeover, the common core was trimmed to about 20% now of each B.A. degree respectively and it is still largely co-taught. The motives for this were not entirely financial. The transdisciplinary nature of the Core implies that professors are teaching in a range of areas, often outside their speciality, which is unpopular among some of the faculty members and also some of the students. Hence, these developments also resulted from internal debates, and not only from financial pressure.

New degrees were introduced to attract new students: the B.A. in Value Studies was renamed B.A. in Humanities, the Arts, and Social Thought, and another B.A., was introduced in Economics, Politics, and Social Thought. There are attempts to capitalize on the flourishing Berlin art scene and to offer many more courses and shorter exchange programmes in the arts (including art practice, theory, and history, and classes on the social and political dimensions of art). Natural sciences still play a minor role. The average class size rose from around 8 in 2012 to around 14 in 2016 and is expected to reach 16.4 by 2019.

Costs and aid. The sticker price increased step by step from 12.500€ to 20.500€ per academic year since 2012. This included room and board for those who lived on campus, priced at around 2000€ in 2010, around 4000€ in 2013, and around 7000€ in 2016 per academic year. While this is a considerable increase over a relatively short period of time, real costs of education provided is estimated by the management at around 40.000 euro/student/year.

During ECLA times, many if not all students were admitted on full scholarships that also covered room and board, and all students were required to live on campus. There are still some full scholarships and a need-blind admission process at BCB, which reduces tuition by 50% on average but does not cover living costs. 80% of first year students and few students of the upper years live in college accommodation now, due to primarily increases in student numbers.

Student body. After an initial fall in application numbers, associated with a name change, student numbers almost doubled from around 80 students in 2012 to ca. 150 in 2016, and are expected to rise to 270 or more by 2019. This allows for a better distribution of costs and increased revenue. As at UWH and ZU, the infrastructure imposes some limits–albeit less so, as the new administration was willing to somewhat compromise the residential character of the college, probably unique in Germany. Adding teaching space is much easier than acquiring new dorms and cafeterias. Yet first steps in that direction have been undertaken through recently received grants. Having a residential character is one of the most important differentiating factors and an important selling point. It expresses a pedagogical core believe in the value of integrating academic and community life. Furthermore, real estate prices in Berlin are rising, steadily and not so slowly, and hence there is also an economic incentive to at least hold on to the land on which the campus is built. It remains to be seen how compatible with each other institutional growth and residential character are in the long run.

Rising tuition increase coincided with changes in student demographics. Tuition is lower than at many American colleges that, since the merger with Bard, BCB might be said to compete with. BCB also tries to attract (mostly) American exchange students, who each and on average bring ca. 1/3 more tuition income than a full time BA student. Both at ECLA and BCB many nations (usually around 40) are represented in the student body, including developing countries. But the relative sizes of the cohorts from different countries shifted: while Eastern European students were well represented at ECLA, today they and students from developing countries are in single digits. German law requires that at least 50% of students qualify for a German degree, which means either German students (a constant but small minority) or holders of small number of Abitur-equivalent secondary degrees. While there is a lot of national, linguistic, and gender diversity, and some racial diversity, too, there seems to be less diversity in terms of class/socio-economic background (in 2014 85.4% students had at least one university educated parent).

Research. Research was never a big focus of the college, whose professors have mostly focused on teaching as well as institutional and curricular development. The WR expects BCB to increase the efforts in this respect in the close future. As of winter 2017, the college has 12 full time professors, three of which are junior professors and plans to hire three more professors in economics, politics, and the arts

125

by fall 2017. 50% of these professors are women and the professors account for 50% of teaching, with 26 adjunct positions (*Lehrbeauftragte*) accounting for the rest.

Management and institutional relations. Between 2003–2011 fundraising was not necessary given the Foundation's support, and administrative staff was rather limited. Later the need for financial sustainability and institutional expansion directed attempts to connect stronger with other Berlin institutions (universities, art spaces, etc.), notably through shared courses or co-organized conferences, in order to make the college more visible in the Berlin and German higher education landscape. Here it might be argued that current leadership is getting closer to the ideals of the 1999–2002 period.

Another way of making itself more attractive to donors has revolved around the term "civic engagement": students are getting money for doing socially engaged projects and the university tries to brand itself as a civically conscious institution. Recently, Bard Annandale matched gifts to create scholarships for nine students from Syria and other crisis regions – so at BCB now as much as 5% of their student body is comprised of refugees. With the instruction in English, refugee students might return to higher education faster than at other institutions that have German proficiency requirements.

Recently introduced summer programmes in German and theatre have turned out to be another powerful source of revenue.

VULNERABLE YET SURVIVING?

In financially challenging times, private universities lacking endowment face the obvious pressure to cut costs and increase revenue. Liberal arts features *sensu stricto*, as well as an *implicit* environment of economic diversity, talented teachers, researchers and students, are undoubtedly at odds with those requirements.

Winning Strategies

The following, overlapping winning strategies were identified:

Diversification of income sources. Depending on a single or few sources of income, especially courted by its founder, poses great risks. Summer schools (BCB), executive education programs (ZU), professionalized fundraising (all three), and new marketing strategies were some examples that we saw at German Private Liberal Education Institutions (GPLEs). Obtaining support from public sources, if possible, might also bring additional income, especially when the subvention goes to teaching activities (psychology at UWH) not research (unless a significant overhead is secured by a university).

Engaging alumni. Institutions increasingly recognize the importance of alumni, especially when they offer financial donations and lobbying pressure in favour of

Table 7.2. Identified strategies employed to mitigate financial pressure by Bard College Berlin (BCB), Zeppelin University (ZU), University Witten-Herdecke (WH)

Field of reaction	Concrete measures	BCB	ZU	WH
Diversification of Income Sources	Undergrad summer schools	Yes	No	No
	Executive education	No	Yes	No
	Professionalized fundraising	Yes	Yes	Yes
	Public funding	No	No	Some
Engaging alumni	In institutional decisions	Growing	Growing	Yes
	As donors	Low	Low	Strong
Stabilizing and democratizing leadership	Statues for leadership changes	Yes	Yes	Yes
	Bind donors to institution, not persons	Yes	Yes	Yes
Strenghtening local ties	Academic	Yes	Yes	Yes
	Cultural	Yes	Yes	Yes
	Economic	Some	Yes	Yes
	Government	Some	Yes	Yes
Selling points	Academic core areas	Expanding	Sustaining	Sustaining
	Signature pedagogies	Kept	Kept	Kept
	Campus life	Reduced	–	–

universities. Even though GPLEs have a relatively short history, they graduated a small yet increasingly able pool of alumni that might offer GPLEs competitive advantage over public institutions. Counterintuitively, this applies also to alumni indebted to the institution through income share agreements.[22] Good alumni network benefits not only in donations, but also in terms of graduate destinations, employability, and reputation of an institution.

Stabilizing and democratizing leadership. Initially, fundraising and management centred around charismatic visionaries, which meant that leadership transition often coincided with financial crisis. Establishment and further stabilisation require different competencies and attitudes, with the latter barring on disenchantment with the revolutionary spirit of the early days. GPLEs should as much as possible have rules in place for stable power transitions changes, encourage donors to identify with the institution rather than one of its leaders, and avoid trust damaging power vacuums, financial intransparencies, and decisions made in top-down manner

Strengthening local ties.   Being firmly integrated into local higher education and research, cultural, and economic landscapes created resiliency-increasing networks in times of crisis, gave visibility and trustworthiness required for donor-acquisition, and made it harder for political actors to withdraw support. Going against the research prestige game of big name research universities, GPLEs have a fair chance of success in attracting students to less academically developed regions. In the future, college networks similar to Five College Consortium in Western Massachusetts might be a viable option for running sustainable colleges/universities at small scale, without the need to duplicate expensive features in closely located institutions.

Sustaining the core area of interest and signature pedagogies.   All GPLEs studied combined a commitment to transdisciplinary education and research with disciplinary concentrations and a set of signature pedagogies that together gave them distinct profiles, broad enough to attract a range of students yet distinct enough to stand out clearly from the higher education landscape. While financial considerations of students comparing them to no-tuition public universities would be the case for any foreseeable future, sustaining predictable financial aid models and keeping prices at bay would be especially important. GPLEs would only survive if they have clear and convincing selling points, be they return on investment or of a more institution-specific character.

LEARNING FROM GPLES

Methodological Note

Studies of GPLEs negotiating their institutional identity and educational mission against the bumpy financial background of higher education in the early 21st century can help us better understand the internal diversity within the liberal education movement. But our use of the "liberal education" label might be seen as controversial.

The methodological discussion on the inclusion criteria is not yet settled. Scholars often find themselves choosing between the Scylla of authoritative, non-defined list (for example ECOLAS) and the Charybdis of highly complex criteria (Godwin, 2013). Previous approaches (curriculum, organization and learning outcomes based) are mostly based on American examples – the tradition of non-vocational undergraduate curricula, enhanced by relatively weak high school preparation, and conscious decision of not offering undergraduate education in many professional programmes. Criteria proposed in this study might offer some suggestions on how to make deductive models more useful, especially in identifying institutions not directly labelling itself as "liberal education" as is the case of most GPLEs. As researchers, we plea for more caution in treating "grassroots" liberal education programmes in European countries together with branch campuses and bubble institutions operating under American law on European soil (the case of well-established American Universities). However, the example of BCB might be a case in counter-point.

Further Research

The most interesting issue, yet undetectable given our methodology, that emerged from our study were changes in the campus climate and leadership styles.[23] It became clear from the interviews that often the institutional growth and crises meant (different kinds of) changes in the institutional culture or spirit, especially affecting 'academic artisans' that serve at the administrative and community backbone of a college without being acknowledged as they perform less research (Brew, Boud, Namgung, Lucas, & Crawford, 2016). Further work, especially of an ethnographic kind, would be needed to understand fully the nature of such change and their effects. What seems clear to us so far is that they both express and respond to developments in the self-image of the institutions and their positions, perceived and actual, as members on the edge of the German higher education and broader cultural landscape.

One key aspect to studying how a place's culture and spirit changed would be to look at how the crises are reflected in the self-presentation of the institutions' histories. UWH, which also has had the most time pass since its crises, offers a fairly comprehensive history of itself on its website. ZU and BCB offer less comprehensive versions of their history. BLS, which has not yet known any major crises like the other places offers almost no information on its history, despite being of comparable age, as if through a lack of marking events nothing gave rise to historical self-awareness.[24] BCB did have an internal working-through process that included institutional efforts to write and preserve its history (which one of the authors was heavily involved with). Such internal processes of reflecting on larger structural shifts are important to make the best possible use of the learnings that the crises offer, to keep perspective and clarity regarding the university's mission, and keep all stakeholders engaged towards its goals.

Secondly, attempts at developing more liberal education are not always successful, while "nature and causes of failure may be just as illuminating as those of success" (Tight, 2012, p. 287). One case to be studied would be Humboldt-Viadrina School of Governance, which declared bankruptcy in 2014 after five years of teaching, despite support from high profile organisations and political figures.[25] But also in the successful cases we looked at, full evaluative, longitudinal studies based on prolonged ethnographic work, could give a fuller picture regarding the price of survival (in terms of student experience, course design, assessment, and evaluations, diversity, graduate destinations, faculty identification, etc.), and the dynamics of internal struggles between different visions and values, with special reference to unfulfilled hopes and rejected plans. While our focus has been on identifying resiliency-increasing winning strategies, those pathways seem especially promising.

Wider Relevance of GPLEs

In a sector plagued by long-term austerity, learning how to survive without selling your academic soul can be of relevance to other countries and types of institutions.

Survival strategies of GPLEs also dovetail with at least three bigger themes in higher education research.

GPLEs provide an example of diversification of HE system, but through the less travelled by path (by private institutions) of academically valuable and broad programmes (Altbach, Reisberg, & Wit, 2017). An important part of their operation is devoted to an alternative to employability, standardization, and the comparability mantra of the Bologna Process. Strategies advanced by GPLEs during austerity are especially important as they were proven effective by institutional survival, and hopefully sustaining their liberal education features.

With a weaker research profile, GPLEs position themselves against both public universities and non-liberal privates by focusing on their signature strengths. One of them is pedagogy. GPLEs belong to a sector that first fostered child-centered pedagogies and student-centered learning, and was more flexible in implementing and experimenting on it. Now it seems that GPLEs might become more successful in reminding public universities of their responsibility for creating more welcoming and effective learning environment. In many countries, including the UK, Norway and Germany, governments took recently more active role in appreciating (and regulating) learning conditions, which slowly become less an autonomously designed feature of higher education institution and more a policy target.

Finally and provocatively, we would argue that when research is well integrated and diversity treated seriously, GPLEs might be said to provide a better environment for well-rounded education or seminar-based Bildung, than their public counterparts.[26]

NOTES

[1] First mentions of contemporary European liberal education (Gillespie, 2001; Rothblatt, 2003) were followed by more comprehensive article by Marijk van der Wende (2011) dealing with regional phenomenon, and case studies of institutions/countries (Kirby & van der Wende, 2016; Peterson, 2012). Kara A. Godwin (2013) conducted an exploratory and comparative study of liberal education outside the U.S., that located 52 programs in Europe. Current number, according to those criteria, would be over 70, however one might be reminded that most studies above did not exclude American universities that are only located in European cities.

[2] Only two public universities in Germany offer liberal education programs. Both started in 2012: Freiburg University College of Liberal Arts and Sciences (Eschenbruch, Gehrke, & Sterzel, 2016), and Leuphana University Lüneburg Studium Individuale. More information on both programs, as well as the German landscape for selective/honors programs, can be found in (Wolfensberger, 2015).

[3] Touro College Berlin and NYU Berlin do not meet the fifth criterion.

[4] BLS is a law school and hence a professional school, included in our sample because of mandatory *studium generale*, which can include subjects such as "philosophy; history, politics & society; art & culture; nature & technology" to which one afternoon per week is set aside, for all undergraduate students, for this broader liberal learning. A broad coaching & mentoring programme (*studium personale*) and internships (*studium professionale*) further complement the degree.

[5] Most numerical values, internal policy changes and plans described in the paper are based on: Wissenschaftsrat reports on UWH (2005, 2011), ZU (2009), BCB (2017), BCB college brochures from 08/09, 10/11, 14/15, 16/17; ZU brochures from 2016/17, ACQUIN accreditation reports (ZU: 2013, BCB: 2013, 2015); and the university homepage.

[6] JUB at one point had to let go a sizable fraction of their administrative personnel.

[7] Anthroposophy, the philosophical school founded by Rudolph Steiner and philosophical background to his Waldorf pedagogy as well as several kinds of heterodox medicine, is an important intellectual background for UWH. A humanism with an esoteric touch, it combines elements of Christianity, German Idealism, and Eastern religious and philosophical thought among other things. Software AG Stiftung is one of the main donors of UWH and the anthroposophist movement in Germany

[8] See also: (Schily, 1993).

[9] Software AG Stiftung now holds 51% of UWH shares, with university foundation, student company, alumni and other bodies as further shareholders. Current numbers can be found https://www.uni-wh.de/universitaet/universitaetsleitung/gesellschafter/

[10] On the windy history of project based learning see (Servant, 2016).

[11] Similarly to the growing popularity of pragmatic liberal education or practical liberal arts in the US (Brint, Riddle, Turk-Bicakci, & Levy, 2005; Paris & Kimball, 2000).

[12] JUB has tried it in the early 2000s but given up on the idea, because, unlike UWH, many of their alumni returned to their non-EU home countries and were hard to reach in cases of default. Given the changed geopolitical situation and the rise in connectivity brought about by the internet age, we think that, rightly designed, it might be able to meet this problem today, help ensure wide accessibility of liberal education, and deserves more scholarly attention.

[13] The new admissions process is modelled after Studienstiftung des Deutschen Volkes, which offers merit-based scholarships and networking opportunities for carefully chosen candidates.

[14] 'Business' here translates 'Wirtschaft,' which includes both business (*Betriebswirtschaft*) and economics (*Volkswirtschaft*) as its two branches.

[15] Similarly to a plan adopted in the fall of 2016 by Vassar College (US), in which faculty teaching load was reduced from 5 to 4 courses per year, in exchange for additional tutoring tasks.

[16] Interestingly, one respondent mentioned absences as a factor effectively reducing class sizes

[17] Notably, the party affiliated Konrad Adenauer Stiftung (CDU), Friedrich Ebert Stiftung (SPD), Hanns Seidl Stiftung (CSU), Friedrich Naumann Stiftung (FDP), Heinrich Böll Stiftung (Greens), and Rosa Luxemburg Stiftung (Left), the church affiliated Evangelisches Studienwerk Vil igst and Cusanuswerk, the meritocratic Studienstiftung des Deutschen Volkes, as well as the union-associated Hans Böckler Stiftung, and the entrepreneurial Stiftung der Deutschen Wirtschaft.

[18] Doppelabitur year mean on in which two age cohorts simultaneously graduated from high school due to school reform in Germany.

[19] CAJEF was supporting liberal education initiatives in CEE, first through "Artes Liberales Association" (1996–2001) and to this day in Warsaw and Bratislava.

[20] MA programmes are expected to start no sooner than 2021.

[21] Bard offers joint degrees with AUCA in Kyrgyz Republic, Smolny College in Russia and Al.-Quds in Palestine.

[22] WR has especially commended UWH for integrating alumni into various aspects of university life.

[23] For example, in terms of institutional governance and culture, one might wonder how leadership might be an occasion to challenge the dominant narrative. At ZU, Jansen enjoyed a reputation of highly valuing student input and engagement, and students generally had a feeling that they truly shared in the ownership of the place. A year after the crisis, the institution called a general assembly, which was designed to inform everyone about the state of the university. Many students felt that they were told that they "don't have anything to say" and that subsequently the bottom line became all-important decision making factor. At the same time, others point to the fact that a lot of student input had been only nominal even well before the crisis, as important decisions were made by a small leadership team around Jansen. Changes in the spirit of the place might thus be only limitedly reflected in changes in institutional arrangements.

[24] JUB, on the other hand, which is currently undergoing a reform, also has virtually no information on its history on the website.

[25] Among other liberal education developments in Europe, reasons for closure were either political (European Humanities University in Minsk) or related to negative accreditation (Academia Vitae in Deventer); despite being on the margins of higher education, no institution (to the best of our knowledge) was unable to continuously attract enough students to survive.

[26] Frank et al. distinguishes five sub-categories of private higher education in Germany. The ones analyzed in this paper fall under "Humboldtian", who "work on a comparable academic level like the specialists, but, differently from those, place the emphasis on multi- and interdisciplinarity, with the goal of developing transdisciplinary competences in research and teaching." (Frank, Hieronimus, Killius, & Meyer-Guckel, 2015, p. 6).

REFERENCES

Altbach, P. G., Reisberg, L., & Wit, H. de. (2017). *Responding to massification: Differentiation in postsecondary education worldwide*. Hamburg: Hamburg Transnational University Leaders Council.

Berndt, C. (1999, November). Konrad Schily Der Geist von Herdecke. *Bild Der Wissenschaft*.

Brew, A., Boud, D., Namgung, S. U., Lucas, L., & Crawford, K. (2016). Research productivity and academics' conceptions of research. *Higher Education, 71*(5), 681–697. Retrieved from http://doi.org/10.1007/s10734-015-9930-6

Brint, S., Riddle, M., Turk-Bicakci, L., & Levy, C. S. (2005). From the liberal to the practical arts in American colleges and universities: Organizational analysis and curricular change. *Journal of Higher Education, 76*, 151–180.

Eschenbruch, N., Gehrke, H.-J., & Sterzel, P. (2016). University college freiburg: Toward a new unity of research and teaching in academia. In C. W. Kirby & C. M. van der Wende (Eds.), *Experiences in liberal arts and science education from America, Europe, and Asia: A dialogue across continents* (pp. 91–108). New York, NY: Palgrave Macmillan US. Retrieved from http://doi.org/10.1057/978-1-349-94892-5_7

Frank, A., Hieronimus, S., Killius, N., & Meyer-Guckel, V. (2015). *Die rolle und zukunft privater hochschulen in deutschland*. Essen.

Gillespie, S. (2001). Opening minds: The international liberal education movement. *World Policy Journal, Winter*, 79–89.

Godwin, K. A. (2013). *The global emergence of liberal education: A comparative and exploratory study*. Boston College.

Godwin, K. A., & Altbach, P. G. (2016). A historical and global perspective on liberal arts education: What was, what is, and what will be. *International Journal of Chinese Education, 5*, 5–22. Retrieved from http://doi.org/10.1163/22125868-12340057

Grant, G., & Riesman, D. (1978). *The perpetual dream: Reform and experiment in the American college*. Chicago & London: University Of Chicago Press.

Huisman, J., & Vught, F. van. (2009). Diversity in European higher education: Historical trends and current policies. In *Mapping the higher education landscape book: Towards a European classification of higher education* (pp. 17–37). Twente: Springer Netherlands.

Kimball, B. A. (1995). *Orators & philosophers: A history of the idea of liberal education*. (R. Orrill, Ed.). New York, NY: College Entrance Examination Board.

Kirby, W. C., & van der Wende, M. C. (Eds.). (2016). *Experiences in liberal arts and science education from America, Europe, and Asia*. New York, NY: Palgrave Macmillan US. Retrieved from http://doi.org/10.1057/978-1-349-94892-5

Norgaard, T., & Hajnal, P. (2014). Value studies and democratic citizenship. In J. N. Reich (Ed.), *Civic engagement, civic development, and higher education: New perspectives on transformational learning* (pp. 41–46). Washington, DC: Bringing Theory to Practice.

Nussbaum, M. C. (1998). *Cultivating humanity: A classical defense of reform in liberal education*. Cambridge,MA: Harvard University Press.

Nussbaum, M. C. (2012). *Not for Profit: Why democracy needs the humanities*. Princeton: Princeton University Press.

Paris, D. C., & Kimball, B. A. (2000). Liberal education: An overlapping pragmatic consensus. *Journal of Curriculum Studies, 32*(2), 143–158. Retrieved from http://doi.org/10.1080/002202700182682

Peterson, P. M. (2012). *Confronting challenges to the liberal arts curriculum: Perspectives of developing and transitional countries*. New York, NY: Routledge.

Rothblatt, S. (2003). *The living arts: Comparative and historical reflections on liberal education*. Washington, DC: Association of American Colleges and Universities.

Schily, K. (1993). *Der staatlich bewirtschaftete Geist: Wege aus der bildungskrise*. Düsseldorf, New York, NY: ECON.

Servant, V. (2016). *Revolutions and re-iterations: An intellectual history of problem-based learning*. Erasmus University Rotterdam.

Tight, M. (2012). Levels of analysis in higher education research. *Tertiary Education and Management*, *18*(3), 271–288. Retrieved from http://doi.org/10.1080/13583883.2012.700461

van der Wende, M. C. (2011). The emergence of liberal arts and sciences education in Europe: A comparative perspective. *Higher Education Policy*, *24*, 233–253.

Wolfensberger, M. V. C. (2015). Germany: Foundations supporting talents. In *Talent development in European higher education* (pp. 179–211). Cham: Springer International Publishing. Retrieved from http://doi.org/10.1007/978-3-319-12919-8_12

Daniel Kontowski
Department of Education Studies and Liberal Arts
University of Winchester
and
Institute of Sociology
University of Warsaw

David M. Kretz
Department of Philosophy
École Normale Supérieure

SANDRA HASANEFENDIC, MARIA TERESA PATRICIO
AND FRANK G. A. DE BAKKER

8. HETEROGENEOUS RESPONSES OF PORTUGUESE POLYTECHNICS TO NEW RESEARCH POLICY DEMANDS

INTRODUCTION

In this chapter, we examine the contrasting organizational responses of two polytechnics in Portugal to new research policy demands in higher education. The research demands were developed as part of the new European policy agenda aimed at transforming the European Union into the most competitive and dynamic knowledge economy in the world (Amaral & Magalhães, 2004). Polytechnic institutes and Universities of Applied Sciences were asked to "accommodate societal demands by linking professional practice and education through innovative research" (De Weert & So, 2009, p. 34). Research was expected to be innovative by promoting cohesion within the region and engaging local industry in short-term projects (Hasanefendic et al., 2016), while at the same time advancing the professional curriculum (Jongbloed, 2010). Despite calls for distributive knowledge production through research, recent studies have shown that rather basic research practices still seem to be dominant in some polytechnics (Holmberg & Hallonsten, 2015), and that even when research is interpreted as applied, short-term and regionally relevant in national higher education settings, polytechnics seem to be responding to these new demands in different ways, leading to the heterogeneity of organizational responses (see Hasanefendic et al., 2016).

Different organizational responses within higher education systems have been examined mostly from a policy perspective. Studies have, for instance, looked at how European policies and global trends have been disseminated and adopted in national higher education systems (e.g. Patricio, 2010) and accounted for differences due to national specificities (e.g., Amaral et al., 2013). At the same time, recent work has stressed how internal organizational attributes, such as organizational identity (Fumasoli & Stensaker, 2013) or tradition (Sam & van der Sijde, 2014) also influence organizational responses to new policy demands. Collectively, these analyses of the ways in which higher education organizations have responded to new policy demands, have reinforced the idea that heterogeneity is a result of differences across national higher education systems. At the same time, organizational heterogeneity has also been explained as a result of organizational attributes which function as

R. Deem & H. Eggins (Eds.), The University as a Critical Institution?, 135–153.

filters of new policy demands and contribute to differences within the same higher education systems (e.g., Fumasoli et al., 2015). Notwithstanding the importance of these different perspectives, we argue that these studies tend to underestimate the role of the national higher education field and the way it shapes organizational responses. Recent research indicates that institutional players in a national higher education field are playing a significant role in shaping organizational experiences, while also contributing to heterogeneous organizational responses (e.g., Hüther & Krücken, 2016; Scott & Biag, 2016; Frølich et al., 2013).

Drawing on neo-institutional theory, a field is defined in this chapter as an aggregate of institutions (field actors) and organizations "that partake of a common meaning system and whose participants interact more frequently and fatefully with one another than with actors outside the field" (Scott, 1995, p. 56). It is characterized by institutional pluralism where organizations are faced with multiple institutional prescriptions from different field actors (Meyer & Höllerer, 2016). Organizations, therefore, are expected to adhere to institutional prescriptions from diverse field actors. This is relatively unproblematic as long as these prescriptions are congruent, compatible or harmonious as this makes the field stable by advancing clear regulatory, normative and cognitive frameworks (Greenwood et al., 2011). However, field actors may also disagree on what is desirable organizational behavior, especially in times of change, in which case incompatibility and contradiction among different institutional prescriptions will be a consequence, leading to organizational experience of complexity in the field (Greenwood et al., 2011). Following these insights, we inquired as to how the organizational experience of the conditions in the Portuguese higher education field influences polytechnic responses to the new research policy.

To address this research question, we interviewed and analyzed the responses of teaching staff, Deans of Schools, Directors of courses and study programs, and the Presidents of two polytechnics in Portugal. Their responses showed that the higher education arena was experienced as a complex field characterized by a lack of consensus among the main field actors. The complexity of the field was also manifest at the macro level of analysis with regard to discrepancies in the legal framework and the ambiguity of research and funding practices. Policy ambiguities and uncertainties were reflected at the micro level in individual behavior, further contributing to the complexity of the field. Through the presentation of two case studies, we illustrated different strategic responses of polytechnics as either "wannabes" or hybridizers. These two responses were enabled by the experienced field complexity and represented organizational aspirations for strategic positioning in the field. This study hoped to contribute to the higher education literature by referencing organizations as strategic entities that strategize and maneuver within a complex field.

The remainder of the chapter is divided into five sections. The following section discusses the theoretical context, whereas the subsequent sections present our research setting, findings, discussion and conclusion, with a future research agenda.

THE HIGHER EDUCATION FIELD: COMPLEXITY AND
ORGANIZATIONAL RESPONSES

The higher education field is composed of diverse posts-secondary educational organizations oriented towards multiple teaching, research and third stream missions while serving a wide range of students (Scott & Biag, 2016; Popp Berman & Paradeise, 2016). These organizations operate in highly institutionalized environments (Scott & Christensen, 1995) and are driven by cultural, cognitive, normative and regulative prescriptions (Harris, 2013). These prescriptions are provided or formulated by field actors who constrain or support higher education organizations in accomplishing their goals, while providing resources and legitimacy (Harris, 2013; Scott & Biag, 2016). These actors are national or international regulatory groups, governmental agencies, funding agencies, professional and trade associations, special interest groups, and the general public, among others (DiMaggio & Powell, 1983). Over time, this field is said to become influenced by a set of isomorphic regulatory (e.g., defined by law, rules and regulations at the macro level), normative and cognitive (internalized by individuals in daily work practices at the micro level) prescriptions that guide action and ensure legitimacy, eventually leading to organizational homogeneity (DiMaggio & Powell, 1983). Institutional isomorphism refers to the way that organizations become more similar because they co-exist in similar environmental conditions and follows the same rules and norms to attain legitimacy (Dacin, 1997). For example, higher education organizations in Europe were expected to implement the Bologna structure and to modernize teaching and research practices in order to contribute to the development of the European Higher Education Area (Teixeira, 2016).

To remain competitive, national governments enforced the mechanisms of Bologna in the national higher education fields in the form of regulatory prescriptions such as laws and policies, as well as through national systems of funding, evaluation, accreditation and other quality assurance mechanisms to control academic programs (Cardoso et al., 2015). These prescriptions were enforced in order to "fine tune" the behavior of higher education organizations, and they were applied to universities and polytechnics alike. As a result of these isomorphic pressures, the common assumption was that the organizations in the higher education field would respond to these new demands, guided by the dominant and coherent regulatory prescriptions, which in turn would lead to similar organizational outcomes (Scott, 1995).

However, fields do not always provide coherent and dominant regulatory, or normative and cognitive frameworks for organizations to follow in order to secure legitimacy in response to a new demand; fields can also be spaces for contestation and disputed arenas (Zietsma et al., 2017). This means that field actors provide contradictory, unclear and even misleading prescriptions for organizations to follow regarding the new demand, which affects the dominant and coherent understanding of regulatory, normative and cognitive frameworks, while contributing to incompatibilities between them (Greenwood et al., 2011). In these instances, organizations experience their fields as complex, face identity ambiguity and may engage in interest-driven struggles with field actors to make sense of the process (Hoffman, 2001). They may dispute different interests that are relevant for achieving their own specific organizational goals, leading to heterogeneity of organizational responses to the new demand (e.g., Bertels & Lawrence, 2016).

Considering the multiplicity of new demands entering the higher education field with globalization and neo-liberal policies, and with the implementation of national policies concerning funding, research and governance to stimulate European and global competition, it can be expected that polytechnics and universities experience their higher education field as increasingly complex. Scrutinizing the higher education field as a domain in which organizations engage in reinterpretations of the field and see opportunities to define and follow their own interests simultaneously, is a useful avenue to explore in aiming to understand heterogeneous organizational responses in higher education. Toward this end, we explore how two Portuguese polytechnics responded to a new research policy by investigating how they experienced specific field conditions in which they are embedded and how this experience shaped their responses.

RESEARCH SETTING

Portuguese polytechnics originated in the 1970s as a way to train the labour force, through the mergers of smaller industrial or commercial institutes, and thus help qualify the under-educated Portuguese population (Leão, 2007; Urbano, 2011). Higher education was no longer a privilege of the wealthy and few, but rather became an opportunity for many to contribute to the economic and social development of the country (Simao et al., 2004). Since then, 15 public Portuguese polytechnics and five non-integrated schools have provided alternatives to a traditional university education (A3ES, 2012). Polytechnics and non-integrated schools have been training students for professions and providing education based on the practical application of theoretical knowledge for several decades (see Hasanefendic et al., 2016). Recently, however, the Government has required polytechnics to undertake research activities. So as to not confuse the research activities of polytechnics with those of universities, the legislation enacting the requirement identified research for polytechnics in the context of applicability, usability and transferability of knowledge to societal actors (e.g., Law n° 49/2005; Law n° 62/2007; Decree Law n° 207/2009). However, and in spite of the explicit policy requirement, the government delayed introducing mechanisms to promote this research practice in Portuguese polytechnics. This means that research is still largely defined within the context of universities by other field actors such as accreditation and funding agencies, which are oriented towards scientific production for the advancement of knowledge. In this context, research is still measured by the number of publications, number of citations and the impact factor of journals. Whereas legal measures and policy discourse in Portugal encourages diversification of research roles, missions and practices between the university and polytechnic sectors, the mechanisms to foster this diversification are absent (Fonseca, 2001; Urbano, 2011), and in their absence the ambiguity of research practice is furthered. This situation has led polytechnics to respond to the new research mandate in different ways.

CASE SELECTION AND DATA COLLECTION

In order to explore how heterogeneity emerged in such a context and what role the field played, we studied the general perceptions of research policy in the higher education field, as well as research practices, at two polytechnics in Portugal. The first polytechnic was situated in a metropolitan urban area close to research universities (PA), whereas the second polytechnic was the major tertiary education provider in a rural part of the country (PB). We chose these two polytechnics as we expected perceptions toward research to be different and the reasons for this difference to be more pronounced. It was hoped that this purposive sampling could help highlight the role of field complexity.

The data were collected between 2014 and 2015 by observations and on-site visits in order to develop a more holistic understanding of the phenomena under study (Dewalt & Dewalt, 2002). We used observations to gain better insight into the context and conditions of the two organizations (see Figure 8.1)

Semi-structured interviews – 19 in Polytechnic A and 21 in Polytechnic B – were conducted which took place in six Schools in Polytechnic A and four Schools in Polytechnic B. We interviewed teaching staff, Directors of Programs, Deans of Schools, Pro Presidents and Presidents and Vice Presidents of each polytechnic. The Schools are organized according to discipline (e.g. engineering, music and arts, health, management of technology, agriculture). Interviews lasted between 50 and 100 minutes. The goal was to interview a diverse group so as to achieve greater validity of the data obtained. The second source of data consisted of government legislation, higher education regulations, official website data, online journals and newspaper articles. Both interview and documental data were analyzed by using the Atlas.ti qualitative data software.

The process of data analysis was iterative (Lincoln & Guba, 1985), following a constant comparison technique (Glaser & Strauss, 2012). The aim was to capture respondents' experiences, views and interpretations of the polytechnics, their experience of the higher education field and their new mission of research in the national higher education field. Open coding was conducted by labelling and paraphrasing quotations; as the data was analyzed, additional concepts and codes were applied, suggesting that the phenomenon was more complex than expected. For example, whenever we found quotations such as "society values university education higher" or "we are perceived as lower quality and second hand institutions," these were coded as the "underdog position of a polytechnic". This was not one of our initial concepts from theory, but it bore relevance to the specific case. Some of these open codes were analytical, whereas others were descriptive, and referred to concrete events, activities, or people.

SOURCES	TYPOLOGY OF DATA		DATA USE
Participant observation and on-site visits	65 pages of written notes (2 A4 notebooks)		Familiarization with the organizational context. Identification of the research setting and interviewees. Understanding of time spent on research in relation to other activities. Understanding the workplace context and differences between the two cases. Validation of findings from the interviews about research practices in both organizations.
Interviews (98% have PhDs and 2% have some sort of professional experience)	**Polytechnic A** (6 female)	**Polytechnic B** (9 female)	In depth understanding of the norms and values underpinning the polytechnic sector and research practice. Understanding of the changes in the polytechnic sector and in comparison to universities. Perceptions on the developments and importance of polytechnics in broader societal terms. Collecting perceptions about the role of research as defined in the law and other regulations, the practice of research at the polytechnic, and how it might have changed their traditional way of work.
Teaching staff and/or Presidents and Vice Presidents of Scientific Councils in their respective Schools (usually dual roles)	13	9	
Deans of Schools/Vice Deans (some still teach)	3	8	
Vice Presidents, Pro Presidents of the Polytechnic	3	4	
Documental data Laws and Decree-Laws	Law n°5/73 of the 25 of July; Decree-Law n.°402/73 of the 11 of August; Decree-Law n.°427-B/77 of the 14 of October; Decree-Law n.°513-T/79 of the 26 of December; Law n.°46/86 of the 14 of October; Law n.°54/90 of the 5 of September; Law n°62/2007 of the 10th of September and Decree-Law n.°207/2009.		Triangulate data and support information emerging from interviews.
Website data	http://www.a3es.pt/; http://www.fct.pt/index.phtml.pt		
Online newspapers	Público, Expresso, TSF Radio Noticias		

Figure 8.1. Typology of data

Once this stage was done, we proceeded by naming or renaming the codes, adding new ones, or removing others, eventually merging several codes into families or second order categories (Gioia et al., 2013). The last step in our analysis involved the establishment of central categories or aggregate dimensions and relating them to other second order categories (see Figure 8.2). Reliability was assured by using multiple data sources, and validity was checked via continuous analysis of data or by going back and forth between interviews and other types of data sources (Glaser & Strauss, 2012).

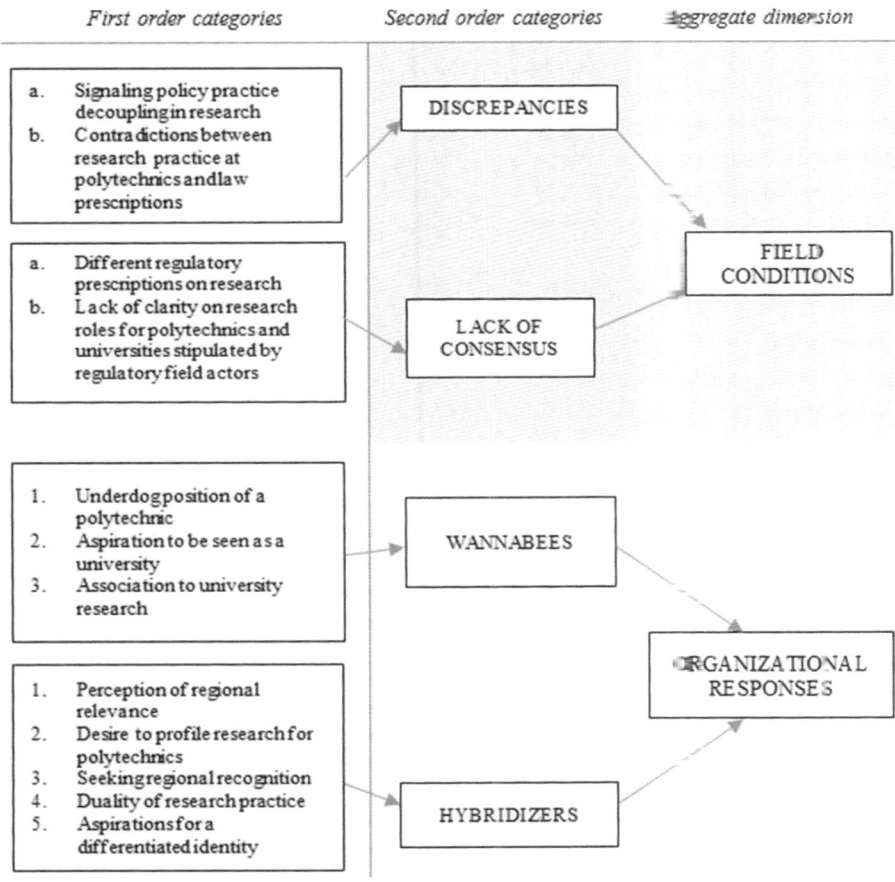

Figure 8.2. Data structure

FINDINGS

Field Conditions

The findings of this chapter start by detailing the respondents' experience of the higher education field. The following two field conditions, discrepancies and lack of consensus, were explicit in analysing the respondents' answers to questions regarding the new research policy.

Discrepancies

From the start, respondents emphasized a discrepancy between prescriptions stemming from regulatory field actors that monitor and promote research activities in polytechnics and the practices and norms concerning research which guide individual behavior in organizations. For example, research was for the first time broadly defined as a task for polytechnics in Decree Law n° 49/2005, with the specific aim of differentiating universities from polytechnics, as seen in the following translated section:

> University education aims to promote research and knowledge creation, seeking to ensure solid scientific and cultural preparation and technical training for the performance of professional activities;

> Polytechnic education aims to promote applied research focused on understanding and solving real problems, and to provide solid cultural and technological skills of higher education quality. It seeks to foster innovative and critical thinking and produce scientific knowledge of theoretical and practical implications or with direct applications to the professions. (Decree Law n° 49/2005).

The current Decree Law n° 207/2009 enforced the 2005 disposition about applied research at polytechnics by stipulating that all teaching staff at the polytechnics were required to do research which creates "cultural value and involves experimental design" (Art. 2A). In terms of research duties, the Decree further underlined that the teaching staff at polytechnics should "develop cultural and scientific knowledge through research projects which are both scientific and technical and attend to the needs of society" (Art. 30A). These regulatory prescriptions provided guidelines for infusing work practices with norms and values for polytechnic teaching staff and managers to follow. They also served to differentiate polytechnics from universities in a binary higher education system and thus provide legitimacy. Yet this was not what actually happened.

Our respondents were highly influenced by developments in the university setting and transposed the practices acquired there to the polytechnic sector, in teaching and later also in research. One respondent emphasized: "I taught at the university in 1991 and I use the same method to teach here. So with respect to teaching there is no difference and in terms of research for me there is no difference" (PB, Interview 13). When polytechnics were created, they hired graduates with bachelor's degrees from universities and started offering classes (observation and field notes). As another respondent argued, "people training here are also formed at universities. They had to do a PhD in a university. When they came back to the polytechnic, they naturally wanted to make their subject more university-like" (PA, Interview 7), and they did the same when research became an official mission, which means that it is "the university that formed the polytechnic education" (PB, Interview 6).

The respondents mentioned that they were not able to provide up to date "professionalized" courses and that their link with the professions was generally weak. Despite the focus on professions, practicality and problem-solving activities in teaching and research, which should serve the needs of society and ensure "closeness with the professional field through research" (PA, Interview 16), there were "actually no differences with the universities" (PB, Interview 5) in terms of research as the law(s) defined with regard to teaching practices at polytechnics. This also proved critical in shaping research practices that were influenced by the training and tradition of research transmitted by universities. Therefore, it is not unusual that our respondents emphasized that they could not "understand what they (the Law) want from us" (PB, Interview 15) and that they "only know what we learnt at universities" (PA, Interview 17).

Lack of Consensus among Regulatory Field Actors

When research was first introduced as an official mission of polytechnics in Portugal, it was stipulated as 'applied' and distinct from the type of research that was carried out at universities. Research was defined within the framework of practical application, whereby "projects with regional industry, community outreach activities and problem solving practices" (Noticias de Instituto Politecnico de Lisboa, 2 June 2011) were stimulated. As with other polytechnics in Europe, research was supposed to improve the educational provision of professionalized practices through interaction with regional industries (Kyvik & Lepori, 2010). However, this newly identified role for polytechnics was not understood in the same way by all regulatory actors in the Portuguese higher education field, which jeopardized its legitimacy. Our respondents were very clear about the contradictions between the way Decree Law n° 207/2009 defined research and the way the current *Statute on Teacher Careers at Polytechnics*, regulated by the same Decree Law n° 207/2009 undermined this research role. As one respondent underlined:

I need to do research, the academic type. If I apply for any other job in academia, or at another polytechnic, I will lose out if I do not have papers published. But the same Law tells me to do research projects with companies which in most cases cannot and do not result in publications. (PA, Interview 6)

The current *Statute on Teacher Careers at Polytechnics* also stipulated that when members of the teaching staff are following career paths leading to promotion to other categories and the earning of higher titles, they must show scientific qualities that are measured by high impact publications in international journals. One respondent mentioned: "If you do not have publications, you do not have enough to advance in your career" (PA, Interview 6). This regulation thus legitimized publications as research outputs relevant for advancement in an academic career, thereby seemingly contradicting the desired outputs of research as an applied, practical and problem-solving activity.

Further, one respondent mentioned that "the type of research they want us to do is bullshit; I mean, they say one thing, but then they evaluate me on something else" (PA, Interview 5). For instance, the National Accreditation Agency, which is responsible for the approval and evaluation of polytechnic undergraduate and graduate programs, as well as the Portuguese Science and Technology Foundation, evaluated and measured scientific quality predominantly based on publications. For example, in order for Master programs to obtain accreditation, the National Accreditation Agency expected that polytechnic teaching staff involved in these programs have both doctoral degrees and a proven research record. The number of publications measures this research record. One respondent explained: "To get a course accredited, you need to have a certain number of PhDs in the course, and the publications matter then as well. So we need to do it" (PB, Interview 1).

When the polytechnic teaching staff applied for funding through the Portuguese Science and Technology Foundation, "the funding and evaluation criteria seemed to evaluate based on publications" (PB, Interview 5). An academic "has to take into account what the funding agency and the national system want. So we have to publish. We can only be successful if we are recognized by these institutions" (PB, Interview 6).

Our respondents stressed that "the Government seems to be forcing us to do things differently from universities" while "the funding agency only cares about publications, or research experience" (PA, Interview 11). For example, one respondent explained that it was important that she had "academic experience" when seeking a grant: "The Portuguese Science and Technology Foundation will not give a grant just to a teacher from a polytechnic; they need to see that you have a researcher profile and that you know how to do research in a university way" (PA, Interview 15). Polytechnics have to "compete with universities for research money; there is no special call just for polytechnics" (PB, Interview 1).

A respondent from PA described this lack of consensus on research for polytechnics among regulatory field actors this way: "Whereas the funding agency, the accreditation and the career statute assess and evaluate research production based on generally accepted scientific criteria", by contrast, "the Law aims for diversification by defining research as practical, project based" (PA, Interview 11). Generally, aiming to develop research as prescribed by law is difficult, as the national accreditation and funding agencies only classify polytechnic practices as "good or excellent" if they can "show publications potential and do not consider that I worked on projects with companies in the region" (PA, Interview 11 . The problem is that these field actors did not legitimate the "other" output so polytechnics refused to do it.

Organizational Responses

Experiencing discrepancies and lack of consensus in the field about research influenced our respondents' practice of research. In fact, our findings showed that the respondents from the two polytechnics were practicing research differently from one another. Their heterogeneous responses were not exclusive, but signalled organizational strategies enabled by the complex experiences they encountered in the field.

Wannabes

Throughout the interviews and based on the field notes of the first author, PA respondents were consistent in showing that the way they did research was the same as universities. They further justified their research activities by referring to the prescriptions stemming from the *Statute on Teacher Careers at Polytechnics*: "When we are evaluated for our performance [or] research or want to advance in the career, we follow the same rules as universities" (PA, Interview 16), while on other hand, they undermined the current stipulations in the laws about research at polytechnics. Lack of consensus in the field enabled the choice to reject some prescriptions while attending to others. Additionally, they emphasized that they have done their PhDs, and were a part of university research centers as one of the respondents explained: "My research group is in a university so we do whatever they do. So we follow their group and lines of thought and publish together" (PA, Interview 17).

The PA respondents interviewed in our study seemed to have been highly influenced by the norms and values that prevail in universities and emphasized that they had to "produce indicators that are accountable for measuring research. which are publications in scientific journals" (PA, Interview 7). They underlined that their organization financially encouraged this output and that it is crucial to "publish in scientific journals. We stimulate this." (PA, Interview, 17). The majority of our PA respondents emphasized that, in an effort to be considered a university, their organization promoted research activities that increased scientific excellence, and matched universities:

> We incentivize paper publications; we give a prize to the author that had best publications or was most cited. We also encourage doing a doctoral degree for teachers. (PA, Interview 16)

In this sense, the patterns of attempting to show they do the same research as universities while not actually being called such prejudices them in the field as they are seen as less valuable and even eventually marginalized by society, indicating a "wannabe" (a colloquial combination of the words "want to be") conformity, as highly popularized by Tuchman (2009). "Wannabe" conformity refers to attempts by universities to achieve success in a corporatized world of higher education (Tuchman, 2009). It also points to an overarching logic of compliance in higher education. Respondents stressed that they wanted to be called 'universities' since they practice the same research and emphasized that currently they are not considered to be as good as universities because "the culture is not aware that polytechnics are as good as universities" (PA, Interview 4).

The President of PA polytechnic recently highlighted that polytechnics should seek equality with universities, not just in practice but also in law, and confirmed that "PA has met all the conditions necessary to be granted the status of a university" (Diario de Noticias, February 2015). This would suggest that PA wanted to minimize the discrepancies experienced in the field and assimilate to universities. PA also recently abandoned their membership in the Portuguese Polytechnics Coordinating Council (CCISP – Conselho Coordenador dos Institutos Superiores Politécnicos). In line with this statement, the PA President reasoned that withdrawal from the Portuguese Polytechnic Coordinating Council was necessary because they were very different from other polytechnics and were more like a university. Abandoning the Council, therefore, was considered a necessary "strategic move" in order to express their determination in becoming recognized and legitimated as a university, thereby removing the existing cultural or societal prejudice against them as a polytechnic.

Hybridizers

Respondents from PB emphasized that their research practices were influenced by university norms and values:

> Our teaching staff has studied at a university, and they all did their PhDs in the university. So this has definitely influenced the way they do research. And also, the recognition of research followed that; so to recognize that what you are doing is scientific and good you have to do classical university research. So what our teachers were expected to do is publish papers and have PhDs. So you see, it is both their tradition – that is how they were trained – and it is also the environment that reinforces and legitimizes university-type research. This is not our evaluation. This is system evaluation…This is what matters for them. So we need to do it… (PB Interview 1)

At the same time, our respondents also emphasized that they are doing "other" research which reinforced projects with local companies and, in particular, impacted the community and region in which the polytechnic is situated:

> Well, some 10 years ago, when the research became an official mission and we had to all do PhDs, etc., we were doing research that was serving the purpose

of universities ... But now our teachers have to look at the region. We have a few quite good groups working in applied research in different areas, food technology and agriculture, also technology linked to the development of agriculture.... (PB, Interview 4)

As the only educational provider in the region, or as one of the members of the teaching staff calls it: "a polytechnic off the beaten track" (idiomatic translation from Portuguese "um politecnico no meio de nada"; PB, Interview 10), PB was described as a polytechnic which did not have to compete directly with universities, but rather shared a social responsibility to its region:

We are very open to the community.... I think this is very important and is the main objective of this polytechnic. We want to improve things in the region and construct new companies and industries. (PB, Interview 10)

A member of the teaching staff argued, "the biggest difference in the type of research we do here and the one they do at universities is that we accept to do research that is important for solving the problems of small industry and companies in our region" (PB, Interview 6). This respondent furthered this argument by specifying that the goal of such research is to help "companies in a short period of time, not in ten or twenty years. If we specify that applied research is something that is valuable for companies some ten years later, then we will not have any advantage. If we think of applied research as short term research with immediate application, then we are contributing a lot". Research at PB was, therefore, described as problem solving "and economically and socially developing the region" (PB, Interview 4). For example, one respondent explained how:

We tend to investigate things that are concrete, that the community needs, where we can give answers to local problems. Research in a polytechnic is the development of scientific activity that responds to problems found in the region. The one who identifies the problems can be the teacher, as our teachers are very close to the region and usually have some connection with the economic aspect of it – either via a relative or a friend or are themselves involved in the production. Or the problem can also be identified by the producer, the outside community, or both. (PB, Interview 15)

The emphasis in this research is the combination of the scientific approach and community relevance, as seen in the following response:

Well, we do a lot of research and publish a lot, and this research is always related to our region and regional products. We have a website in English where we make all of our research available to the public. (PB, Interview 9)

Almost all PB respondents referred to "collaboration with local companies" (PB, Interview 5) and "integration of traditional ways of doing research with practice, or practical research. We are crossing some boundaries, but this is difficult"

(PB, Interview 12). This difficulty was related to funding, as it supported university or scientific research and output. What the respondents emphasized is that they felt they had to simultaneously concede to both the prescriptions about research practice stemming from the laws, and the rules as stipulated by other regulatory field actors concerning research such as the funding agency or the *Statute on Teacher Careers at Polytechnics*. They undertook practical, applied research in collaboration with local industries in the region and did scientific research to obtain funding and advance in their careers. This indicated what we refer to as hybridity.

Whereas respondents felt this was an obligation due to specific field conditions, they also emphasized that this integration of practical and scientific research was a way for them to be "different from universities" and positon themselves in the field as "regionally oriented or solving problems of local companies in our region" rather than competing against universities in the field (PB, Interview 1; also TSF Radio Noticias, 28th of August, 2015). Respondents from PB contended, "the polytechnics are motors of regional development as they make sure these remote rural areas advance. But they are also dependent on the region" (PB, Interview 8). As one member of the teaching staff reported: "People are aware that if we do not do community outreach work, maybe the institution will have to close" (PB, Interview 6).

These reactions from our respondents reveal that the region itself, as an economically, socially and territorially unique area, was seen as an important actor in the field. Region is an important source of legitimacy and resources for the functioning of PB. Regional funding is also an important means for ensuring this type of practical, applied and regionally embedded research.

DISCUSSION

To date, there has been substantial empirical evidence that responses by higher education organizations to new policies are varied or heterogeneous (Berg & Pinheiro, 2016, Canhilal et al., 2015). Yet most higher education literature considers that higher education organizations either filter new policies due to organizational attributes or adopt them irrespective of the conflict or incompatibilities in national higher education fields (also see Frølich et al., 2013). By adapting a theoretical framework to analyze the dynamics and interplay between actors and organizations, we sought to apply insights from neo-institutional field theory and recent work on complexity in fields to offer a more comprehensive understanding of the conditions influencing organizational behavior in higher education. We examined how polytechnics in Portugal responded to new research policy demands by focusing on the organizational experience of field conditions as influencing heterogeneous organizational responses. In this way we heeded the call for more empirical studies on how higher education organizations interpret and respond to their environments (e.g., Frølich et al., 2013; Lepori, 2016).

Our analysis revealed that complexity in a higher education field was experienced in two distinct ways. First, there were discrepancies between field frameworks. The analysis revealed a discrepancy between laws which prescribe rules for polytechnic organizations (and their research practice) and normative and cognitive prescriptions which guide the teaching staff at the polytechnic in their daily work practices. These prescriptions were not compatible. This indicated a lack of connection, or a "disassociation", of individuals in polytechnics from the rules and regulations prescribed in the law. This finding coincides with recent work by Bertels and Lawrence (2016) and Lepori (2016). Their work shows how individuals' views on a new demand might not correspond with those of the regulatory field actors. For instance, different individuals might have different understandings of the policy because of the backgrounds, experiences, etc. which shape their normative and cognitive frameworks. But this understanding might be incompatible with how regulatory field actors define the new policy. Such incompatibilities indicate micro and macro level factors contributing to complexity in the field (Degn, 2016). In other words, complexity at the field level is exacerbated by discrepancies between prescriptions at macro-levels (stemming from regulatory field actors) and the micro-level that guide the behaviour of individuals and give meaning to their work practices.

Furthermore, the field was also characterized as lacking consensus as regulatory field actors enforced ambiguous institutional prescriptions regarding research for the polytechnic sector. This made it virtually impossible to develop a coherent regulatory field framework concerning the new practice and underpin it with normative and cognitive prescriptions that would guide organizations in this new task. A coherent regulatory field framework is essentially underpinned by normative and cognitive prescriptions that encourage or reflect consistent organizational behaviour and provide field stability (Smith & Tracey, 2016). This indicates that uncertainty and ambiguity generated at field level resulted in a framework deficiency for organizations seeking legitimacy and recognition, enabling, however, several ways of attaining legitimacy (see also Raaijmakers et al., 2015). All these factors contribute to complexity in the field.

This analysis also explains the different strategic ways in which polytechnics responded to complexity in their field. Our analysis shows how PA emulated those organizations in the field considered "legitimate" and having research practices legitimated by some (but not all) regulatory field actors. PA followed this practice because it aspired to become a university, and therefore followed the university model, making clear that they do the same type of research as universities. Complexity in the field allowed PA to make such strategic rational choices based on its "best interest"- a practice we termed 'wannabe'.

On the other hand, PB conducted "legitimate" research, similar to universities, but also developed other types of research related to regional issues and solving regional problems, as recommended by government policy and legislation. In this way, PB compromised and conceded to prescriptions stemming from regulatory field actors, unlike PA which conformed to only those prescriptions which were also legitimate for universities. PB saw the region as an additional source of resources and legitimacy; we termed this "hybridizing." Rather than opting for one institutional prescription, PB integrated and incorporated different prescriptions and sources of legitimacy. In this way PB strategically positioned itself in the field and maneuvered different institutional prescriptions.

In the wider literature, strategizing and manoeuvring have been identified as key elements in response to changes in the legal, social and political environments (Frølich et al., 2013; Delmas & Toffel, 2008; Smets et al., 2012). But so far, higher education studies have been approached mostly from the perspective of universities (Frølich et al., 2013). Strategizing in higher education has been related to keeping up with national and international competition by incorporating global trends at universities, and thereby acquiring acceptability as a national higher education player in the field (Frølich et al., 2013). This leads to the incorporation of similar elements by universities and points towards convergence as a response to new policy demands (e.g., Morphew et al., 2016).

But the Portuguese polytechnics studied engaged in strategizing and defined their own research missions. We argue that the experience of complexity at the "local" field level enabled polytechnics to differently strategize and define their responses to policy demands. These strategic responses, while enabled by the experience of complexity in the field, seem to have been influenced by the organizational interest in positioning in such a field. Position in a field has been connected to strategizing, and is also found in complex fields (Greenwood et al., 2011). For instance, higher education organizations might use complexity in their fields to strategically advance their position in the national higher education field (see Kodeih & Greenwood, 2014). Similar findings are emerging in the work of other higher education scholars working on universities. For instance, a working paper by Cattaneo et al. (2017) on competition and diversification at Italian universities in the post-2008 financial crisis points out that even universities do not necessarily adopt similar strategies when coping with global external demands and may even adopt quite different strategies, depending on local competition. This work seems to point to the importance of local field-level dynamics in shaping organizational strategies in response to new, especially global, demands.

CONCLUSION

This study contributes to the understanding of how conditions in the higher education field influence organizational responses to new policy demands. First, we have shown that organizations can experience their higher education field in a complex manner, based on macro-micro incompatibilities and the multiplicity of legitimacy sources. Second, we explored two distinct organizational responses to the emerging research policy demands in a complex field: assimilating ("wannabes") and hybridizing. These organizational responses resulted from different manoeuvring strategies to new research policy demands. More responses are likely since complexity in fields can give rise to divergent responses, requiring organizations to pay more attention to local dynamics by further developing strategic aptitudes and capacities.

Raynard (2016) argued that complexity could either be purposeful or be a consequence of field actors who seek to appropriate the stability or purposefully prevent the stability from being achieved in the field. Revealing the sources of complexity in detail was beyond the scope of our study as we focused on heterogeneous organizational responses to field-level changes. Nevertheless, it is an interesting issue for further research in studies of higher education. Future research that looks into more cases in similar fields and explores different responses, as well as that which investigates the dynamics of complexity in higher education fields is encouraged.

Our study also raises questions relevant for policymakers. Higher education policy has been greatly influenced and defined at the European or international level. National or local field conditions have tended to be relegated to a secondary role or even ignored. But national field conditions have consequences for the implementation of policy. Complexity on the local field-level seems to allow higher education organizations to be more flexible, encouraging strategic potential and action based on organizational interest and interrelation with local actors. The capacity of an organization to strategically deal with uncertainty and ambiguity brought about by complexity in fields can be an advantage in the dynamic and changing atmosphere of global higher education (Hüther & Krücken, 2016).

Policies defined at supranational levels will not necessarily yield similar impacts or have the same results when applied in varied and multiple areas. Rather, these policies will be interpreted within the limitations and context of the organizations and their interests as they strive to retain their role as strategic agents in their local fields (also see Cattaneo et al., 2017). This means that policymakers should shift from fostering universal policy solutions that promote higher education competitiveness at global levels to designing policies that take into account more local field dynamics and organizational dimensions.

REFERENCES

Amaral, A., & Magalhães, A. (2004). Epidemiology and the bologna saga. *Higher Education, 48*(1), 79–100.

Amaral, A., Jones, G. A., & Karseth, B. (Eds.). (2013). *Governing higher education: National perspectives on institutional governance* (Vol. 2). Dordrecht, NL: Springer Science & Bus ness Media.

Berg, L. N., & Pinheiro, R. (2016). Handling different institutional logics in the public sector: Comparing management in Norwegian universities and hospitals. In R. Pinheiro, L. Geschwind, F. O. Ramirez, & K. Vrangbaek (Eds.), *Towards a comparative institutionalism: Forms, dynamics and logics across the organizational fields of health care and higher education* (pp. 145–168). Emerald Group Publishing Limited.

Bertels, S., & Lawrence, T. B. (2016). Organizational responses to institutional complexity stemming from emerging logics: The role of individuals. *Strategic Organization, 14*(4), 336–372.

Canhilal, S. K., Lepori, B., & Seeber, M. (2016). Decision-making power and institutional logic in higher education institutions: A comparative analysis of European universities. In R. Pinheiro, L. Geschwind, F. O. Ramirez, & K. Vrangbaek (Eds.), *Towards a comparative institutionalism: Forms, dynamics and logics across the organizational fields of health care and higher education* (pp. 169–194). Emerald Group Publishing Limited.

Cardoso, S., Tavares, O., & Sin, C. (2015). The quality of teaching staff: Higher education institutions' compliance with the European standards and guidelines for quality assurance—the case of Portugal. *Educational Assessment, Evaluation and Accountability, 27*(3), 205–222.

Cattaneo, M., Horta, H., Malighetti, P., Meoli, M., & Paleari, S. (2017). *The relationship between competition and programmatic diversification*. Working paper.

Dacin, M. T. (1997). Isomorphism in context: The power and prescription of institutional norms. *Academy of Management Journal, 40*(1), 46–81.

Degn, L. (2016). Academic sensemaking and behavioural responses – exploring how academics perceive and respond to identity threats in times of turmoil. *Studies in Higher Education.* Retrieved from http://dx.doi.org/10.1080/03075079.2016.1168796

Delmas, M. A., & Toffel, M. W. (2008). Organizational responses to environmental demands: Opening the black box. *Strategic Management Journal, 29*, 1027–1055.

DeWalt, K. M., & DeWalt, B. R. (2002). *Participant observation.* Walnut Creek, CA: Altamira Press.

de Weert, E., & Soo, M. (2009). Research at universities of applied sciences in Europe: Conditions, achievements and perspectives. Center for Higher Education Policy Studies (CHEPS), University of Twente. The Netherlands. https://sites. google. com/site/uasnet/home, haettu, 21, 2011.

DiMaggio, P., & Powell, W. W. (1983). The iron cage revisited: Collective rationality and institutional isomorphism in organizational fields. *American Sociological Review, 48*(2), 147–160.

Frølich, N., Huisman, J., Slipersæter, S., Stensaker, B., & Bótas, P. C. P. (2013). A reinterpretation of institutional transformations in European higher education: Strategising pluralistic organisations in multiplex environments. *Higher Education, 65*(1), 79–93.

Fumasoli, T., & Stensaker, B. (2013). Organizational studies in higher education: A reflection on historical themes and prospective trends. *Higher Education Policy, 26*(4), 479–496.

Fumasoli, T., Pinheiro, R., & Stensaker, B. (2015). Handling uncertainty of strategic ambitions—The use of organizational identity as a risk-reducing device. *International Journal of Public Administration, 38*(13–14), 1030–1040.

Gioia, D. A., Corley, K. G., & Hamilton, A. L. (2013). Seeking qualitative rigor in inductive research: Notes on the Gioia methodology. *Organizational Research Methods, 16*(1), 15–31.

Glaser, B. S., & Strauss, A. (2012). *The discovery of grounded theory: Strategies for qualitative research,* 7th Ed. New Brunswick, USA, and London, UK: Transaction Printing.

Greenwood, R., Raynard, M., Kodeih, F., Micelotta, E. R., & Lounsbury, M. (2011). Institutional complexity and organizational responses. *The Academy of Management Annals, 5*(1), 317–371.

Harris, M. (2013). Understanding institutional diversity in American higher education. *ASHE Higher Education Report, 39*(3). John Wiley & Sons.

Hasanefendic, S., Heitor, M., & Horta, H. (2016). Training students for new jobs: The role of technical and vocational higher education and implications for science policy in Portugal. *Technological Forecasting and Social Change, 113*(part B), 328–340.

Hoffman, A. J. (2001). Linking organizational and field-level analyses the diffusion of corporate environmental practice. *Organization & Environment, 14*(2), 133–156.

Holmberg, D. & Hallonsten, O. (2015). Policy reform and academic drift: Research mission and institutional legitimacy in the development of the Swedish higher education system 1977–2012. *European Journal of Higher Education, 5*(2), 181–196.

Huisman, J. (2008). Shifting boundaries in higher education: Dutch *hogescholen* on the move. In J. S. Taylor, J. Brites Ferreira, M. de Lourdes Machado, & R. Santiago (Eds.), *Non-university higher education in Europe* (pp. 147–167). Dordrecht, NL: Springer.

Hüther, O., & Krücken, G. (2016). Nested organizational fields: Isomorphism and differentiation among European universities. In E. Popp Berman & C. Paradeise (Ed.), *The university under pressure* (Research in the Sociology of Organizations, Vol. 46, pp. 53–83). UK: Emerald Group Publishing Limited.

Jongbloed, B. (2010). The regional relevance of research in universities of applied sciences. In S. Kyvik & B. Lepori (Eds.), *The research mission of higher education institutions outside the university sector* (pp. 25–44). Dordrecht: Springer.

Kyvik, S., & Lepori, B. (Eds.). (2010). The research mission of higher education institutions outside the university sector: Striving for differentiation (Vol. 31). Springer Science & Business Media.

Leão, M. T. (2007). *O ensino superior politécnico em Portugal: Um paradigma de formação alternativo.* Santa Maria da Feira: Edições Afrontamento.

Lepori, B. (2016). Universities as hybrids: Applications of institutional logics theory to higher education. In J. Huisman & M. Tight (Eds.), *Theory and method in higher education research* (pp. 245–264). Emerald Group Publishing Limited.

Lincoln, Y. S., & Guba, E. G. (1985). *Naturalistic inquiry* (Vol. 75). Newbury Park, CA: Sage.

Manning, K. (2012). *Organizational theory in higher education*. New York, NY: Routledge.

Meyer, R. E., & Höllerer, M. A. (2016). Laying a smoke screen: Ambiguity and neutralization as strategic responses to intra-institutional complexity. *Strategic Organization, 14*(4), 373–406.

Morphew, C. C., Fumasoli, T., & Stensaker, B. (2016). Changing missions? How the strategic plans of research-intensive universities in Northern Europe and North America balance competing identities. *Studies in Higher Education*. Retrieved from http://dx.doi.org/10.1080/03075079.2016.1214697

Patricio, M. T. (2010). Science policy and the internationalisation of research in Portugal. *Journal of Studies in International Education, 14*(2), 161–182.

Popp Berman, E., & Paradeise, C. (2016). Introduction: The university under pressure. In E. Popp Berman & C. Paradeise (Ed.), *The university under pressure* (Research in the Sociology of Organizations, Vol. 46, pp. 1–22). UK: Emerald Group Publishing Limited.

Raaijmakers, A. G., Vermeulen, P. A., Meeus, M. T., & Zietsma, C. (2015). I need time! Exploring pathways to compliance under institutional complexity. *Academy of Management Journal, 58*(1), 85–110.

Raynard, M. (2016). Deconstructing complexity: Configurations of institutional complexity and structural hybridity. *Strategic Organization, 14*(4), 310–335.

Sam, C., & van der Sijde, P. (2014). Understanding the concept of the entrepreneurial university from the perspective of higher education models. *Higher Education, 68*(6), 891–908.

Scott, W. R. (1995). *Institutions and organizations*. Thousand Oaks, CA: Sage

Scott, W. R., & Biag, M. (2016). The changing ecology of US higher education: An organization field perspective. In E. Popp Berman & C. Paradeise (Eds.), *The university under pressure* (Research in the Sociology of Organizations, Vol. 46, pp. 25–51). UK: Emerald Group Publishing Limited.

Scott, W. R., & Christensen, S. (1995). *The institutional construction of organizations: International and longitudinal studies*. Thousand Oaks, CA: Sage.

Smets, M., Morris, T. I. M., & Greenwood, R. (2012). From practice to field: A multilevel model of practice-driven institutional change. *Academy of Management Journal, 55*(4), 877–904.

Smith, W. K., & Tracey, P. (2016). Institutional complexity and paradox theory: Complementarities of competing demands. *Strategic Organization, 14*(4), 455–466.

Teixeira, P. (2016). Two continents divided by the same trends? Reflections about marketization, competition, and inequality in European higher education. In E. Popp Berman & C. Paradeise (Eds.), *The university under pressure* (Research in the Sociology of Organizations, Vol. 46, pp. 489–508). UK: Emerald Group Publishing Limited.

Tuchman, G. (2009). *Wannabe U: Inside the corporate university*. Chicago, IL: Chicago University Press.

Urbano, C. (2011). A (id) entidade do ensino superior politécnico em Portugal: da Lei de Bases do Sistema Educativo à Declaração de Bolonha. *Sociologia, Problemas e Práticas*, (66), 95–115.

Zietsma, C., Groenewegen, P., Logue, D., & Hinings, C. (2016). Field or fields? Building the scaffolding for cumulation of research on institutional fields. *Academy of Management Annals*, annals-2014.

Sandra Hasanefendic
ISCTE-IUL, School of Sociology and Public Policy, Lisbon
and
Vrije Universiteit Amsterdam, Faculty of Social Sciences
Department of Organization Sciences

Maria Teresa Patricio
ISCTE-IUL, School of Sociology and Public Policy, Lisbon

Frank G. A. de Bakker
IÉSEG School of Management (LEM-CNRS 9921), Lille

153

PART 3

HIGHER EDUCATION POLICIES AND PRACTICES ON TEACHING QUALITY AND EXCELLENCE, RESEARCH AND THE STUDENT EXPERIENCE

MARIA J. MANATOS, MARIA J. ROSA AND CLÁUDIA S. SARRICO

9. THE PERCEPTIONS OF QUALITY MANAGEMENT BY UNIVERSITIES' INTERNAL STAKEHOLDERS

Support, Adaptation or Resistance?

INTRODUCTION

Concerns with quality in higher education are not new; however, it was mainly since the late 1980s that the logic of accountability became inseparable from the higher education sector and the concerns with quality became more visible and relevant for universities, government and society as a whole. The demands for economic efficiency due to resource constraints; the increasing role of market regulation; the "erosion of trust" in universities associated with the rise of managerialism and the new public management (Massy, 2003); and the massification within the higher education sector, led to the need of universities to justify the expenditure of public funds and to demonstrate "value for money" (Deem, 1998; Rosa & Amaral, 2007).

Similarly "academics are encouraged 'to do more with less' and be more accountable for scarce resources" (Becket & Brookes, 2008, p. 46). The pressures come both from outside and inside universities. Externally the pressures are exerted by funding bodies and external quality assurance agencies. Internally, the pressures are exerted by managers and administrators on academic and non-academic staff in universities (Deem, 1998).

In Portugal, the European developments in higher education, driven by new public management and new managerialism context, boosted the deep process of change of Portuguese higher education. Since the mid-1990s "there has been a change of emphasis from governing to governance (…), leading to tensions between institutional autonomy and the need for regulation, by governments, to ensure the achievement of policy objectives" (Rosa & Amaral, 2014, p. 154). However, it was only in 2007, that the higher education sector in Portugal witnessed substantive developments, setting up the conditions, structures and organisation of a more rigorous system of evaluation for higher education in compliance with the European exigencies, namely the Standards and Guidelines for Quality Assurance in the European Higher Education Area (ESG) (Rosa & Sarrico, 2012).

The idea of quality management in universities tends to raise different degrees of acceptance, support and adaptation, which can play an important role in facilitating or hampering the implementation of quality management systems in these organisations (Cardoso, Rosa, & Santos, 2013; Manatos, Sarrico, & Rosa, 2015; Newton, 2002).

R. Deem & H. Eggins (Eds.), The University as a Critical Institution?, 157–172.

Assuming that the positions from the main universities' internal stakeholders on quality management are essential for the success of the implementation of the quality management systems in universities, it is essential to understand their perceptions on this topic (Stensaker, Langfeldt, Harvey, Huisman, & Westerheijden, 2011; Watty, 2006). It is well known from the literature (Manatos et al., 2015; Rosa, Tavares, & Amaral, 2006; Stensaker et al., 2011) that stakeholders' involvement in quality management relates to their degree of resistance and/or acceptance towards quality management, so it seems interesting to see how far their involvement can lead to resistance to or support for quality management.

The purpose of this paper is to discuss the perceptions of the main internal stakeholders in universities regarding the quality management systems of universities and to understand their degrees of support, adaptation or resistance. We also intend to understand how far the perceptions regarding quality management vary according to the type of stakeholder and their degree of involvement with quality management. Furthermore, we aim to discuss whether the perceptions on quality management vary according to the position in the academic hierarchy. Previous research indicates that "front-line academics" have "less positive views of quality or the quality system" than academic managers (Newton, 2002, p. 46).

LITERATURE REVIEW

The Perceptions of Academics on Quality Management: Support, Adaptation or Resistance

Academics tend to show "different degrees of acceptance, support and adaptation to the quality assurance idea, policies and implementation procedures" (Cardoso et al., 2013; Newton, 2002; Westerheijden, Hulpiaub, & Waeytens, 2007).

Newton (2002, p. 46) identifies different views from academics regarding quality in higher education, which also correspond to the limitations academics tend to point out in the quality management systems: (i) quality as "ritualism and tokenism", meaning quality as compliance with requirements as priority and enhancement as secondary; (ii) quality as "impression management", meaning the "stage-managed" preparations for external assessment; (iii) quality as a "burden", particularly "administrative and cost burden", in the words of Laughton (2003, p. 309), and" "part of an inspectorial compliance culture"; (iv) quality as "failure to close the loop", meaning the exclusion of key areas; (v) quality as "suspicion of management motives" or, as argued by Harvey (2006, p. 290) "manifestation of managerialist control", monitoring and controlling the academic work and weakening the academic autonomy; (vi) quality as "lack of mutual trust", emphasising the accountability of front-line academics; (vii) quality as "a culture of getting by" where front-line academics, constrained by lack of time, deal with confusing demands. The lack of time to deal with the quality requirements and the bureaucracy associated with the quality management procedures are indeed a weakness stressed by academics and one recurring factor for their resistance to quality management (Harvey, 2006; Laughton, 2003; Newton, 2002).

Moreover, academics complain about their little involvement in the development of the quality management procedures (Cardoso et al., 2013; Loukkola & Zhang, 2010), and also about the quality procedures themselves, claiming that they are reductionist, incapable of grasping the essence of the educational process and not entirely reliable (Cardoso et al., 2013; Laughton, 2003).

It is also interesting to observe that academics tend to differentiate the improvements in the quality management systems from the improvements in quality (Newton, 2002). Harvey (2006) claims that academics, when questioned about the main impacts of external quality management in higher education, underline the improvements in the quality procedures, namely "performance indicators", "review process", "internal quality units and formal processes" rather than improvements in the quality of the university and its mission, namely teaching and learning and research and scholarship.

This "concern" of academics that the "quality initiatives emphasise processes rather than outcomes" seems to be related to a gap between rhetoric and reality regarding quality management. Hence, there seems to be a "gap between what staff would like the initiatives to achieve and what they think they have achieved" which lead us to conclude that academics "perceive the initiatives as being more about assurance than enhancement" (Lomas, 2007, p. 410).

Furthermore, academics perceive quality as a philosophy that is in "contradiction to the core values of academic culture, and ultimately as a subversion of academic identity" (Laughton, 2003, p. 318). Bell and Taylor argue that (2005, p. 239) "academics as a community do not identify with quality as a worthwhile project through which identity can be formed."

Still, there are also academics that seem to show a growing acceptance and support of quality management, with a positive perception of its introduction, namely in the case of Portugal (Cardoso et al., 2013; Rosa & Sarrico, 2012). Kleijnen et al. (2011, p. 149) state that academics believe in the benefits of quality management and particularly that "quality management results in improvement and not only results in control."

The acceptance of quality management activities by academics also seems to depend to a great extent on the level of 'control' they involve and on the level of 'academic autonomy' they enable. "Academics in general see self-evaluation and quality assurance as means to administer their everyday life as long as academics' autonomy to their own work is cherished and controlling mechanisms are avoided" (Huusko & Ursin, 2010, p. 868).

Some academics neither resist nor support quality management, but rather adapt to it, meaning they "reluctantly [collaborate] in order to prevent more unpleasant or problematic professional outcomes" (Cartwright, 2007, p. 298). In this sense, academics are "resilient compliers" who "combine passive resignation (..) with mostly silent resistance. They deliver the information needed and apply the rules,

159

but try to avoid becoming known as vassals of the system" (Sousa, Nijs, & Hendriks, 2010, p. 1454).

One final issue regarding academics perceptions of quality management is that those performing management functions and involved in quality management activities tend to have a more optimistic view of such activities (Bell & Taylor, 2005; Manatos et al., 2015; Newton, 2002; Rosa et al., 2006; Stensaker et al., 2011).

The Role of Students in Quality Management: The Benefits of an Active Participation

The participation of students in the quality management systems of universities has been a crucial element in the development of quality management in Europe specially since the years 2000s. However, one cannot find extensive literature on the topic.

Assuming that the students are one of the main stakeholders of higher education, it is clear that they can give crucial information in assessing its quality (Cardoso, Santiago, & Sarrico, 2012a; Harvey, 2003; Leckey & Neill, 2001; Stensaker et al., 2011; Trowler, 2005). Therefore, "students' representations should be taken into account" in order to "to align quality assessment systems with the expectations of one of the institutional groups most interested in the improvement of higher education quality" (Cardoso, Santiago, & Sarrico, 2012b, p. 293).

However, and despite the increasingly important role attributed to students, they "have no universally accepted part in the evaluation of the education which they receive" (Kogan, 1993, p. 22).

According to Mourad (2013, p. 359), "there are a lot of challenges in front of the students' active participation in the quality assurance activities." On the one hand, the exclusion of students from an active intervention on the quality management systems of their universities seems to lead to a low level of awareness from students. According to Cardoso and colleagues (Cardoso et al., 2012a, p. 125), "this lack of awareness brings in to question the effectiveness of assessment as a device for promoting institutional accountability."

On the other hand, students often perceive quality management activities as "useless", "wasting of time", "not clear" and "not transparent" (Mourad, 2013, p. 359). Students are indeed sceptical regarding the capacity of quality management systems to generate positive results (Kogan, 1993; Stensaker et al., 2011). This sceptical position seems to be related to the lack of information about the results of the quality management systems and the changes derived from them. Although it can be argued that students do not develop effective strategies to access the information provided by universities concerning the results of the quality management systems, the literature shows that universities do not adopt a clear and transparent position regarding the dissemination of concrete data on quality management (Cardoso et al., 2012a; Harvey, 2003; Leckey & Neill, 2001).

The scepticism and the low interest students frequently show regarding quality management seem also to be linked to a low interest on institutional matters in general (Bateson & Taylor, 2004; Tavernier, 2004).

Students, however, perceive some benefits from quality management system: image, reputation and credibility of the university, on the one hand; and continuous improvement and enhancement of the educational quality through the students' evaluation of the faculty and the courses (Mourad, 2013).

Furthermore, students who are involved in quality management activities believe that "their awareness about (…) the internal quality assurance system enhance their learning experience (…), self-development (…) and self-satisfaction due to participating in the decision making process within the university" (Mourad, 2013, p. 359).

In this context, "the challenge universities now seem to face is to be creative and to engage in new and diverse strategies aimed at informing students of the assessment process and its consequences" (Cardoso et al., 2012a, pp. 133, 134).

METHODOLOGY

A country case study was undertaken, which includes three embedded university case studies. Universities A, B and C (designated as UA, UB and UC below) were the first universities in Portugal with an internal quality management system certified by A3ES – Agency for Assessment and Accreditation of Higher Education (in 2013, for a period of 6 years). These cases can be defined as paradigmatic (Flyvbjerg, 2006) or extreme cases (Gerring, 2007). We believe that it is interesting to explore the perceptions of the main internal stakeholders of the universities which in principle have well developed and consolidated quality management systems, since they were the first ones to have their quality management systems certified.

The university case studies are all different in terms of size and location. This choice ensures a diversified sample, able to empirically base the research. To further diversify the study, the contrasting study areas of Engineering, Language and Literature, and Education were investigated in the different institutions.

We have conducted semi-structured interviews with different internal stakeholders. We interviewed academics with different involvement levels in the internal quality management systems and with different hierarchical positions in the organisational structure, from top managers responsible for the development of the quality management systems, to academics without management functions, who have to deal with the systems on a daily basis. We also interviewed non-academics involved in quality management activities, who were part of the operational bodies for quality, and students. We consider that the academics with low levels of involvement in quality management are the ones who do not participate either in specific bodies responsible for the management of their quality management systems, or in operational structures that coordinate the quality management area, while the academics with high levels of involvement in quality management are the ones who make part of at least one of these strategic or operational bodies.

Academics without management functions and students were interviewed in panels of 3 to 5 people. In total, we did 23 individual interviews and 9 panel interviews.

The original interview script did not include questions regarding the standpoints of the interviewees regarding quality management. The interviews were aimed at understanding whether universities are developing their different quality management systems comprehensively and integrating them in their broader management and governance systems, covering different processes, organisational levels and the principles underlying the definition of quality management (Manatos, Sarrico, & Rosa, 2017).

However, the different positions in favour and against quality management arose in almost every interview, emerging as new research dimensions. Thus, the results of the study presented here are a case of serendipity (Konecki, 2008). In this research we analised the perceptions of our interviewees regarding quality management, by identifying the discourses associated with their different positions, namely resistance, adaptation or acceptance, which constitute our main categories of analysis; and by finding the reasons given by the interviewees for such positions, which constitute our subcategories of analysis: lack of communication, lack of information, sense of uselessness, in the case of resistance; resilient compliance, in the case of adaptation; and self-reflexion, improvement of procedures, improvement of universities' quality, in the case of acceptance.

RESULTS

Different Stakeholders, Different Perceptions

Firstly, our interviews show that the discourses of top managers are not always in line with the discourses of other academics. This 'misalignment' seems to be mostly motivated by the lack of knowledge of the academics not directly involved in the quality management activities, about the quality management system.

Academics without management functions and even some academics with management functions but with low levels of involvement in quality management activities demonstrate some lack of knowledge regarding the different aspects of the quality management system, namely:

a. how the results, especially from student surveys, are analysed: "If there is a group of people who will reflect about the results? I don't think so" (Academic from the programme of the Informatics Engineering, UC).
b. who analyses the results: "Certainly, the coordinators of the programme must have access to all the results, I am not sure" (Academic from the programme of Informatics Engineering panel, UA).

c. the work from the quality offices: "I believe that there are several ways to collect and analyse the information, and I think there is some group which does that work, but I don't know for sure how the data is analysed" (Coordinator of the programme of Informatics Engineering, UA).

The academics with management functions tend to know more about the quality management system and to have a more positive view about it. Nevertheless, even these academics can reveal some lack of knowledge and have no concrete opinion about the topic. More than holding management functions, it is the involvement in quality management activities that seems to play a major role in the perceptions of academics and of other internal stakeholders. Academics, as well as non-academics closely related to the development of the quality management system have more knowledge about it and, as we will see, also a more positive opinion of it.

It is also interesting to notice the differences regarding the perceptions of quality management in higher education in general. The less involved in quality management activities the interviewees are, the less integrated their perceptions of quality management are. The academics who are less involved in quality management activities tend to have a more limited vision of quality, mainly focusing: (a) on the quality of academics (as professors) and of students (as learners and, in the end, as professionals), stating that "a learning process with quality, a programme with quality and a department with quality will produce good professionals" (Coordinator of the programme of Informatics Engineering, UA); or less frequently (b) on the relationship between teaching and learning and research: "teaching and learning should always go hand in hand with research (…) we should improve research to improve teaching" (Academic from the programme of Basic Education, UC).

The interviewees who are more involved in quality management activities more frequently define quality as a "a multidimensional, a multilevel concept and a dynamic concept" (Responsible for Quality at Rectory, UB), considering other processes in higher education: "the quality is a broad concept and approaches different aspects of our activity in different areas, namely, the teaching and learning activity (…); the research and the technological development (…); the administrative procedures and services (…); the services to society and the transfer to the companies of what is produced in the university" (President of the Strategic Body for Quality, UA). Simultaneously, they highlight the importance of approaching different processes as a 'requirement' of a true quality management system: "We don't qualify our system as a quality assurance system, but as a quality management system, because it is not limited to the conformities… it is broader than that …it involves continuous improvement and all the processes of the school" (Responsible for the Operational Body for Quality, UA).

For students the notion of quality management is centred on their learning experience. Consequently, the quality of academics, of teaching in general, and of the resources and services to support learning are the most focused topics: "The quality management in higher education should guarantee the conditions necessary for students to learn what they should in their areas (…) and good professors" (Student from the programme of Basic Education, UC).

Globally, the testimonies from academics and students show that the perceptions about quality management, in a broader sense, and specifically about the quality management system in their universities differ according to the position these different stakeholders occupy in the quality management system, to their experience regarding the implementation of quality management in their universities, and to the level of involvement in quality management activities. In general, a low involvement in quality management activities is linked to less knowledge about quality management and to a more sceptical opinion, as it will be explained below.

Adaptation and Resistance of Academics to Quality Management

The academics and the non-academic staff highly involved in the development of quality management in their universities tend to highlight the benefits of its development and implementation: "the university largely benefits from a holistic and formal quality system and from strategic plans which include the component of quality" (Responsible for Quality at Rectory, UB). Some academics less involved in quality management activities also mention the importance of the quality management system: "for professors (...) [the system] is a crucial tool to prepare, for example, the reports for the A3ES evaluation. We prepare all the documentation for the evaluation of our programmes on the basis of the information given by the [quality management] system. That is why it is an indispensable tool" (Academic from the programme of Language and Literature, UB).

Globally, the academics who are less involved in quality management seem to show adaptation to the idea of quality management and to the quality management systems of their universities, in particular. This "adaptation" translates into the way academics have to deal with the quality management system, by "feeding" it on a daily basis.

However, they seem to "adapt" to the system at the same time that they emphasise its shortcomings and express their resistance to it.

In fact, the resistance to quality management seem to be the predominant standpoint of the academics who are less involved in quality management activities. Different motives for such resistance stand out in the interviews.

Frequently, academics resist change and novelty, at least at the beginning. In the three universities, the process of development and implementation of a formal quality management system is relatively recent and this resistance is felt with high intensity. "At the beginning, the quality management system found many resistances, partly because, as in any innovative procedure, things did not go well" (Academic from the programme of Informatics Engineering, UB).

Some academics perceive the quality management activities as a mean to control their work rather than to improve it. Regarding student surveys about courses and their lecturers, the academics state that their only goal is "to assess the professor ... I don't see any other goals ... Are there people who analyse the results? I don t think so!" (Academic from the programme of Informatics Engineering, UC).

Furthermore, and considering the student surveys as one of the most important instrument assessing teaching and learning, some academics do not recognise them as a proper instrument to assess their performance. One academic from the programme of Informatics Engineering of UC, argues that: "most of the students (and there are only few students who answer the survey), are not thorough and are not conscious about the consequences of their answers. I even think that the way they answer the surveys is careless and negligent. (...) How can a student assess the subject or the professor if he/she is never in the class? (...) When a student attends 10% of the classes and gives his/her opinion saying that the professor is bad, what does that mean (in the assessment process)? That is why I never care about those surveys or about what the students say about me."

In addition, the quality management system is seen as extra work which will take up the time of academics, who should be occupied with teaching and research: "The system is useful, but it cannot make life of academics and non-academics hell. We cannot forget that the academics are paid to teach and do research. We cannot pay (well) to academics to insert data in online systems" (Academic from the programme of Language and Literature, UB). Over time, some academics started to realise the advantages of the system and accede to their requirements. Nevertheless, these different factors seem to have led to the lack of motivation to actively participate in the quality management system.

Some academics also emphasise the inflexibility of the quality management system. As some academics say: "Sometimes, it seems that the system was not built to help us. The system should serve us and not the other way round. And sometimes, it seems that we have to serve the system" (Academic from the programme of Language and Literature, UB).

The lack of communication between the top management bodies and representatives who develop the quality management system and the academics who have to deal with it on a daily basis, together with the insufficient diffusion of the main goals and strategies of the quality management system seem also to justify the resistance of academics to quality management. In UB, an academic from the programme of Informatics Engineering states that: "There is a gap between decision making up there and down here, and several times, the decisions are not explained."

The lack of communication and the insufficient diffusion tend to drive the lack of knowledge of the academics about the quality management system. Some academics are unaware of the goals, procedures and the expected results from the quality management system, knowing only the procedures which make part of their daily activities. As the Coordinator of the programme of Education from UC states: "Maybe a greater proximity between the pro-rectory for quality and the programme directors would help ... maybe this should be the way ahead." Such unawareness seems to drive more sceptical and negative positions regarding the quality management system.

Student Resistance to Quality Management

Besides academics, students also show resistance to the quality management system. First of all, students show resistance to answering the surveys which assess courses and their lecturers. They emphasise specific motives for their resistance. On the one hand, they fear being penalised by the academics, despite the fact that the questionnaires are, in principle, anonymous. However, when the subjects have few students, it is not difficult to identify the students according to their answers: "even if the questionnaires are anonymous, (…) there are few students and the professor can know who answered" (Student from the programme of Language and Literature, UB).

On the other hand, there is a sense of uselessness. Often the students do not understand the goals of the surveys, since they do not see corrective measures to improve the elements which are pointed out as negative: "Honestly, I do not know what the university does with the questionnaires and if the university takes into account our opinion" (Student from the programme of Basic Education, UC).

The resistance of the students is also linked to a lack of interest and laziness, which is highlighted by academics, but also by the students: "there are students who do not answer because they are lazy and they are not interested, even when the professors encourage the students to answer" (Student from the programme of Language and Literature, UB).

Actually, universities are facing problems regarding the participation of students in the surveys, and some of the universities are considering adopting measures, either positive (awards) or negative (penalties), in order to increase the participation rates of the students. In University B, the responsible for quality at rectory emphasises the positive incentives: "We chose not to penalise the students, by for example, preventing them to apply, but to award the students who were more participative in the system, adding that information to their diplomas."

The Support of Non-Academics to Quality Management

Although we have interviewed a small number of non-academics, all of them highly involved in quality management activities, it is interesting to note that they present a similar perspective regarding quality management. In general, they support the quality management systems of their universities, consensually perceiving them as "useful" and contributing to the "overall improvement of the university."

It is also interesting to observe that the interviewed non-academics, who are highly involved in quality management activities, tend to believe that the academics and the students accept or at least adapt to the quality management systems, as the statement of the Coordinator of the Operational Body for Quality from UB shows: "I think it [quality management system] was already internalised and accepted and people start to understand that it can be bureaucracy but it can also be useful. It only depends on the way people use the instrument and the system. (...) In my point of view, people already face it as something that belongs to them and they want to participate and contribute to it, because (...) they know that they have a way to show their opinion and that will pass to those who make decisions."

However, some also acknowledge the resistance from academics and students to quality management especially in the beginning of its implementation: "there were much resistance to the process. Things moved forward and then stopped, and they moved forward again and they stopped again ... The quality culture is something that we have been built over time, because there are people that face it as a bureaucracy and not as an opportunity to improve" (Member of the Operational Body for Quality, UC).

They also emphasise the involvement and participation of academics in the quality management system: "There is a high involvement, everybody participates, professors, students (...). There is involvement, participation, exchange of information, etc." (Coordinator of the Strategic Body for Internal Audit, UA).

It is also interesting to highlight the statement of the Responsible for the Operational Body for Quality in UA which highlights the increasing participation of the students, but recognises that their participation should be even stronger: "The students have been increasingly involved in all the bodies, they are called to become part of the Council for Quality, in the evaluations, etc., but we are far from giving them the importance that I believe they deserve."

Globally, it seems that the non-academic staff highly involved in the quality management systems support them and emphasise their importance. They also seem to be aware of the resistance of the academics and the reasons for it as well as of the need of a higher involvement, particularly from the students.

Notwithstanding, they seem to have a more positive perspective regarding, not only the position of academics and students with respect to quality management, but also their participation and involvement in the system, then the position that academics and students effectively show.

CONCLUSIONS

Our research aimed to understand the perceptions of the main internal stakeholders of the quality management systems in place in their universities

The perceptions seem to differ mainly according to their involvement in the quality management system. On the one hand, those with low involvement in quality management activities tend to have less knowledge and a more pessimistic perception of quality management. On the other hand, those more directly involved in the quality management system seem to have a deeper knowledge of the quality management system of the universities and also a more optimistic view of such activities, as corroborated by the literature (Bell & Taylor, 2005; Manatos et al., 2015; Rosa et al., 2006; Stensaker et al., 2011). Hence, the (low or high) involvement in quality management activities can influence not only the acceptance, adaptation or resistance to quality management but also the level of awareness and knowledge of the quality management system in universities. The two seem to be connected, since a low level of awareness regarding quality management seems to be related to a more sceptical position.

The lack of awareness and knowledge of quality management seems to be, in turn, related to a gap in the communication between top managers who develop the quality management systems and the other academics who deal with them daily (Kleijnen et al., 2011), and also to little involvement of academics in the development of quality management systems (Cardoso et al., 2013). Furthermore, we argue that the lack of knowledge regarding quality management, the gap in the communication between different hierarchical levels, and the low involvement of academics, can also explain the misalignment between the discourses of the different stakeholders with different hierarchical levels and with different involvement levels in the quality management process.

This is an interesting but not surprising conclusion. It is however surprising how, after so many years of quality management in universities and so much research on the topic, there is still a gap in the communication and information regarding quality management, which potentially hampers the implementation of effective quality management systems. It is surprising how universities and their management bodies did not yet learn that communication and information are key elements for effective quality management, which contributes to the improvement of the quality of universities and their processes. As stated by Mourad (2013, p. 361), it is crucial that those responsible for quality management have "the social skills to communicate effectively with faculty members and students."

These aspects represent some of the motives for the resistance of academics to quality management identified in our research. In addition, academics state that they should be focused on teaching and research and not on meeting the requirements of the quality management system (Newton, 2002). It seems that the academics view quality as "ritualism and tokenism" (Newton, 2002). They also consider that quality management activities aim to monitor and to control their activities rather than to improve them. In this sense, quality is seen as "suspicion of management motives" or "manifestation of managerialist control", monitoring and controlling the academic work and weakening the academic autonomy (Cardoso et al., 2013; Harvey, 2006; Newton, 2002). Some academics are also sceptical about student surveys as a proper instrument to assess their work, since students are not "trained assessors" (Leckey & Neill, 2001; Nasser & Fresko, 2002).

Nevertheless, while academics express their resistance and highlight the limitations of the system, they also seem to "adapt" and "resiliently comply" to the quality management systems, meeting their requirements (Newton, 2002; Sousa et al., 2010).

Besides academics, students also show resistance, particularly in answering the surveys which assess the courses and their lecturers, either because they fear to be penalised, or because they do not understand the surveys' aims and doubt that they will change or improve their university and their experience as students, as previous research also indicates (Mourad, 2013; Stensaker et al., 2011). The lack of interest to participate in these surveys is also common among students. The low participation rates of students are a problem which universities are trying to solve, namely by adopting rewarding or penalising measures. In this regard, Mourad (2013, p. 361) argues that "there should be an announcement of the recognition and reward system for student participation in quality assurance activities. The reward could be in the form of personal development, international exposure, training and support, financial payment."

Consequently, and like previous research, our study indicates that despite the "rationale of providing students with better information on the quality of teaching and learning" behind most quality management systems, students seem to be the group with less information regarding quality in higher education (Stensaker et al., 2011, p. 479).

In this context, stimulating the participation and the engagement of students in the quality management systems and improving the information and communication about their development and implementation are perhaps some of the greatest challenges for the future of quality management in higher education, at the risk of "questioning the legitimacy of the whole process" (Stensaker et al., 2011, p. 479).

However, students are not the only group of internal stakeholders who lack information and participation regarding the quality management system. As stated above, academics with low involvement levels in the quality management process are less informed and more sceptical and need to be involved and engaged.

In general, the resistance to quality management systems in universities seems to be mainly related both to a lack of information and to a lack of communication regarding the quality management systems among the academics and the students with low involvement levels in quality management activities.

Regarding the perceptions of the internal stakeholders on quality management, we found no significant differences between the three universities or even between scientific areas. We observed differences in their perceptions particularly according to their roles, positions, experiences and involvement in the quality management process.

Since our sample involves the first Portuguese universities to have a certified quality management system, presumably those more experienced in the development and the implementation of quality management systems, we can conclude that even those universities still face the same problems regarding the acceptance and engagement of their internal stakeholders with regard to their quality management systems.

Ours and similar research invite the discussion on the quality management systems which are being developed and implemented in the European Higher Education Area, particularly about their design and objectives. As Stensaker and colleagues (2011, p. 476) argue: "there is a real danger that quality assurance schemes can be accused of not being very efficient and of targeting processes stimulating bureaucracy, organisation and regulation more than addressing issues that are central in the minds of the academic staff and students."

Furthermore, Watty (2006, p. 298) highlights the importance of listening to the various stakeholders in universities, arguing that if policy-makers do not recognise "the legitimate voices of various stakeholders (…) in their discussions about quality improvement and quality assurance policies for higher education (…) there is a risk for universities that the large amounts of resources (…) dedicated to quality assurance and quality improvement programmes, result in little more than an exercise in compliance and form-filling."

Consequently, "universities must invest in staff development as well as students training" and "educate students and faculty members about their roles in the quality assurance process." Particularly, universities must treat students "as partners" and increase "their participation in the decision making process" so that they understand "they are having an impact on the university" (Mourad, 2013, p. 361).

Since our research is based on three case studies, it cannot be representative of other universities. For this reason, it would be interesting to understand what is happening in other universities (Portuguese or from other countries), how their quality management systems are being developed and which (if any) resistance they are facing. It would also be interesting to monitor the development of the quality management systems of these three universities in the next few years, in order to understand if the resistance from the different internal stakeholders persists or if it is being overcome over time.

Furthermore, since the support, adaptation and resistance to quality management systems of universities are emerging dimensions from a study with different research dimensions and goals, it would be useful to develop another study specifically based on the standpoints of the different internal stakeholders regarding quality management, in order to raise specific questions on the topic and consequently deeply explore and understand some of our results.

REFERENCES

Bateson, R., & Taylor, J. (2004). Student involvement in university life – beyond political activism and university governance: a view from Central and Eastern Europe. *European Journal of Education, 39*(4), 471–483.

Becket, N., & Brookes, M. (2008). Quality management practice in higher education – What quality are we actually enhancing? *Journal of Hospitality, Leisure, Sport and Tourism Education, 7*(1), 40–54.

Bell, E., & Taylor, S. (2005). Joining the club: the ideology of quality and business school badging. *Studies in Higher Education, 30*(3), 239–255.

Cardoso, S., Santiago, R., & Sarrico, C. S. (2012a). The impact of quality assessment in universities: Portuguese students' perceptions. *Journal of Higher Education Policy and Management, 34*(2), 125–138.

Cardoso, S., Santiago, R., & Sarrico, C. S. (2012b). The social representations of students on the assessment of universities' quality: The influence of market- and managerialism-driven discourse. *Quality in Higher Education, 18*(3), 281–296.

Cardoso, S., Rosa, M., & Santos, C. (2013). Different academics' characteristics, different perceptions on quality assessment? *Quality Assurance in Education, 21*(1), 96–117.

Cartwright, M. (2007). The rhetoric and reality of "quality" in higher education – an investigation into staff perceptions of quality in post-1992 universities. *Quality Assurance in Education, 15*(3), 287–301.

Deem, R. (1998). 'New managerialism' and higher education: The management of performances and cultures in universities in the United Kingdom. *International Studies in Sociology of Education, 8*(1), 47–70.

Flyvbjerg, B. (2006). Five misunderstandings about case-study research. *Qualitative Inquiry, 12*(2), 219–245.

Gerring, J. (2007). *Case study research: Principles and practices*. Cambridge: Cambridge University Press.

Harvey, L. (2003). Student feedback [1]. *Quality in Higher Education, 9*(1), 3–20.

Harvey, L. (2006). Impact of quality assurance: Overview of a discussion between representatives of external quality assurance agencies. *Quality in Higher Education, 12*(3), 287–290.

Huusko, M., & Ursin, J. (2010). Why (not) assess? Views from the academic departments of Finnish universities. *Assessment and Evaluation in Higher Education, 35*(7), 859–869.

Kleijnen, J., Dolmans, D., Willems, J., & van Hout, H. (2011). Does internal quality management contribute to more control or to improvement of higher education? A survey on faculty's perceptions. *Quality Assurance in Education, 19*(2), 141–155.

Kogan, M. (1993). The evaluation of higher education: an introductory note. In M. Kogan (Ed.), *Evaluating higher education* (pp. 11–26). London: Jessica Kingsley.

Konecki, K. (2008). Grounded theory and serendipity. *Qualitative Sociology Review, 4*(1), 171–186.

Laughton, D. (2003). Why was the QAA approach to teaching quality assessment rejected by academics in UK HE? *Assessment & Evaluation in Higher Education, 28*(3), 309–321.

Leckey, J., & Neill, N. (2001). Quantifying quality: The importance of student feedback. *Quality in Higher Education, 7*(1), 19–32.

Lomas, L. (2007). Zen, motorcycle maintenance and quality in higher education. *Quality Assurance in Education, 14*(4), 402–412.

Loukkola, T., & Zhang, T. (2010). *Examining quality culture: Part 1 – quality assurance processes in higher education institutions*. Brussels: European University Association.

Manatos, M., Sarrico, C. S., & Rosa, M. (2015). The importance and degree of implementation of the European standards and guidelines for internal quality assurance in universities: The views of Portuguese academics. *Tertiary Education and Management, 21*(3), 245–261.

Manatos, M., Sarrico, C. S., & Rosa, M. (2017). The integration of quality management in higher education institutions: A systematic literature review. *Total Quality Management & Business Excellence, 28*(1–2), 159–175.

Massy, W. (2003). *Honoring the trust: Quality and cost containment in higher education*. Bolton: Anker Publishing Company, Inc.

Mourad, M. (2013). Students' perception of quality assurance activities. *Sustainability Accounting, Management and Policy Journal, 4*(3), 345–365.

Nasser, F., & Fresko, B. (2002). Faculty views of student evaluation of college teaching. *Assessment & Evaluation in Higher Education, 27*(2), 187–198.

Newton, J. (2002). View from below: Academics coping with quality. *Quality in Higher Education, 8*(1), 39–61.

Rosa, M., & Amaral, A. (2007). A self-assessment of higher education institutions from the perspectives of EFQM model. In D. F. Westerheijden (Ed.), *Quality assurance in higher education: Trends in regulation, translation and transformation*. Dordrecht: Springer.

Rosa, M., & Amaral, A. (2014). The Portuguese case: New public management reforms and the European standards and guidelines. In H. Eggins (Ed.), *Drivers and barriers to achieving quality in higher education* (pp. 153–166). Rotterdam: Sense Publishers.

Rosa, M., & Sarrico, C. S. (2012). Quality, evaluation and accreditation: From steering, through compliance, on to enhancement and innovation? In A. Amaral & G. Neave (Eds.), *Higher education in Portugal 1974–2009: A nation, a generation* (pp. 249–264). Dordrecht the Netherlands: Springer.

Rosa, M., Tavares, D., & Amaral, A. (2006). Institutional consequences of quality assessment. *Quality in Higher Education, 12*(2), 145–159.

Sousa, C., Nijs, W., & Hendriks, P. (2010). Secrets of the beehive: Performance management in university research organizations. *Human Relations, 63*(9), 1439–1460.

Stensaker, B., Langfeldt, L., Harvey, L., Huisman, J., & Westerheijden, D. (2011). An in-depth study on the impact of external quality assurance. *Assessment and Evaluation in Higher Education, 36*(4), 465–478.

Tavernier, F. (2004). The students' role in french academic deliberative democracy. *European Journal of Education, 39*(4), 497–505.

Trowler, P. (2005). A sociology of teaching, learning and enhancement: Improving practices in higher education. *Revista de Sociologia, 76*, 13–32.

Watty, K. (2006). Want to know about quality in higher education? Ask an academic. *Quality in Higher Education, 12*(3), 291–301.

Westerheijden, D., Hulpiaub, V., & Waeytens, K. (2007). From design and implementation to impact of quality assurance: An overview of some studies into what impacts improvement. *Tertiary Education and Management, 13*(4), 295–312.

Maria J. Manatos
ISEG Lisbon School of Economics and Management
and Centre for Research in Higher Education Policies (CIPES)

Maria Rosa
Department of Economics
Industrial Engineering and Tourism
University of Aveiro
and Centre for Research in Higher Education Policies

Cláudia Sarrico
ISEG Lisbon School of Economics and Management
University of Lisbon
and Centre for Research on Higher Education Policies

TONE HORNTVEDT AND ELLEN CARM

10. INTERNATIONALIZATION – A TOOL TO ENHANCE INTERCULTURAL COMPETENCE IN HIGHER EDUCATION?

INTRODUCTION

This chapter is based on more than ten years' work with students from Oslo and Akershus University College of Applied Sciences (HiOA) going to countries in the Southern Hemisphere for at least three months during their undergraduate programme. On average the number of students who choose to stay abroad for such a period is around 200. Less than 10% of these are men. We found the gender issue interesting and will comment on this in relation to the different categories of the students' reactions.

These students were drawn from different programmes, but had in common that they would graduate with a practically orientated education as nurses, teachers, social or health care workers. They were sent to countries like India, Cuba, Brazil, Tanzania, Uganda, Namibia, China, the Philippines, and the Dominican Republic and stayed there for at least three months, either working or doing projects, some of which were their undergraduate projects.

One of the major goals of the Oslo and Akershus University College of Applied Sciences (HiOA) is that its students should become familiar with internationalization, whether abroad or in Norway. It is considered important and necessary that intercultural competence is included in the educated student's portfolio. This goal led to a project where we were asked to follow students from the vocational teacher education programme when, for the first time, their programme included a period to be spent abroad in a country in the South. These students are different from the average undergraduate student in that they are older than most students; they have studied previously and are practicing as professionals in their various occupations. They are part-time students and work part-time in their own professional field. They have more social commitments (children, elderly parents, loans, and so on) than the average student. The occupations they represent include electricians, plumbers, carpenters, hairdressers, childcare workers, cooks, etc. Until our pilot project started, it had been impossible to find mature students willing to go abroad. However, when the project was presented to the students, ten were sufficiently interested to consider whether it would be possible for them to be away from home for three months. Eventually, only three of these students (one male and two females) completed the

R. Deem & H. Eggins (Eds.), The University as a Critical Institution?, 173–183.

period abroad. We did a follow-up two years later with one mature female student who found it possible to spend three months abroad. It was these students that we wished to compare with the so-called average student group by looking for similarities and differences in how they coped with the new context.

DESIGN/METHODOLOGY/APPROACH

As indicated earlier, this research is based on more than ten years of observation of students going abroad to the Southern hemisphere. One consequence of such a long study period is that the data was collected using different methods and approaches.

Two main data collecting methods were utilized during this period:

Qualitative Content Analysis

We read and analysed more than 50 theses from different undergraduate programmes. To gain insights into how the students discussed and described aspects of intercultural communication, and thereby intercultural competence, in terms of personal and social phenomena in their theses, a qualitative content analysis was conducted. Content analysis allows the researcher to read and analyse large numbers of texts and to identify trends and patterns at an individual, institutional, or social level (Hesse-Biber & Nagy Leavy, 2011; Krippendorff, 2012; Weber, 1990). In addition, content analysis provides descriptions, analyses and potential solutions to problems related to the case in hand, making it possible to discuss events from a relativistic cultural prospective (Horntvedt & Fougner, 2015). The nature of the trends and patterns searched for and identified depend on the topic of that particular research. In this chapter, we were looking at results that related to the obtaining and enhancing of intercultural competence.

Case Study Approach

We also used the case study approach, and systematically interviewed students before they left Norway, while in the field, and after they returned to Norway. We also interviewed teachers and international coordinators who had been involved with the students both in Norway and in the countries visited. A case study is based upon a constructivist paradigm and built on the premise of a social construction of reality (Berger & Luckman, 2000; Vygotsky, 1996). The case study approach is an empirical inquiry that investigates phenomena within their real-life context (Yin, 2009; Creswell, 2009). As such, it is often used to discover underlying principles (Yin, 2009). A qualitative case study facilitates the exploration of a phenomenon within its context using a variety of data sources. Thus, in this research, the main sources of data were qualitative interviews, field visits and observations, and some documentary reviews.

174

One of the advantages of this approach is the close collaboration between the researchers and participants, which enables the participants to recount their experiences. The participants described their perception of the exchange programme, their role in it, their involvement, and the learning outcomes from this exchange period. The results from these studies, as they relate to intercultural competence, will be presented in the Findings section.

THEORETICAL PERSPECTIVES

Three main sources described in the literature are used for obtaining intercultural competence. One is to draw on theory about human behaviour in different parts of the world; another is the experience one obtains by living in a foreign context, and the third source is the critical analytic approach where the students obtain competence by deconstructing their experiences through knowledge.

We found that de Wit's (2013) theory on the role played by internationalization in achieving intercultural competence in higher education was a helpful approach. One of his basic tenets is that internationalization per se will not necessarily enhance intercultural competence in students. The most important thing is for students to go into a foreign context and meet people from backgrounds different from their own. If they stay more or less isolated in a context similar to that at home, the learning outcome may be zero. This is enhanced if they also spend most of their time abroad in groups with other students either from their own institution or from the same country. Being able and willing to interact with the unknown is, according to de Wit (2013), necessary for obtaining intercultural competence in higher education.

We have chosen Fantini and Termizi's (2006, p. 12) definition of intercultural competence as our key theory in approaching this concept. They define this phenomenon as "a complex of abilities needed to perform effectively and appropriately when interacting with others who are linguistically and culturally different from oneself". Lustig and Koestler (2012) further limit this to occurring in contexts other than one's own. Studies have demonstrated that the most efficient way to enhance intercultural competence and awareness among students is through international practical placements (Barker, Kinsella, & Bossers, 2010; Fitzgerald, 2000; Koskinen & Tossaveinen, 2004).

FINDINGS

This section will be divided into two parts: the first part examines some trends and tendencies that all undergraduate students experience. The second part will deal with the vocational teaching students and what we have found to be particular to them.

Preparing students to become part of an international and intercultural world has become an increasingly essential part of the undergraduate programmes at Oslo and Akershus University College. This is despite the fact that there has been little research into the learning outcomes and problem-solving skills reported by students who have spent part of their education abroad in Southern countries (Barker et al., 2010; Pechak & Black, 2013). According to Garaj, Orkai, Feith and Radwohl (2012) and McAllister, Whiteford, Hill, Thomas and Fitzgerald (2006), we need greater insight into the nature of knowledge construction and the process that leads to students making relevant choices. In our research investigating how students act and react in unfamiliar contexts, we have seen certain patterns that reappear independently of the student group or the programme attended. These patterns have been primarily based on data collected from the undergraduate students. We have seen four different reactions from the students when the context is new and unfamiliar. These patterns are, of course, not closed, and some students have been observed to move between the different responses.

One group of students, fortunately a small group, all of them male, became more racist than before leaving Norway. These expressed racist opinions either in their interviews, conversations with co-students or in project reports. We used the following definition of a racist from the Oxford Dictionary in this chapter because it is simple and to the point. It describes a racist as follows, "a person who shows or feels discrimination against people of other races or believes that a particular race is superior to another". These students said that they found the others to be dirty, unreliable, and less intelligent than themselves. This was seldom expressed directly to people they met, but rather in how they talked about others in discussions with their co-students, told us in interviews or wrote in their reports. As one student said when we asked him why he used shorts and singlet at work while the locals were dressed in black suit, white shirt and tie:" I don't want to be identified with these dressed up monkeys".

A small number of these students felt ashamed of themselves for having these thoughts and feelings, but as they said, this was the way they felt. We think that those students found their own attitude towards others difficult because of their social background. Being born and raised in Norway puts you through a socialization process that tells you that racism is unacceptable, and it is unacceptable to have such attitudes.

All these students took the view that their basic attitudes and feelings towards others from this part of the world were confirmed and sometimes reinforced by their stay abroad and by meeting with the locals in those areas. It seemed that it was more acceptable for the male students to express such negative thoughts out loud than for the female students. This may also have to do with gender socialization in a Norwegian context where, though all children are encouraged to present their opinions, males often turn out more direct and open in the communication than females. Females seemed to use other techniques to react to foreign contexts, and they often ended up in the second group.

The second group became xenophobic because everything was different from the way it was at home. They constituted around one third of the total number of the students and they were all female. Male students may have felt this way, but they never talked openly about it. We used the Oxford Dictionary as the source for our definition of xenophobia; "dislike or prejudice against people from other countries". These students had difficulty interacting with the locals, not because they were racist but because the context seemed frightening, and they did not have the skills with which to handle their new context. They became paralysed and isolated themselves from what was happening around them. Engebrigsten (1988), in her research on families living in countries in the South while the husbands were working as representatives of Norwegian NGOs, describes how the wives became obsessed with washing. They washed everything including objects and clothes already washed by the house cleaners. They felt that everything around them was dirty. This happened even with those women who considered themselves liberal and open-minded. Gullestad (2002) describes this phenomenon, saying that although Norwegian society is characterized by openness to experiences from outside their society, the reality is that people become uneasy when foreign elements enter their society. Our findings revealed that the same thing seems to happen when certain Norwegians go abroad to live in foreign contexts.

Bakic-Miric (2008) describes a phenomenon called "cultural noise", saying that a culture's symbolic meanings and symbolic values can easily just be heard as cultural noise when an individual is not prepared to respond to them. Perceiving cultural noise has the potential to break down communication completely One student, who became so anguished that she more or less isolated herself inside her room, was asked by her co-students to go home to Norway. She didn't want to do that because it felt like a failure, she said. She went to a tourist place nearby and stayed there for a period with her husband and then returned to her co-students. For her, this worked, as she said: "I got slowly used to all the strange things in an environment that looked more like other tourist places I have visited before". Even though we try to prepare our students for what they are going to meet, we know that it is impossible to prepare anyone for what real life feels like.

A third group, as anthropologists describe it, "went bush". These were not many, but one or two each year ended up in this category. They were both males and females. They lost their ability to see both their native culture and the foreign culture; they jumped straight into the new society wanting to be assimilated as soon as possible. They forgot why they were in this society, that they had assignments to complete, and responsibilities in their native country. Their co-students often tried to "wake them up from this dream", but seldom succeeded. They found the new context to be so much more open, inclusive and warm than their native culture, which they now described as being superficial and too concerned with material goods. "Norway is such a cold country where nobody greets you on the street, nobody seems to care about strangers, only their own families and closest friends But here, everybody greets you, is curious about you, wants to talk to you and take care of you even though you are a stranger" one of the students told us when she left her co-students and went to live with her new boyfriend's family. Some of these students remained in or returned later to this new society. Some even married and had children there. This phenomenon is described by Hofmann in her book "The White Massai".

The fourth group managed to balance their own culture with the possibilities available in the new context. They compared their impressions and made the best out of every situation. They were creative and flexible and searched for challenges and possibilities. We found both male and female students in this category. If they landed up in situations that were difficult or felt impossible to handle, they rolled up their sleeves and tried to find ways to cope. They were network builders and open-minded. They had what Jones (2013) describes as the necessary qualities for developing intercultural competence. An example is one group who arrived in an institution where they were supposed to spend the next three months, but nobody knew they were coming. This group rearranged themselves mentally, asked to talk with the boss in the institution and explained their situation. The boss listened to them and together with him they managed to find a new place to stay. Another example is a female student who came to a university on strike. She went downtown in the city and talked to people and found herself a place to work while waiting for the university to re-open again. As she said; "I cannot just wait until something happens, then I might wait forever, I have to solve this myself so that I learn something from this period." She learned a lot by building a social network around her while searching for a place to work.

When we started the most recent project with students from the vocational teacher education programme, we wanted to explore whether these students would react, cope and handle their period in the South differently from the regular students. These students were older and accustomed to handling adult challenges and responsibilities. They also had long experience from working in their original occupations. Their backgrounds were, in these ways, very different from those of the younger students.

Even though the number of students we were able to follow was very low (because of difficulties in finding students who wanted to go abroad), we found that they fell into some of the categories described above. It seemed as though age and earlier experience did not make a difference; it was the personality and personal qualities of the students that made the difference. None of the vocational teacher students we followed had racist tendencies, but we did find xenophobia, passivity, fear, insecurity, unwillingness, and indifference. However, we also found activity, creativity, flexibility, and the courage to find solutions to difficult situations and experiences.

One particular event made it easy for us to study how the students coped with unexpected events. When they arrived at the university in the South, there was a protracted strike going on, so nobody could meet them and instruct them as to what to do. From this, we could see how each of the students experienced, coped with, and reflected on the fact that they were left on their own. We were also able to see how their emotions and thoughts about this were expressed and we got some insights into how this influenced their opinions about their new context. For two of the students, this strike opened the possibility of getting to know the society outside the university and to build social networks independent of their status as students. For the third student, this led to passivity and reinforcement of her/his feeling of strangeness and difference. This student expressed a feeling of being lost in an unknown world. All the vocational teacher students commented on the fact that they had been left alone when they arrived in the new context, but the active ones coped with this feeling completely differently from the more passive one.

One aspect of Norwegian society and culture that may not be familiar to everyone is the huge impact of the "ideology of sameness". This was defined in the Norwegian governmental White Paper no 49 (1996–1997): "the ideology of sameness must still to the greatest extent be an objective to secure citizens the same opportunities, and the same civil and political rights and duties, independent of background". This idea is central to the social democracy of Norway (Eriksen & Sajjad, 2011; Gullestad, 2002). Sameness in this context has its base in the Latin meaning of identity as idem, ergo "the same". One is primarily identified through the group one belongs to and is treated as one of the group and not as an individual. Everyone has the same possibilities, rights and duties as everyone else. This leads to a particular meaning for 'sameness', which does not refer to equality, but to a kind of similarity. One is expected to treat everybody in the same way, independent of status, background, culture, religion, ethnicity and so on.

This ideology is so incorporated into the Norwegian students' thinking that it affects their stay abroad. When they feel lost in an unknown world, where people are different, treat them differently, and relate in a more hierarchical way than they are accustomed to, they lack the tools to cope and to re-establish their security and stability in the new context. As we saw from the material studied, while some students managed to cope in these situations, many did not. Possibly these experiences of insecurity might, in some cases, lead to xenophobia and racism as a kind of defence. These reactions may become tools for survival, although they are tools that negated the possibility of obtaining and enhancing intercultural competence.

One could say that students in such situations go through a process of "othering" the local people that they meet. By "othering" we mean "the process of perceiving or portraying someone or something as fundamentally different or alien" (Wiktionary, 2016). "Othering" leads to "otherness": "the quality of being not alike; being distinct or different from that otherwise experienced or known" (Wiktionary, 2016). This may lead to the other being seen in contrast to one's self. This way of considering the other is expressed in the dichotomy of "us and them". Our understanding of the other, othering and otherness is based on ideas of social construction: we construct the other as a contrast to ourselves (Said, 1979). This process seems to give us an identity and through that a feeling of security. One knows to which group one belongs and which people are different from oneself. This is a phenomenon described as "the ethnocentric syndrome" (Axelrod & Hammond, 2003; Brown, 1988). Our congenital need is to construct in-groups and out-groups (Tajfel, 1970) to create some security and order in a chaotic world.

We also saw what might be a natural connection between the students' insecurity and the way in which the local infrastructure and the relationship between the cooperating institutions functioned. The more ineffective and uncertain these functions seemed to the students, the more their inborn capacity to cope with the unknown was expressed. Nearly all the students expressed that at times they felt abandoned by both their home institution and the local institution. But there were significant differences in how they coped with this feeling of isolation. The most active and independent students saw this as a way of developing their own learning experiences: they went out, talked to people, explained what they wanted, and found places where they could stay and learn new things; while the more passive students became very frustrated and scared. They had no energy or will to redefine their situation; instead they stayed in their lodgings and waited for something to happen.

The more grounded vocational teacher students reacted in the same way when, due to the strike, they were left to themselves. One of the students coped with the situation by finding herself a place where she could learn some things she wanted to learn; another used this period to participate in the local culture, while the third one felt very uncomfortable and became passive and dissatisfied with the whole going abroad programme .There was one aspect in which the vocational teacher education students were different from the undergraduate students, namely which part of their competence portfolio they used when abroad. The undergraduates all worked in fields where they could use their knowledge and earlier experience from their bachelor education, whether they were nursing students, social work students, teacher students, etc. However, the vocational teacher students presented themselves first in terms of their original education and occupations. They wanted to work in the capacity of hairdresser, electrician, child and youth worker, and so on. Only one of them found, for a short period, status as a vocational teacher student. The fact that the students selected and preferred their earlier profession instead of taking the opportunity to act as teacher students surprised some of the local teachers and supervisors. Several of them commented that they had expected the students to want to teach in the vocational education institutions, but when they found that this was not what the students wanted, they let them do as the students themselves wished. One might wonder why the students chose to remain in their former professions rather than taking the opportunity to experience their role as teacher in a new setting. It might have to do with the fact that they were adults, with many years of working experience, and they wanted to appear competent rather than insecure and new in their role as teachers. This might also have to do with the status and power balance. We never asked them about this, but this might make an interesting theme for a future research project.

We have met hundreds of students in connection with our work with students going abroad. The meetings have been of different quality, with some just happening in passing, while others have been formalised as debriefing situations, and others have been interviews or conversations. However, even though some of the students have had painful and life changing experiences; some have found the experience very boring; some have been afraid; while others have fallen in love; we have never met one student who regretted going abroad. Even those students who had racist tendencies did not regret it. They had experienced a validation of their earlier opinions and as a couple of them said; "seen huge fantastic animals and beautiful nature".

In the students' feedback and reports, all have expressed the view that they learned a great deal about themselves. Nearly all of them spoke about personal growth, but almost none spoke about learning outcomes in relation to their future roles as professionals or about enhanced intercultural competence. When asked to reflect on the connection between personal growth and professional practice, they said that they thought they had changed as individuals in ways that would make them better professionals. However, so far, none of students has spontaneously expressed the idea that they had obtained enhanced intercultural professional competence abroad.

We find this rather surprising and a little alarming. Why is this? Are the qualities required in the individual professional fields underdeveloped abroad compared to those of Norway? We do not think so. Are the students so caught up in their own way of thinking about their future profession that they really do not perceive what is happening in the places they visit? Are their expectations about their own learning potential set so low that they do not recognise that they are learning something new? There are many questions and challenges here that need to be discussed with other people committed to this kind of internationalization.

In conclusion, we found that while most of the students experienced personal growth through being abroad, many of them were unable to transfer this personal growth into professional intercultural competence. They were not aware of this. It seems that they constructed a barrier between themselves as individuals and themselves as future professionals. Tearing down this barrier might be a necessary part of a debriefing process when the students return to their home institution.

CONCLUSION

From our point of view, the impact of these findings will mainly affect the relationships between the professionals and those who use their services. In recent times, most societies have become increasingly intercultural, ecumenical, and inter-ethnic, and professionals need the skills to cope with the challenges arising in such societies. The more aware and well informed we can make the students for their stay abroad, the more skills the students will be able to bring to their interactions with people from all over the world. This may lead to fewer negative experiences and to improved communications between professionals and the people they serve than we see at present (Horntvedt, 2016; Daae-Qvale, 2016; Sørheim, 2000).

As far as we have been able to discover from the literature, our project is original. Firstly, it describes four reaction patterns among students going abroad to countries in the South, the racist-, the xenophobic-, the "gone bush"- and the interculturally competent group. Secondly, it makes a distinction between ordinary undergraduate students and vocational teacher students and compares their ability to cope in new contexts. One goal of our study was to discover whether these adult students would obtain intercultural competence more easily than the younger students. The results of this research show that the two groups were similar in most ways, with most of the differences being based on personality rather than on age or former experience.

REFERENCES

Axelrod, R., & Hammond, R. A. (2003, April 3–6). *The evolution of ethnocentric behavior.* Paper delivered at Midwest Political Convention, Chicago.

Bakic-Miric, N. (2008). Re-imaging understanding of intercultural communication, culture and culturing. *Journal of Intercultural Communication, 9.* Retrieved December 29, 2014 from http//www.immi.se/intercultural

Barker, A., Kinsella, E. A., & Bossers, A. (2010). Learning in international practice placement education: A grounded theory study. *The British Journal of Occupational Therapy, 73,* 29–37.

Berger, P. L. og., & Luckman, T. (2000). *Den samfunnsskapte virkelighet. [The Social Construction of Reality].* Bergen: Fagbokforlaget.

Brown, R. J. (1988). *Group processes: Dynamics within and between goups.* Oxford: Blackwell.

Creswell, J. (2009). *Research design: Qualitative, quantitative and mixed methods approaches.* London: Sage.

Daae-Qvale, I. (2016). Profesjonsidentitet i et flerkulturelt helsevesen: Paradokser, grenser og ambivalens. *Scandinavian Journal of Intercultural Theory and Practice, 3*(1), 1–19.

de Wit, H. (2013). Internationalisation of higher education, an introduction on the why, how and the what. In H. de Wit (Ed.), *An introduction to higher education internationalisation.* Milan: Vita e pensiero.

Engebrigtsen, A. I. (1988). *Med NORAD – i Afrika: Identitetshåndtering og virkelighetsforståelse blant nordmenn i Zambia.* Magisteroppgave fra Universitet i Oslo. Institutt for Sosialantropologi.

Eriksen, T. H., & Sajjad, T. A. (2011). *Kulturforskjeller i praksis.* Oslo: Gyldendal akademiske.

Fantini, A. E., & Tirmizi, A. (2006). Exploring and assessing intercultural competence. In *Final report, world learning publications.* Paper 1. St. Louis: Washington University.

Fitzgerald, M. (2000). Establishing cultural competency for health professionals. In V. Skultans & J. Cox (Eds.), *Anthropological approaches to psychological medicine.* London: Jessica Kingsley.

Garaj, E., Orkai, A. H., Feith, J. H., & Radvohl, E. G. (2012). Some aspects of cultural diversity and learning styles in international higher education. *Practice and Theory in Systems of Education, 7,* 273–278.

Gullestad, M. (2002). *Det norske sett med nye øyne.* Oslo: Universitetsforlaget.

Hesse-Biber, S., & Nagy Leavy, P. (2011). *The practice of qualitative research.* Los Angeles, CA: Sage.

Hofmann, C. (2006) *The white masai.* New York, NY: HarperCollins Publishers.

Horntvedt, T. (2016). *Interkulturelt helsearbeid.* Drammen: Forlaget Vett & Viten.

Horntvedt, T., & Fougner, M. (2015). Critical incidents and cultural relativism: Tools for survival in a foreign context? *Reflective Practice 2015.* London/NY: Tyler & Francis Group.

Jones, E. (2013). Internationalisation and student learning outcomes. In H. de Wit (Ed.), *An introduction to higher education internationalisation.* Milan: Vita e pensiero.

Koskinen, L., & Tossaveinen, K. (2006). Studying abroad as a process of learning intercultural competence in nursing. *International Journal of Nursing Practice, 10,* 11–120.

Krippendorf, K. (2012). *Content analysis: An introduction to its methodology.* Thousand Oaks, CA: Sage.

Lustig, M. W., & Koester, I. (2010). *Intercultural competence: Interpersonal communication across cultures.* Boston, MA: Allyn & Bacon.

Mc Allister, L., Whiteford, G., Hill, B., Thomas, N., & Fitzgerald, M. (2006). Reflection on intercultural learning: Examining the international experience through a critical incident approach. *Reflective Practice, 7,* 367–381.

Pechak, C., & Black, J. D. (2013). Benefits and challenges of international clinical education from a US-based physiotherapist faculty perspective. *Physiotherapy Research International, 18*(4), 239–249.

Said, E. W. (1979). *Orientalism.* Vintage Book Addition.

Sørheim, T. A. (2000). *Innvandrere med funksjonshemmede barn i møte med tjenesteapparatet.* Oslo: Gyldendal Akademiske.

Tajfel, H. (1970). Experiments in intergroup discrimination. *Springer Nature, 223,* 96–102.

Vogotsky, L. S. (1996). Interaksjon mellom læring og utvikling. In E. L. Dale (Ed.), *Skolens undervisning og barnets utvikling.* Oslo: ad Notam Gyldendal.

Weber, R. P. (1990). *Basic content analysis* (2nd ed.). Newbury Park, CA: Sage.

Wiktionary- the free dictionary (15 July 2016).

Yin, R. K. (2009). *Case study research: Design and methods* (4th ed.). Thousand Oaks, CA: Sage Publications.

Tone Horntvedt
Institute for Internationalization and Interpreting, Oslo
and
Akershus University College of Applied Sciences

Ellen Carm
Institute for Internationalization and Interpreting, Oslo
and
Akershus University College of Applied Sciences

MONIA ANZIVINO AND MICHELE ROSTAN

11. UNIVERSITY STUDENT PARTICIPATION IN OUT-OF-CLASS ACTIVITIES

Consequences for Study Career and Academic Achievement

INTRODUCTION

Student university experience is not limited to class attendance In fact students may be involved in various out-of-class activities implying both horizontal interaction with peers and vertical interaction with faculty. The participation in these activities may influence both students' performance and career.

The theory of involvement (Astin, 1984, 1993) include many out-of-class experiences among the factors that affect learning outcomes. Living in a residence hall, academic involvement, student-faculty interaction after class, athletic involvement, socialization and participation in student organizations or in a fraternity or sorority, are some of the experiences that could promote learning. Further, academic and social involvement – or engagement – is considered one of the most important conditions favouring student persistence and graduation (Tinto, 1975, 1997, 2010). In several research works conducted in different contexts and with different methods, the interaction with peers is positively associated with study success measured by various indicators.

Using a qualitative approach, Kuh (1993, 1995) provides a picture of the positive outcomes that students associate with out-of-class experiences. Results show that out-of-class activities contribute to personal development enhancing the "capacity for critical thinking, personal reflection, competence and self-direction" (Kuh, 1993, p. 300). In particular, peer interactions are "mentioned frequently as instrumental to the development of interpersonal competence, humanitarianism, and cognitive complexity" (Kuh, 1995, p. 134). Peer interaction is a major concern in the discussion on "learning beyond the curriculum". Using a narrative approach, the role of peer learning in the process of becoming a university student, adapting to the institutional, social and cultural rules, is emphasized (Havnes 2008).

Other studies are carried out using quantitative methods They investigate the association between students' involvement in various activities and study outcomes considering several aspects of their interaction with peers.

The study by Nicpon et al. (2006), based on Tinto's model of academic persistence (1993), shows the great importance of peer relationships in deciding to persist. Students who are satisfied with their social relationships feel less isolated and more

R. Deem & H. Eggins (Eds.), The University as a Critical Institution?, 185–216.

supported, and are more likely to persist. Although the indicators used in this study are mainly psychological and are not focused on out-of-class activities, its findings are useful to understand the importance of social integration for students' career. Also relying on Tinto's framework, Meeuwisse et al. (2010) show that both formal and informal relationships with peers and faculties are important to develop a sense of belonging, in turn connected with study progress.

Using data from the 2008 National Survey on Student Engagement (NSSE), Webber et al. (2013) examine the relationship between engagement in curricular and co-curricular activities – including conversation with peers and work with other students during and outside classes – and study success measured by cumulative grades and students' levels of satisfaction with their college experience. Authors find that higher levels of engagement are associated with better results: students who report more frequent involvement in academic and social activities accumulate higher grades and express higher levels of satisfaction.

In their analysis of NSSE data, Carini et al. (2006) find that many measures of student engagement – including the quality of the relationship with other people in the university and student-faculty interactions – are positively, although weakly, related to various aspects of academic performance, such as critical thinking and grades. Student engagement in various activities appears to be especially beneficial for students with lower ability or belonging to minority groups. For instance, Kuh et al. (2008) show that students' involvement in educationally purposeful activities has a greater impact on academic achievement and persistence for disadvantaged students.

Some studies focus on learning communities as an opportunity for peer interaction. Participating in a learning community favours working with others, critical enquiry and reflection, communication and articulation of knowledge, understanding and skills, managing learning and how to learn, self and peer assessment, which in turn affect study success (Boud et al., 2001). Further, the participation in a learning community is positively associated with numerous indicators of study success, such as positive perceptions of college environment, self-reported gains, and satisfaction with college experience. It also promotes involvement in academic and social activities that extend beyond the classroom fostering social integration and connection with an affinity group of peers, which are important factors for study success (Zhao & Kuh, 2004).

A vast body of literature covering several decades (Pascarella, 1980; Kuh & Hu, 2001; Pascarella, 2006) shows that students' interaction with faculty is also associated with positive student outcomes. These studies consider a wide range of outcomes varying from academic achievement and institutional persistence to personal development and satisfaction with higher education. Student persistence from first to second year is one of the major focuses of concern (Pascarella & Terenzini, 1977; Pascarella & Terenzini, 1978). Further, academic achievement measured in terms of grades is often taken into consideration (Pascarella & Terenzini, 1978; Endo & Harpel, 1982; Kim & Sax, 2009). Several aspects of the interaction between students and faculty are investigated the frequency of it (Pascarella & Terenzini, 1977; Pascarella & Terenzini, 1978; Endo & Harpel, 1982; Cotton & Wilson, 2006; Kim & Sax, 2009), the nature of the interaction – for instance, social or academic (Cotton & Wilson, 2006), formal or informal (Pascarella & Terenzini, 1977; Pascarella & Terenzini, 1978; Endo & Harpel, 1982) – and its contents including both academically focused matters and matters having a broader scope (Pascarella & Terenzini, 1978; Endo & Harpel, 1982; Cox & Orehovec, 2007). For many reasons, attention focuses on students' contact with faculty beyond the classroom. In fact, out-of-class interaction is deemed to be a crucial aspect of students' integration or involvement in the life of colleges and universities (Tinto, 1975), it is considered as an important element of the socialising function of higher education institutions through the action of individual faculty members (Pascarella, 1980) and a crucial part of an institutional environment promoting student retention and institutional completion (Tinto, 2010). Some studies cover a rather short length of time – 1–2 academic years – focusing on freshmen students (Pascarella & Terenzini, 1977; Pascarella & Terenzini, 1978) while others extend the analysis to longer periods of time including also more mature students (Endo & Harper, 1982; Cotton & Wilson, 2006). Both quantitative and qualitative approaches characterise the study of student-faculty interaction. Relying on multivariate analysis, quantitative studies investigate both the general positive effects of student-faculty interaction on outcomes (Pascarella, 1980) and its conditional effects looking at different patterns of interaction for various subgroups of students (Pascarella, 2006; Kim & Sax, 2009). In both cases the association between interaction and outcomes is controlled by various individual and contextual characteristics. Qualitative studies explore not only the frequency of student-faculty interaction but also its complex nature trying to shed light on its determinants, to reveal the processes that underlie the contact between faculty and students outside the classroom, and to identify different types of interaction (Cotton & Wilson, 2006; Cox & Orehovec, 2007). Finally, information on student-faculty interaction is gathered either within a single campus (Pascarella & Terenzini, 1978) or from more than one (Kim & Sax, 2009).

Although results from these studies document an overall positive association between out-of-class interaction with faculty and student outcomes, divergent or different evidences are also reported. Sometimes out-of-class interaction with faculty is associated with academic achievements measured in terms of grades (Pascarella & Terenzini, 1978) while in others informal student-faculty interaction and academic achievement were found to be unrelated (Endo & Harpel, 1982), possibly because two different lengths of students' career were considered in the investigation. According to some authors, only the interaction with faculty in specific areas such as the discussion on intellectual or course related matters and on matters related to students' future career have a positive effect on student outcomes (Pascarella & Terenzini, 1977) while others argue that almost every type of interaction between faculty and students can have positive effects (Cox & Orehovec, 2007).

All these studies – either focusing on the horizontal interaction with peers or the vertical interaction with faculty – mainly refer to the Anglo-Saxon context leaving it open the question on which factors are taken into consideration when studying students' outcomes in other contexts.

In the Italian context, recent contributions on several aspects of university students' career and performance have adopted a multivariate approach. These studies have mainly focused on several measures of dropout and withdrawal (Aina, 2013; Belloc et al., 2010; Agasisti & Murtinu, 2016; Clerici et al., 2015; Ghignoni, 2017; Meggiolaro et al., 2015; Triventi & Trivellato, 2009), degree completion and time to complete degree courses (Aina et al., 2011; Agasisti & Murtinu, 2016; Clerici et al., 2015; Meggiolaro et al., 2015; Triventi & Trivellato, 2009), and formative credits acquisition (Agasisti & Murtinu, 2016). Student outcomes have been related to various students' individual characteristics (Aina et al., 2011; Belloc et al., 2010; Clerici et al., 2015; Ghignoni, 2017; Meggiolaro et al., 2015; Triventi & Trivellato, 2009), several characteristics of their families (Aina et al., 2011; Aina, 2013; Ghignoni, 2017; Triventi & Trivellato, 2009), university facilities, endowments and human resources (Aina et al., 2011; Ghignoni, 2017), financial aid for students through the provision of grants (Agasisti & Martinu, 2016), and labour market conditions (Aina et al., 2011; Ghignoni, 2017). In these studies students' experience within or outside the classroom, including interaction with peers and/or faculty is not taken into consideration.

As a consequence, we would like to contribute to the study of university student outcomes in the Italian context using previous studies as a term of reference and bringing into the analysis a rather neglected aspect of student experience. Thus, this chapter aims at exploring the relationship between students' involvement in extra-curricular and out-of-class activities and two aspects of their academic performance: the regularity of their study career and their academic achievement. It also deals with the different participation in extra-curricular or out-of-class activities according to students' characteristics.

The paper is based on the study of a large random representative sample of students attending a comprehensive institution covering both undergraduate and graduate courses, and a wide range of study fields. Further, it investigates students' university experience and its outcomes profiting from the opportunity to match individual survey data on students' characteristics and behaviours with a vast array of administrative data on students' career.

Our research questions are the following:

1. Is students' involvement in out-of-class activities associated with their academic performance?
2. Which individual characteristics can favour or hinder students' participation in out-of-class activities?

We answer these questions looking at the case of the University of Pavia.

THE UNIVERSITY OF PAVIA

Pavia is a small city with 70,000 inhabitants 40 km south of Milan, the regional capital of Lombardy, one of the more populated and rich Italian regions. The University of Pavia was established in 1361 and until the 20th century has been the only university in the area of Milan and in Lombardy. Todays within the region there are 13 universities, 7 of which are located in Milan. Seven institutions, including Pavia University, are state universities.

Currently, some 24,000 students study at the University of Pavia. About 21,500 students attend short first cycle courses (55%), that is undergraduate or Bachelors' programmes, long first cycle (28%) and second cycle (16%) courses, that is graduate programmes equivalent to Masters'. The rest are doctoral students and students attending advanced specialised courses, especially in medicine.

Students can choose study courses from a wide range of disciplines. First and second level courses' students may be divided into four groups: science and technology (26%), health sciences (30%), social sciences, business and law (33%) and the humanities (11%).

Less than 10% of the students are from Pavia; about 55% of them come from other places within Lombardy, while 35% come from outside the region. Class attendance is very high (90–95%). According to the results of the student survey we have carried out, almost half of attending students commute every day to reach their classrooms. Those who live in the city during term can be divided into three groups: long-term living-in students generally coming from another region (26%), short-term living-in students going back home for the week end (20%), and town citizens (8%). Most of the long and short-term living-in students find accommodation in Pavia renting an apartment (75%), while the rest benefit from the existence of a "college system".

Pavia is one of the very few university cities in Italy hosting a system of special institutions – called "collegi" – providing students with both housing, educational and leisure services. "Collegi" are not colleges in the Oxbridge sense of the term yet they are neither mere residence halls. There are three types of "collegi". Firstly, there are four so-called historical or independent colleges, two of which are very old and reputed institutions. Admittance to these colleges is based on merit. To enrol, students must have obtained very good grades at their secondary school final examination and need to pass an entry examination. Further, to maintain a post within the college, students need to have a grade point average of at least 27/30. Secondly, there are 12 colleges that are owned and managed by a special agency of the University called "Ente per il diritto allo studio" (EDISU). Admittance to these colleges is mainly based on need, while to maintain a post in college beyond first year students must accumulate a certain amount of university formative credits. Finally, there are three private colleges more or less directly associated with the Catholic Church with their own rules.

DESIGN, METHODS, DATA COLLECTION AND LIMITATIONS

In order to answer our research questions, we rely on two sets of data: data from a student survey and administrative data. The student survey was carried out in the academic year 2014–2015.[1] A standard questionnaire (in Italian and English) was administered online to a representative stratified and random sample of the entire student population, excluding doctoral students and students attending advanced specialised programmes. The sample included 6,761 students and – thanks to several reminders by both e-mail and SMS and a communication campaign through old and new media – it was possible to collect information on 2,186 respondents, with a response rate of 32.3%. The questionnaire addressed various thematic areas, including students' university experience (the choice of Pavia University, attendance & learning, the use of some university facilities), their relationship with the city (accommodation & housing, mobility & transportation, leisure & sport activities, social & cultural activities, security) and some personal characteristics (employment & work, family background, time budget).

Table 11.1. Comparing student sample's and population's characteristics (%)

	Actual sample	*Student population 2014/2015*
Gender		
Female	63.5	55.7
Male	36.5	44.3
Age		
19–21 years-old	35.0	29.3
22–23 years-old	29.2	28.9
24–25 years-old	19.9	21.2
25–30 years-old	10.4	13.5
Over 30	5.5	7.1
Study cycle		
Short first cycle courses	53.8	55.4
Long first cycle courses	25.4	27.6
Second cycle courses	19.6	15.8
Other	1.2	1.2
Study field		
Architecture & engineering	14.2	14.2
Science	14.4	12.0
Health sciences	26.0	29.8
Social sciences	26.8	24.0
Law	7.3	9.2
Humanities	11.4	10.9
N	2,186	20,923

Other relevant data on respondents' secondary education, academic performance and career were retrieved from the University's administrative data warehouse and merged with survey data.

The student sample was selected according to two stratification criteria: study cycle and study field. Study cycle included three categories: short first cycle courses (i.e. Bachelors'), long first cycle courses (i.e. mainly EU regulated programmes) and second cycle courses (i.e. Masters'). Study fields were grouped into six categories: architecture & engineering, science, health science, social sciences, law, and humanities. Although the actual sample fits quite well, the student population's characteristics by study cycle and study field (see Table 11.1), it must be noted that women and younger students are slightly over represented in it.

Before illustrating data analysis and results some limitations of the study are worth mentioning. Firstly, it refers to a single case. Thus, any generalisation of its findings to the Italian higher education system is premature. In order to develop further studies on the relationship between students' involvement in out-of-class activities and study performance, the case of Pavia should be compared to more similar other cases according to the characteristics described in the previous section. Secondly, although available, information on secondary school final exam grades has not been included in the analysis. This variable, known to influence student success, was not included because of some missing values in the administrative data, problems with the reliability of final grades in assessing secondary education attainments and difficulties in collecting relevant data. Thirdly, the student survey was not intended to study the relationship between out-of-class activities and academic performance, so the research instrument didn't include questions on individual attitudes and expectations, and personal satisfaction and interests. Thus, important elements affecting our dependent variables were not available. Finally, as we collected cross-sectional data, and not longitudinal ones, we had to limit our analysis to exploring the association between relevant phenomena, and we can say little on causal relations between variables. As it will be shown, sometimes the impact could be supposed but not proved.

DATA ANALYSIS

In order to answer our research questions, data analysis was carried out in two stages. First, we looked at the relationship between students' participation in out-of-class activities and study performance relying on linear regression models. These models were used to: (a) explore the bivariate relationship between students' involvement and academic outcomes; (b) control this relationship by numerous individual and contextual variables.

In the second stage of the study, we utilized linear regression models to see whether some aspects of students' involvement were related to relevant individual characteristics.

In stage one of the analysis, we created two dependent variables measuring study performance and five independent variables measuring students' participation in out-of-class activities. Further, we selected or created a number of control variables (Astin, 1984; Endo & Harpel, 1982; Kim & Sax, 2009; Kuh, 1995; Kuh et al., 2008; Meeuwisse et al., 2010; Pascarella, 1980; Thiele, 2016; Tinto, 2010; Zhao & Kuh, 2004). In stage two of the analysis, variables on students' involvement in out-of-class activities took on the role of dependent variables while control variables were used as independent variables.

All these variables are presented briefly below and more extensively in the Appendix (Tables 11.4–11.6).

Academic Performance

In order to study two aspects of student performance, namely study regularity and academic achievement, we retrieved from the administrative dataset information on credits earned by each individual student and on her or his grades.

Study regularity is measured by the ratio between the credits earned by students at the end of the academic year and those they were expected to obtain according to course regulations. The ratio ranges between 0 and 100.

Academic achievement is measured by the mean of the grades of the exams passed by students within the end of the academic year. We consider this measure as their grade point average ranging between 0 and 30.

Student Involvement

The survey asked students to indicate the frequency with which they were involved in some activities that represent two dimensions of students' participation in the university experience, the interaction with peers and that with faculty. Four of the five dimensions concern the relationship with peers and the remaining one is about the relationship with teachers.

To study the relationship with peers, survey data provide different indicators, aggregated into four constructs, namely:

- Studying with peers;
- Leisure activities;
- Living together;
- Social and political commitment.

For each of these constructs we have built an additive index on the basis of appropriate items measured on Likert scales, except for living together with peers which consists of a single variable in three categories: living with the family or alone, living with peers in a private apartment, living with peers in a college or student residence. We had to distinguish those who live in a private apartment from those who live in college because the requirements to stay in college affect students' performance, as it is necessary to have a minimum grade point average and/or a minimum numbers of credits.

To study the relationship with faculty, survey data provide only two indicators conflated into a single construct: out-of-class communication with faculty. Also in this case, the indicators were measured on a Likert scale and summed to obtain an overall index.

Control Variables

Each model of regression is controlled by numerous variables. Some of these variables do not require much explanation as they are widely used in sociological studies. In the literature, gender, age, family background, nationality and the type of secondary education are recognized as factors that influence both the participation in student life and study performance. Other selected variables are directly related to study career. The number of years of enrolment, i.e. the length of the career, the year of course enrolment (1st, 2nd, etc.), the field of study and programme's cycle are factors that shape student's university experience. Class attendance, employment status, residence in the city of Pavia and study hours, are other factors that influence students' chance to get socially involved "on campus" and the academic outcomes they achieve.

RESULTS

The results of the bivariate analysis[2] show significant differences between each index measuring students' involvement in extra-curricular and out-of-class activities and the two outcome variables, regularity and achievement. Participation in out-of-class activities with either peers or faculty is associated with higher regularity rates and grade point averages.

Then, we tested whether differences found in the bivariate analyses were robust enough to remain significant controlling for other students' characteristics. We ran five linear regression models for each of the two dependent variables and we estimated the net impact of students' involvement on academic outcomes. In Table 11.2 we show the regression coefficients for each controlled model while the complete models are shown in the Appendix (Tables 11.7 to 11.11).

Involvement in Out-of-Class Activities and Academic Performance

As we look, firstly, at the relationship between students' interaction with peers and study regularity, we can see that studying with peers is associated with study regularity and the relationship remains significant after controlling for various students' personal characteristics and academic attributes.

Table 11.2. Linear regression coefficients on study performance

	Regularity rate	Grade point average
Studying with peers	2.419**	.224
Leisure activities with peers	3.631**	.356
Living together:		
• in apartment	3.377	.568
• in a "collegio"	10.295***	1.579***
• not living with peers	0	0
Social and political commitment	.977	−.055
Out-of-class communication with faculty	5.095***	.352

**p-value<0.05; ***p-value<0.001

The more frequently students are involved in out-of-class shared study activities, the higher is their regularity rate, that is the number of credits they have gained compared to those they were expected to obtain according to course regulations.

Spending free time with peers participating in leisure activities – cultural and recreational initiatives organized by students unions or students groups, practicing sports at the university sport club, simply meeting friends and other students – is connected to study regularity as well, and the relationship remains significant after controlling for students' characteristics. The more students get together in leisure activities, the higher is their regularity rate.

As evident from bivariate analysis, living together with peers is related to study regularity. However, including control variables within the model, the relationship loses its significance. While living with peers in an apartment doesn't make a difference compared to living alone or with parents, staying in a "collegio" does make a difference but this depends on college requirements. As mentioned before, in order to maintain their post in a college, students must acquire a certain number of credits every year. As a consequence their career is more regular.

While social and political commitment appeared to be related to study regularity in the bivariate analysis, controlling for various students' characteristics the relationship fades away.

As far as the relationship between students' interaction with faculty and regularity is concerned, out-of-class communication with faculty – talking with a professor outside the class or office hours and communicating with faculty by e-mail – is also related to regularity.

The more frequently students interact with faculty the higher is their study regularity rate. It has to be noted that – as shown by the value of the B coefficient and the level of significance – this relationship appears to be stronger than those with peers.

Turning to the relationship between interaction with peers and academic achievement, we see that, although studying with other students appeared to be significantly related to academic achievement in the bivariate analysis, the relationship loses its significance including control variables in the analysis. The same holds true for the participation in leisure activities and social and political commitment.

As it was for the relationship between living together and study regularity, living together and academic achievement appear to be related only when students stay in college. But, again, this is likely due to the fact that some colleges require students to maintain a high grade point average throughout their entire academic career.

Finally, out-of-class communication with faculty is associated with students' academic achievement. The more frequently students interact with faculty the higher is their grade point average. It has to be noted that this is the only aspect of students' out-of-class experience positively – although rather weakly – related to their academic achievement.

Students' Characteristics and Involvement in Out-of-Class Activities

In order to answer our second research question, we now turn to the analysis of the relationship between some personal characteristics of students and of their study programmes, and their involvement in out-of-class activities.

There are only three aspects of student involvement, which are significantly associated with students' academic performance. They are: (a) studying with others, (b) participation in leisure activities, and (c) interaction with faculty.

For each of these aspects we tested whether involvement is associated with some of the individual characteristics deemed important in the literature. In order to estimate the net impact of each of them, we ran three linear regression models, one for each aspects of students' involvement associated with students' performance.

To the general overview of the results of this analysis (see Table 11.3; full models are reported in the Appendix, Table 11.12), we can add that students who are over 25 – likely being late in completing their studies – are less involved in studying with peers and in leisure activities, than their younger colleagues. On the contrary, as students grow up, their out-of-class communication with faculty increases. Further, as students progress in their study career their involvement in studying with peers, leisure activities and out-of-class communication with faculty grows.

Parents' education is associated with involvement in leisure activities and out-of-class communication with faculty, but it isn't associated with students' participation in shared study activities.

The characteristics of study programmes are associated with students' participation in out-of-class activities. Architecture and engineering students are more involved in out-of-class shared activities of study than students of any other field. Law students are the least involved in this activity. On the contrary, architecture and engineering students are less involved in leisure activities than their colleagues from the humanities and the social sciences, while no significant relationship is reported for students from the health sciences, science and law.

Table 11.3. Summary of the results of the linear regressions on the involvement in out-of-class activities: is the relationship significant?

	Studying with peers	Leisure activities	Out-of-class communication with faculty
Gender	No	No	No
Age	Yes	Yes	Yes
Nationality	No	No	No
Parents' socioeconomic status	No	No	No
Parents' education	No	Yes	Yes
Type of secondary education	No	No	No
Field of study	Yes	Yes	Yes
Study cycle	Yes	Yes	Yes
Year of course enrolment	Yes	Yes	Yes
Residential status	Yes	Yes	Yes
Employment status	No	No	No

Students from the humanities, science, architecture and engineering are more involved in out-of-class communication with faculty than their colleagues from law, while no significant difference is reported for students from the health and the social sciences.

Compared to commuters, students living in Pavia during term have more chance to study with their peers, get involved in leisure activities and communicate with faculty.

According to the results of the student survey, some relevant characteristics of the students, such as gender, type of secondary education, employment status during studies, and nationality are not related to the three considered aspects of students' involvement in out-of-class activities. Finally, parents' socioeconomic status is neither related to the two considered aspects of students' horizontal interaction with peers nor to their vertical interaction with faculty.

CONCLUSIONS AND IMPLICATIONS

Looking at the results of data analysis on students' interaction with peers and faculty, we can come to some conclusions often supporting findings from previous researches.

First, studying with peers is associated with students' career regularity measured in terms of credits. Although the survey didn't collect detailed information on the ways students study together, it is likely that studying with others provide individuals with useful resources to meet their course's credits requirements, or nevertheless to take and pass exams, accumulating credits. Studying with peers may give students the opportunity to acquire or to increase their skills in managing learning and to understand how to learn. It may also help them to manage their study time more effectively and to give pace and order to their study providing as well practical and psychological support in preparing and taking exams (Boud, 2001; Kuh, 1993, 1995; Kuh et al., 2008; Meeuwisse et al., 2010).

Second, a higher rate of study career regularity is also as sociated with a more intense participation in leisure activities. We haven't questioned students on the contents of these activities, but it may be that meeting frequently with peers at social, recreational and cultural events, or practicing a sport with classmates and other fellow students provide the individual with useful information on lessons' contents, assignments, handouts, study materials, tutorship, seminars, practicals and any other relevant information she or he may have missed or misinterpreted. Thus, a high level of integration in students' social life – although focused on non-educational activities – may result in a more regular study career (Astin, 1993; Nicpon et al., 2006).

Third, out-of-class interaction with faculty is associated with study regularity as well (Pascarella & Terenzini, 1977). Although we lack detailed information on this interaction, it may be that students reporting a more intense out-of-class communication with teachers have entered or can enter a virtuous circle. More regular students – those who sit more frequently at exams – get to know more teachers and/or are more easily known by them increasing their chances to talk or to exchange mails with faculty gaining further elements to proceed more rapidly in their career.

The study sheds light also on another aspect of students' performance, namely their academic achievement measured in terms of grades. While students' involvement in out-of-class activities with peers is not associated with their academic achievement, their out-of-class interaction with faculty is (Pascarella & Terenzini, 1978). This two-fold finding opens up to further lines of inquiry. On the one hand, we can speculate on the links connecting out-of-class communication with faculty and better grades. It may be that students search for contacts with faculty because they may lead to higher grades, or that a relationship with a faculty member – no matter why initiated – motivate students to increase the effort they apply to study leading to better grades (Cotten & Wilson, 2006). It may also be that students reporting a more intense out-of-class communication with teachers have entered or can enter a second virtuous circle. More brilliant students may search for extra-contacts with faculty more than other students. If they succeed they may be able to gain more information and advice improving their academic performance; thus, it seem that student-faculty interaction and student outcomes reinforce each other (Pascarella & Terenzini, 1978; Pascarella, 1980). On the other hand, it seems that the two considered aspects of student career, regularity and achievement, depend on different causes. For instance, studying together, i.e. making study activity a collective effort, doesn't translate into better individual achievements. Likely, better grades depend on other factors, possibly related to individual traits.

As we turn to students' characteristics that may foster or hinder their involvement in out-of-class activities, we can come to three conclusions.

First, being a young student, studying architecture and engineering, attending a second cycle course, the advancement in study career – e.g. passing from first to second year – and staying in Pavia during term all favour studying with peers. On the contrary, being more than 25 years old, studying in other fields, attending a first cycle course, and commuting hinder it.

Second, a high level of family cultural capital, being a young student, studying humanities and the social sciences, the progress in study career and living in Pavia during term facilitate the participation in leisure activities, while a low level of cultural capital, being more than 25 years old, studying other disciplines and commuting hamper it.

Third, a high level of family cultural capital, studying humanities and science, attending a second cycle course, the progress in academic career, and staying in Pavia during term, foster out-of-class communication with faculty, while the reverse is true for the opposite categories. Finally, involvement in out-of-class communication with faculty becomes more frequent as students get older (Pascarella, 1980; Cotton & Wilson, 2006).

Two further comments to these conclusions are worth mentioning. First, some individual characteristics, which often result in inequalities and disparities – such as gender, parents' socioeconomic status, type of secondary education, and nationality – are not related to the participation in out-of-class activities (Kim & Sax, 2009). Thus, we can argue that very likely at Pavia University the three sets of out-of-class activities that are associated with study regularity and, at least partially, with academic achievement are largely open to students' participation irrespectively of their individual traits. Second, as approximately half of the students stay in Pavia during term while the other half commutes every day to attend lessons, their residential status appears to be the more evident cleavage differentiating students as far as their participation in out-of-class activities is concerned.

Findings from the study have practical and policy implications. In discussing them we focus on study regularity that is one of the most important elements in the external assessment and public funding of state universities in our country.

The study's results show that there are at least three areas of activity, namely out-of-class study with peers, the participation in leisure activities, and student-faculty out-of-class communication, that deserve special attention by Pavia University and possibly other Italian higher education institutions because being involved in them helps students to keep up with their exams. Targeting these areas with proper policy measures can foster study regularity preventing student departure and the waste of public money invested in human capital development.

Our findings also show that factors favouring or hindering students' participation in out-of-class activities can be divided into two groups. The first includes the characteristics that it is very unlike or impossible for universities to influence such as students' ageing and their parents' education. The second includes characteristics that may be influenced by universities such as students' residential status. Providing students with more opportunities to live in Pavia during term may increase their participation in out-of-class activities enhancing the regularity of their study. As a consequence, measures such as the provision of student residences or social housing for students, enacted directly by the university or negotiated with third parts, should be considered as crucial. Our results also show that cultural and recreational activities should be equally considered important. Measures fostering student residence should be accompanied by initiatives and facilities providing students the opportunity to meet with each other and with faculty beyond ordinary academic activities.

Although the University of Pavia displays some peculiar traits – being located in a "university town" with a proportion of students on inhabitants greater than 10%, having a rather high proportion of long-term living-in student coming from other places, the presence of a "college" system – it is also characterised by a rather high proportion of daily commuters as other Italian universities. Very likely, irrespective of all efforts deemed to enhance students' stay during term, many of them will continue to commute daily either for economic reasons or for other motives. As a consequence, measures providing all students – including commuters – services and facilities to study together, for instance suitable learning spaces, should be considered crucial as well.

Thus, to enhance study regularity, policy measures aimed at increasing student residence "on campus", policy measures targeting the quality of student life outside the university and policy measures targeting the quality of learning inside the university should be pursued together.

NOTES

[1] The authors wish to thank the Centre for Study and Research on Higher Education Systems and the Centre for orientation and job placement of the University of Pavia for funding the survey, and the Disabled students service, and the University administrative services for collaborating to its implementation. Special thanks are addressed to the two thousand students who participated in it.

[2] Please look at B coefficients in the regression models in the Appendix, where we reported both results for bivariate analysis (model 1 in each table) and multivariate analysis (model 2 in each table).

REFERENCES

Agasisti, T., Murtinu, S. (2016). Grants in Italian university: A look at the heterogeneity of their impact on students' performances. *Studies in Higher Education, 41*(6), 1106–1132.

Aina, C. (2013). Parental background and university dropout in Italy. *Higher Education, 65*(4), 437–456.

Aina, C., Baici, E., & Casalone, G. (2011). Time to degree: Students' abilities, university characteristics or something else? Evidence from Italy. *Education Economics, 19*(3), 311—25.

Astin, A. W. (1984). Student involvement: A developmental theory of higher education. *Journal of College Student Personnel, 25*(4), 297–308.

Astin, A. W. (1993). *What matters in college? Four critical years revisited.* San Francisco, CA: Jossey-Bass.

Belloc, F., Maruotti, A., & Petrella, L. (2010). University drop-out: An Italian experience. *Higher Education, 60*(2), 127–138.

Boud, D. (2001). Introduction: Making the move to peer learning. In D. Boud, R. Cohen, & J. Sampson (Eds.), *Peer learning in higher education: Learning from and with each other*. London: Kogan Page.

Clerici, R., Giraldo, A., & Meggiolaro, S. (2015). The determinants of academic outcomes in a competing risks approach: Evidence from Italy. *Studies in Higher Education, 40*(9), 1535–1549.

Cotten, S. R., & Wilson, B. (2006). Student–faculty interactions: Dynamics and determinants. *Higher Education, 51*(4), 487–519.

Cox, B. E., & Orehovec, E. (2007). Faculty-student interaction outside the classroom: A typology from a residential college. *The Review of Higher Education, 30*(4), 343–362.

Endo, J. J., & Harpel, R. L. (1982). The effect of student-faculty interaction on students' educational outcomes. *Research in Higher Education, 16*(2), 115–138.

Ghignoni, E. (2017). Family background and university dropouts during the crisis: The case of Italy. *Higher Education, 73*(1), 127–151.

Havnes, A. (2008). Peer mediated learning beyond the curriculum. *Studies in Higher Education, 33*(2), 193–204.

Kim, Y. K., & Sax, L. J. (2009). Student–faculty interaction in research universities: Differences by student gender, race, social class, and first-generation status. *Research in Higher Education, 50*(5), 437–459.

Kuh, G. D. (1993). In their own words: What students learn outside the classroom. *American Educational Research Journal, 30*(2), 277–304.

Kuh, G. D. (1995). The other curriculum: Out-of-class experiences associated with student learning and personal development. *The Journal of Higher Education, 66*(2), 123–155.

Kuh, G., & Hu, S. (2001). The effects of student–faculty interaction in the 1990s. *Review of Higher Education, 24*(3), 309–332.

Kuh, G. D., Cruce, Ty M., Shoup, R., & Kinzie, J. (2008). Unmasking the effects of student engagement on first-year college grades and persistence. *The Journal of Higher Education, 79*(5), 540–563.

Meeuwisse, M., Severiens, S. E., & Born, M. (2010). Learning environment, interaction, sense of belonging and study success in ethnically diverse student groups. *Research in Higher Education, 51*(6), 528–545.

Meggiolaro, S., Giraldo, A., & Clerici, R. (2015). A multilevel competing risks model for analysis of university students' careers in Italy. *Studies in Higher Education*, published online 29 September 2015, 1–16.

Nicpon, M. F., Huser, L., Blancks, E. H., Sollenberger, S., Befort, C., & Robinson Kurpius, S. E. (2006). The relationship of loneliness and social support with college freshmen's academic performance and persistence. *Journal College Student Retention, 8*(3), 345–358.

Pascarella, E. T. (1980). Student-faculty informal contact and college outcomes. *Review of Educational Research, 50*(4), 545–595.

Pascarella, E. T. (2006). How college affects students: Ten directions for future research. *Journal of College Student Development, 47*(5), 508–520.

Pascarella, E. T., & Terenzini, P. T. (1977). Patterns of student-faculty informal interaction beyond the classroom and voluntary freshman attrition. *The Journal of Higher Education, 48*(5), 540–552.

Pascarella, E. T., & Terenzini, P. T. (1978). Student-faculty informal relationships and freshman year educational outcomes. *The Journal of Educational Research, 71*(4), 183–189.

Thiele, T., Singleton, A., Pope, D., & Stanistreet, D. (2016). Predicting students' academic performance based on school and socio-demographic characteristics. *Studies in Higher Education, 41*(8), 1424–1446.

Tinto, V. (1975). Dropout from higher education: A theoretical synthesis of recent research. *Review of Educational Research, 45*(1), 89–125.

Tinto, V. (1993). *Leaving college: Rethinking the causes and cures of student attrition* (2nd Ed.). Chicago: The University of Chicago Press.

Tinto, V. (1997). Classroom as community: Exploring the educational character of student persistence. *The Journal of Higher Education, 68*(6), 599–623.

Tinto, V. (2010). From theory to action: Exploring the institutional conditions for student retention. In J. C. Smart (Ed.), *Higher education: Handbook of theory and research* (Vol. 25). Dordrecht, the Netherlands: Springer.

Triventi, M., & Trivellato, P. (2009). Participation, performance and inequality in Italian higher education in the 20th century: Evidence from the Italian longitudinal household survey. *Higher Education*, *57*(6), 681–702.

Webber, K. L., Krylow, R. B., & Zhang, Q. (2013). Does involvement really matter? Indicators of college student success and satisfaction. *Journal of College Student Development*, *54*(6), 591–611.

Zhao, C.-M., & Kuh, G. D. (2004). Adding value: Learning communities and student engagement. *Research in Higher Education*, *45*(2), 115–138.

Monia Anzivino
Centre for Study and Research on Higher Education Systems
University of Pavia

Michele Rostan
Centre for Study and Research on Higher Education Systems
University of Pavia

APPENDIX

Table 11.4. Study performance variables

Name of variable	Indicators	Operations
Study regularity	Credits acquired at the end of the academic year	Credits acquired / Credits required x 100
	Credits required by course regulation	
Academic achievement	Grade point average at the end of the academic year	Grades / Number of exams

Table 11.5. Student involvement variables

Name of variable	Indicators	Operations
Studying with peers	Thinking of this academic year experience, how often did you study with…? (Often, sometimes, rarely, never): With my classmates With students from other courses	Assigning a number value (1-never; 2-rarely; 3-sometimes; 4-often) to answer categories. Different indicators are summed and divided by their number.
Leisure activities with peers	How often do you participate in each of the following activities? (Often, sometimes, rarely, never): Meet friends and other students; Take part in cultural and recreational initiatives organized by students unions or students groups; Practice a sport at CUS (the university sport club)	Assigning a number value (1-never; 2-rarely; 3-sometimes; 4-often) to answer categories. Different indicators are summed and divided by their number.
Living together	During term, who do you live with? (Alone; With flatmates, friends, siblings, partner or college fellows; With my parents or other relatives) During term, what is your kind of accommodation? (I rent a room only for myself, I rent a shared room with two or more people, I live in a "collegio", I rent an apartment only for myself, Other)	Recoding indicators into a single variable.
Social and political commitment	How often do you participate each of the following activities? (Often, sometimes, rarely, never): Participate in meetings regarding student and university problems; Taking part in social, environmental or political initiatives (excluding university problems)	Assigning a number value (1-never; 2-rarely; 3-sometimes; 4-often) to answer categories. Different indicators are summed and divided by their number.
Communication with faculty	In your university experience of this year, how often did you… (Often, sometimes, rarely, never): Talk with a professor out of class or office hours; Exchange emails with professors	Assigning a number value (1-never; 2-rarely; 3-sometimes; 4-often) to answer categories. Different indicators are summed and divided by their number.

Table 11.6. Control variables

Name of variable	Indicators	Operations
Gender		
Age		
Nationality		Recoding into a variable with two categories: Italian; Other.
Family socioeconomic status	Profession of father Profession of mother	Computing a single variable considering the highest professional level of either student's father or mother. Recoding the new variable into three categories: lower status, middle status, upper status.
Family educational background	Father's education Mother's education	Computing a single variable considering the highest educational attainment of either student's father or mother. Recoding the new variable into three categories: lower educational attainment, secondary education, tertiary education.
Type of secondary education		Recoding into a variable with two categories: Lyceum; Other school.
Year of course enrolment		
Number of years of enrolling		
Study cycle	Short first cycle courses Long first cycle courses Second cycle courses	
Field of study	Discipline of study courses	Recoding every course into five categories: Architecture and Engineering; Science; Health sciences; Social sciences; Law; Humanities.

(Continued)

Table 11.6. (Continued)

Name of variable	Indicators	Operations
Class attendance	During this academic year, how many courses did you attend, even not regularly? (All the courses related to the exams I want to take; Only few of the courses related to the exams I want to take; None)	Recoding into a variable with two categories: Fully attending classes; Attending few classes or not attending.
Employment status	Did you have a job during this academic year? (Yes, I have a permanent job; Yes, I have an occasional job; No, I have no job)	Recoding into a variable with two categories: Working full time during the academic year; working occasionally/not working during the academic year.
Residential status	Where do you live during term? (In the municipality of Pavia; In another municipality of the Province of Pavia; Somewhere else)	Recoding into a variable with two categories: Living in Pavia; Commuting.
Study hours	Please specify how many hours per week on average do you spend in each of the following activities during term: Studying	

Table 11.7. *Studying with peers and study performance – Linear regression models, bivariate and multivariate estimates for study regularity and academic achievement*

Model	Variable	Regressor	Study regularity B	S.E.	Academic achievement B	S.E.
1	Intercept		62.091***	1.88	23.771***	.345
	Studying with peers index		5.286***	.769	.490***	.140
2	Intercept		20.454**	6.00	14.680***	1.089
	Studying with peers index		2.419**	.740	.224	.134
	Gender	Male	1.253	1.23	.035	.223
		Female	0		0	
	Age		−.179	.185	−.002	.034
	Parents' socio-economic status	Lower	−.891	2.22	−.252	.403
		Middle	.401	1.34	.101	.244
		Upper	0		0	
	Parents' education	Parents with lower educational attainment	−3.699	2.20	−.729	.399
		Parents with secondary education	−2.226	1.36	−.304	.247
		Parents with tertiary education	0		0	
	Type of secondary education	Lyceum	5.082***	1.36	1.248***	.247
		Other schools	0		0	
	Field of study	Science	8.794***	2.23	1.741***	.405
		Health sciences	12.429***	2.21	2.498***	.401
		Humanities	10.853***	2.37	3.283***	.431
		Social sciences	20.430***	1.94	2.670***	.353
		Law	12.561***	3.05	2.600***	.555
		Architecture and Engineering	0		0	
	Study cycle	Second cycle courses	6.079***	1.67	3.890***	.303
			−3.997 2.158		−.122	.391

(Continued)

Table 11.7. (Continued)

			Study regularity		Academic achievement	
Model	Variable	Regressor	B	S.E.	B	S.E.
		Short first cycle courses	0		0	
	Year of course enrolment		7.791***	.689	1.039***	.125
	Number of years of enrolment		−1.904***	.293	−.082	.053
	Study hours		.930	.602	.195	.109
	Residential status	Living in Pavia	3.279*	1.276	.602**	.231
		Commuting	0		0	
	Employ-ment status	Working full time during the academic year	−1.407	1.893	−.152	.343
		Working occasionally /not working during the academic year	0		0	
	Nationality	Italian	11.495***	2.927	1.959***	.531
		Other	0		0	
	Class attendance	Fully attending classes	13.874***	1.536	1.781***	.279
		Attending few classes or not attending	0		0	
	Collegial status	Staying in "collegio"	8.927***	1.933	1.339***	.350
		Not staying in "collegio"	0		0	

***p<0.001; **p<0.01; *p<0.05

Table 11.8. Involvement in leisure activities and study performance – Linear regression models, bivariate and multivariate estimates for study regularity and academic achievement

Model	Variable	Regressor	Study regularity		Academic achievement	
			B	S.E.	B	S.E.
1	Intercept		54.616***	2.096	22.268***	.383
	Leisure activities with peers index		10.466***	1.062	1.401***	.194
2	Intercept		21.040***	5.957	14.698***	1.080
	Leisure activities with peers index		3.631**	1.138	.356	.206
	Gender	Male	1.169	1.232	.027	.223
		Female	0		0	
	Age		−.193	.185	−.002	.034
	Parents' socio-economic status	Lower	−.534	2.224	−.217	.403
		Middle	.470	1.344	.108	.244
		Upper	0		0	
	Parents' education	Parents with lower educational attainment	−3.563	2.202	−.714	.399
		Parents with secondary education	−2.118	1.364	−.293	.247
		Parents with tertiary education	0		0	
	Type of secondary education	Lyceum	5.020***	1.362	1.242***	.247
		Other schools	0		0	
	Field of study	Science	7.967***	2.223	1.664***	.403
		Health sciences	11.882***	2.212	2.446***	.401
		Humanities	9.922***	2.382	3.194***	.432
		Social sciences	19.566***	1.947	2.587***	.353
		Law	11.048***	3.036	2.458***	.550
		Architecture and Engineering	0		0	

(Continued)

Table 11.8. (Continued)

Model	Variable	Regressor	Study regularity		Academic achievement	
			B	S.E.	B	S.E.
	Study cycle	Second cycle courses	6.312***	1.668	3.910***	.302
		Long first cycle courses	−3.982	2.159	−.121	.391
		Short first cycle courses	0		0	
	Year of course enrolment		7.792***	.689	1.038***	.125
	Number of years of enrolment at university		−1.936***	.293	−.084	.053
	Study hours		.947	.602	.197	.109
	Residential status	Living in Pavia	2.218	1.356	.495*	.246
		Commuting	0		0	
	Employ-ment status	Working full time during the academic year	−1.592	1.892	−.169	.343
		Working occasionally /not working during the academic year	0		0	
	Nationality	Italian	11.226***	2.929	1.932***	.531
		Other	0		0	
	Class attendance	Fully attending classes	14.039***	1.534	1.795***	.278
		Attending few classes or not attending	0		0	
	Collegial status	Staying in "collegio"	7.577	1.958	1.208**	.355
		Not staying in "collegio"	0		0	

***p<0.001; **p<0.01; *p<0.05*

Table 11.9. Living together and study performance – Linear regression models, bivariate and multivariate estimates for study regularity and academic achievement

Model	Variable	Regressor	Study regularity		Academic achievement	
			B	S.E.	B	S.E.
1	Intercept		70.124***	.807	24.211***	.147
	Living together	Living together with peers in apartment	8.613***	1.431	1.403***	.260
		Living together with peers in "collegio"	16.827***	2.128	2.856***	.386
		Not living together with peers	0		0	
2	Intercept		28.370***	5.635	15.472***	1.020
	Living together	Living together with peers in apartment	3.377	1.962	.568	.355
		Living together with peers in "collegio"	10.295***	2.473	1.579***	.447
		Not living together with peers	0		0	
	Gender	Male	1.338	1.236	.047	.224
		Female	0		0	
	Age		−.255	.184	−.008	.033
	Parents' socioeconomic status	Lower	−.969	2.230	−.265	.404
		Middle	.256	1.348	.084	.244
		Upper	0		0	
	Parents' education	Parents with lower educational attainment	−4.274	2.209	−.807*	.400
		Parents with secondary education	−2.600	1.369	−.357	.248
		Parents with tertiary education	0		0	
	Type of secondary education	Lyceum	5.002***	1.368	1.232***	.248
		Other schools	0		0	

(Continued)

Table 11.9. (Continued)

Model	Variable	Regressor	Study regularity		Academic achievement	
			B	S.E.	B	S.E.
	Field of study	Science	8.200***	2.229	1.689***	.403
		Health sciences	12.083***	2.219	2.460***	.402
		Humanities	10.705***	2.379	3.280***	.431
		Social sciences	19.933***	1.949	2.616***	.353
		Law	11.330***	3.044	2.488***	.551
		Architecture and Engineering	0		0	
	Study cycle	Second cycle courses	6.560***	1.672	3.939***	.303
		Long first cycle courses	−4.034	2.165	−.125	.392
		Short first cycle courses	0		0	
	Year of course enrolment		7.975***	.688	1.053***	.124
	Number of years of enrolment at university		−1.942***	.294	−.085	.053
	Study hours		1.010	.604	.204	.109
	Residential status	Living in Pavia	1.599	1.847	.286	.334
		Commuting	0		0	
	Employment status	Working full time during the academic year	−1.482	1.899	−.149	.344
		Working occasionally/not working during the academic year	0		0	
	Nationality	Italian	10.790***	2.941	1.850**	.532
		Other	0		0	
	Class attendance	Fully attending classes	14.253***	1.537	1.818***	.278
		Attending few classes or not attending	0		0	

***p<0.001;**p<0.01; *p<0.05*

Table 11.10. Social and political commitment and study performance – Linear regression models, bivariate and multivariate estimates for study regularity and academic achievement

Model	Variable	Regressor	Study regularity		Academic achievement	
			B	S.E.	B	S.E.
1	Intercept		66.265***	1.527	23.660***	.277
	Social and political commitment index		5.771***	.995	.892***	.181
2	Intercept		26.665***	5.673	15.368***	1.027
	Social and political commitment index		.977	.968	−.055	.175
	Gender	Male	1.274	1.235	.039	.224
		Female	0		0	
	Age		−.263	.184	−.009	.033
	Parents' socioeconomic status	Lower	−.875	2.226	−.253	.403
		Middle	.319	1.346	.090	.244
		Upper	0		0	
	Parents' education	Parents with lower educational attainment	−3.753	2.210	−.759	.400
		Parents with secondary education	−2.269	1.367	−.321	.248
		Parents with tertiary education	0		0	
	Type of secondary education	Lyceum	5.089***	1.365	1.254***	.247
		Other schools	0		0	
	Field of study	Science	8.021***	2.230	1.685***	.404
		Health sciences	12.065***	2.216	2.474***	.401
		Humanities	10.240***	2.397	3.270***	.434
		Social sciences	19.772***	1.962	2.647***	.355
		Law	11.173***	3.044	2.491***	.551
		Architecture and Engineering	0		0	

(Continued)

211

Table 11.10. (Continued)

Model	Variable	Regressor	Study regularity		Academic achievement	
			B	S.E.	B	S.E.
	Study cycle	Second cycle courses	6.467***	1.671	3.929***	.302
		Long first cycle courses	−4.133	2.165	−.123	.392
		Short first cycle courses	0		0	
	Year of course enrolment		7.968***	.689	1.062***	.125
	Number of years of enrolment at university		−1.951***	.294	−.085	.053
	Study hours		.955	.604	.202	.109
	Residential status	Living in Pavia	3.486**	1.298	.660**	.235
		Commuting	0		0	
	Employment status	Working full time during the academic year	−1.633	1.897	−.167	.343
		Working occasionally/not working during the academic year	0		0	
	Nationality	Italian	11.580***	2.934	1.958***	.531
		Other	0		0	
	Class attendance	Fully attending classes	14.114***	1.540	1.821***	.279
		Attending few classes or not attending	0		0	
	Collegial status	Staying in "collegio"	8.363***	1.952	1.326***	.353
		Not staying in "collegio"	0		0	

***$p<0.001$; **$p<0.01$; *$p<0.05$

Table 11.11. Out-of-class communication with faculty and study performance – Linear regression models, bivariate and multivariate estimates for study regularity and academic achievement

Model	Variable	Regressor	Study regularity		Academic achievement	
			B	S.E.	B	S.E.
1	Intercept		56.660***	1.994	21.908***	.362
	Out-of-class communication with faculty index		7.168***	.768	1.217***	.139
2	Intercept		20.270***	5.671	14.831***	1.036
	Out-of-class communication with faculty index		5.095***	.774	.352*	.141
	Gender	Male	.916	1.223	.013	.223
		Female	0		0	
	Age		−.315	.183	−.013	.033
	Parents' socioeconomic status	Lower	−.981	2.203	−.258	.402
		Middle	.510	1.333	.106	.243
		Upper	0		0	
	Parents' education	Parents with lower educational attainment	−3.290	2.183	−.706	.399
		Parents with secondary education	−2.143	1.351	−.302	.247
		Parents with tertiary education	0		0	
	Type of secondary education	Lyceum	5.009***	1.351	1.244***	.247
		Other schools	0		0	
	Field of study	Science	7.403**	2.208	1.629***	.403
		Health sciences	11.770***	2.194	2.445***	.401
		Humanities	9.126***	2.365	3.156***	.432

(Continued)

Table 11.11. (Continued)

Model	Variable	Regressor	Study regularity B	S.E.	Academic achievement B	S.E.
		Social sciences	20.357***	1.927	2.655***	.352
		Law	12.923***	3.021	2.595***	.552
		Architecture and Engineering	0		0	
	Study cycle	Second cycle courses	3.803*	1.703	3.742***	.311
		Long first cycle courses	−2.631	2.152	−.029	.393
		Short first cycle courses	0		0	
	Year of course enrolment		6.756***	.707	.973***	.129
	Number of years of enrolment at university		−1.727***	.292	−.070	.053
	Study hours		.836	.598	.190	.109
	Residential status	Living in Pavia	3.449**	1.259	.625**	.230
		Commuting	0		0	
	Employment status	Working full time during the academic year	−2.183	1.879	−.210	.343
		Working occasionally/not working during the academic year	0		0	
	Nationality	Italian	10.997***	2.905	1.925***	.531
		Other	0		0	
	Class attendance	Fully attending classes	13.575***	1.524	1.769***	.278
		Attending few classes or not attending	0		0	
	Collegial status	Staying in "collegio"	7.652***	1.921	1.244***	.351
		Not staying in "collegio"	0		0	

***p<0.001; **p<0.01; *p<0.05*

Table 11.12. Students' characteristics and participation in out-of-class activities – Linear regression models estimates

Variable	Regressor	Studying with peers		Leisure activities with peers		Out-of-class communication with faculty	
		B	S.E.	B	S.E.	B	S.E.
Intercept		2.422***	.106	1.443***	.071	1.723***	.099
Gender	Male	−.003	.036	.036	.024	.060	.034
	Female	0		0		0	
Age	21-22 years old	.045	.055	−.001	.036	.267***	.052
	23-24 years old	−.027	.070	−.003	.046	.484***	.066
	25-30 years old	−.223**	.081	−.146**	.053	.404***	.076
	Up 30 years old	−.783***	.112	−.426***	.074	.207*	.105
	19-21 years old	0		0		0	
Nationality	Italian	−.016	.085	.064	.057	.122	.080
	Other	0		0		0	
Parents' socio-economic status	Lower	−.010	.066	−.077	.043	.041	.062
	Middle	−.035	.040	−.030	.026	−.029	.037
	Upper	0		0		0	
Parents' education	Parents with lower educational attainment	−.114	.065	−.103*	.043	−.173**	.062
	Parents with secondary education	−.058	.040	−.068*	.026	−.065	.038
	Parents with tertiary education	0		0		0	
Type of secondary education	Lyceum	.004	.040	.042	.026	.034	.038
	Other schools	0		0		0	
Field of study	Science	−.296***	.065	.069	.043	.164**	.061
	Health sciences	−.139*	.065	.082	.043	.068	.061

(Continued)

215

Table 11.12. (Continued)

Variable	Regressor	Studying with peers		Leisure activities with peers		Out-of-class communication with faculty	
		B	S.E.	B	S.E.	B	S.E.
	Humanities	−.163*	.070	.196***	.046	.270***	.066
	Social sciences	−.174**	.057	.124**	.038	−.070	.054
	Law	−.562***	.089	.064	.059	−.356***	.083
	Architecture and Engineering	0		0		0	
Study cycle	Second cycle courses	.186**	.061	.085*	.040	.353***	.057
	Long first cycle courses	.038	.063	.011	.042	−.211***	.060
	Short first cycle courses	0		0		0	
Year of course enrolment		.044*	.020	.047**	.013	.107***	.019
Residential status	Living in Pavia	.186***	.036	.482***	.024	.110**	.034
	Commuting	0		0		0	
Employment status	Working full time during the academic year	−.102	.055	−.004	.036	.087	.052
	Working occasionally/not working during the academic year	0		0		0	

***p<0.001; **p<0.01; *p<0.05

ANDREA KOTTMANN

12. UNRAVELLING TACIT KNOWLEDGE

Engagement Strategies of Centres for Excellence in Teaching and Learning

INTRODUCTION

In the recent years at higher education institutions in Europe the establishment of Centres for Excellence in Teaching and Learning (CETL) has become widespread. Mostly institutions use these centres to implement and coordinate activities improving the quality of teaching and learning, new teaching technologies or to train their teachers. While some institutions establish these centres from their own funds, others use national funding schemes such as the Norwegian SFU scheme, the German Quality Pact for Teaching or the (already terminated) CETL scheme by HEFCE.

Research on CETL so far, in particular research done on the HEFCE CETLs, stated that CETLs have had difficulties in promoting activities aiming to improve the quality of teaching and learning. According to Saunders et al. (2008) this is due to the low acceptance and legitimacy of the pedagogical knowledge generated by CETLs, among academic staff. Further, due to the lack of an engagement strategy CETLs also had difficulties in changing teaching practices for a larger group of teachers or reaching out to a wider teaching and learning community (Saunders et al., 2008, p. 5).

This paper will investigate what engagement strategies of current CETLs look like and how they are able to gain more acceptance for pedagogical knowledge. It will argue that developing a shared understanding and shared value for high quality teaching is a key prerequisite to engaging teachers in CETL activities and motivating them to change their teaching practices. To be successful activities aiming to develop shared understandings and values of teaching, need to adapt to teachers' daily practices and help them unravel and reflect their tacit teaching knowledge. The paper will further argue that the implementation of a CETL is crucial for the success of its engagement strategy. Therefore, it aims to identify factors and hindrances for developing shared values and a shared understanding of high quality teaching.

To this effect, a CETL in Norway and a CETL in Germany will be compared. The selected cases are highly contrasting. The Norwegian CETL is located in a mono-disciplinary and relatively small higher education institution. It is one of the CETLs funded by the Norwegian SFU programme. The CETL is not an

R. Deem & H. Eggins (Eds.), The University as a Critical Institution?, 217–235.

independent department, but has been integrated as a project into the already existing organizational structures of the institution. The German CETL, on the other hand, is an independent service department at the central level of the university funded mainly by institutional resources.

The remainder of this paper is organized as follows: the second section will discuss CETLs and the different ways they have been implemented. Further, the section will investigate why shared values and understandings are key to a successful engagement strategy of a CETL. The third section will report on to what extent shared values and understandings with regard to teaching and learning have been established among teachers in the two cases under review. Further, the CETLs' engagement strategies will be analysed. In the final section, the paper will summarise important factors in and hindrances to a successful engagement strategy.

CETLS AND THEIR ROLE IN DEVELOPING A SHARED UNDERSTANDING OF TEACHING AND LEARNING

Current teaching cultures in higher education can be described as strongly individualized, i.e. teaching often happens as a solitary and private endeavour of the academic. Teachers are often alone in front of their class and there is no sharing of teaching tasks, i.e. teachers are responsible for any task such as developing syllabus, preparing teaching material, doing lectures and assessing students' achievements. The scholarship of teaching and learning, i.e. a methodological and reflective approach to teaching based on learning theories and other didactical knowledge rarely plays an important role. More frequently, teaching is based on the teachers' experiences such as their own experiences of being taught or on tacit knowledge they developed in a trial-and-error process throughout their careers. Academic staff may not routinely share experiences, results and teaching methods with their colleagues. Teachers are also often reluctant to use new methodologies or technologies in their teaching, as they lack sufficient knowledge about how to use them. There is often no peer review of teaching activities. Furthermore, feedback of students provided through evaluations does not stimulate a thorough and methodological reflection on teaching activities. Finally, though some teachers take part in initial courses introducing them to higher education teaching, there is often no continuous development or professionalization of teaching competencies.

Current research, however, indicates that a more collaborative teaching culture picking up characteristics of research cultures, such as collaboration, collegiality, continuous development of teaching competencies, peer review, documentation of results and feedback as well as a scholarly approach to teaching do strongly support enhancement activities in teaching and learning. In particular, studies done by Mårtensson and Roxå made clear that teachers who have the opportunity to exchange ideas about their teaching practices in social networks are more likely to develop beliefs and values related to teaching (Mårtensson & Roxå, 2016b, p. 176). Exchanging with others in significant interactions helps develop teacher identity.

A more recent study shows that within these networks, micro-cultures are established that have some positive impact on teachers' engagement and motivation for teaching as well as for the prestige and status of teaching and learning activities. This is in particularly true for networks that strongly support teachers. Teachers involved in significant networks that provide little support for them do not engage in teaching and learning activities as strongly; at these institutions teaching and learning typically has less prestige (Mårtensson & Roxå, 2016a). The institutional culture or context also impacts on the orientations of teachers. In institutions promoting more learning-oriented approaches, academic staff more often engage in these kinds of teaching practices (Mårtensson & Roxå, 2016b, p. 133). Overall, in their study, the authors distinguish between strong and developing micro-cultures. Strong micro-cultures resemble to some extent Wenger's communities of practices (Wenger, McDermott, & Snyder, 2002): key characteristics are 'strong internal trust intense interactions, information sharing, and commitment to the group's enterprise a shared history, and interest in collaboration' (Mårtensson & Roxå, 2016b, p. 136). These strong cultures stimulate a high engagement of teachers in high quality teaching. Developing micro cultures, however, create 'a shared desire to do something new _ and thus are helping to develop such cultures (Mårtensson & Roxå, 2016b, p. 136).

In their paper, Mårtensson & Roxå do not address how networks of teachers get established and how they are implemented at the institutional level. They focus more on the individual enculturation of teachers and how they develop their teaching identity. This paper will take a different perspective and investigates how CETLs facilitate the communication among teachers to establish strong or developing micro cultures of teaching and learning. It will further argue that the way CETLs are established at higher education institutions is crucial to their impact.

What Are CETLs?

To date, the research literature has not yet elaborated a definition of CETL, though excellence initiatives have been examined (Pruvot & Estermann, 2014). Research studying the impact of CETLs often build on an implicit understanding of CETL as central level departments providing services and activities that seek to promote the enhancement of teaching and learning through the work of education professionals or specialists. This implicit idea is also picked up here. CETL will be understood as "'nodes' of teaching- and learning-focused activities, whose purposes are to enhance quality (and sometimes excellence) in teaching practices and to invest in that practice in order to increase and deepen its impact across a wider teaching and learning community" (Kottmann, Huisman, Brockerhoff, Cremonini, & Mampaey, 2016; Saunders et al., 2008). CETLs, however, have been established very differently at different higher education institutions (Challis, Holt, & Palmer, 2009; Raaheim & Karjalainen, 2012; SQW, 2011; Webler, 2012). Kottmann and Cremonini (2017) distinguish between CETLs as central organizational units and CETLs as networks of teachers at department or faculty level.

CETLs as Organisational Units

To facilitate organisational learning, some higher education institutions implement CETLs as service units that are located at the central administration level. These centres provide services for the whole institution. Mostly these units are assigned to stewardship of the university leadership, for example the vice-rector for teaching and learning. The CETLs typically have their own staff who are often educational specialists and do not much engage in other teaching or in research. Their main area of activity is to promote the improvement of teaching and learning at their institution. Such promotion activities include, for example, the didactical trainings of academic staff, individual coaching of teachers or coordinating and running teaching development projects. These centres also engage in the dissemination of knowledge of teaching and learning processes by running education days, lecture series, publications on good practices or through websites.

Recent research states that CETLs can help establish a number of collaboration opportunities. Among these are *inter alia* enhancing networking and collaboration within the institution as well as outside the institution. They provide staff with the opportunity to try out, develop and study (innovative) teaching methods. They can support the institution in developing a cross-institutional profile in teaching and learning, i.e. shared goals and ideas about high quality teaching. Further, CETLs can have an important role in raising the institutional engagement for teaching and learning and thus improve the status of teaching and learning. Finally, CETLs often get engaged in professional training of academic staff, in particular in didactical training (Bélanger, Bélisle, & Bernatchez, 2011; Challis et al., 2009; Gosling & Turner, 2014; Lieberman, 2005; Raaheim & Karjalainen, 2012; Saunders et al., 2008; Webler, 2012).

A key feature of these centres is that they take a strongly individualized approach to promoting the improvement of teaching and learning. There is an overwhelming sense that strengthening the individual competences of teachers will improve the teaching and learning at the institution as a whole. The centres often do not focus on teachers as groups or developing a more collaborative culture in teaching and learning, i.e. developing shared understandings of good teaching and learning, which could be helpful for engaging teachers in high quality teaching and learning. Rather, it is argued that individual teachers who have successfully run an innovative teaching projects will act as role models and motivate other teachers to also engage in the improvement of their teaching practices.

The literature also defines a number of factors that make CETLs successful in stimulating higher education institutions to engage in improving teaching and learning (Gosling & Turner, 2014; Saunders et al., 2008). Those CETLs that are included in the strategic planning of the institution and are also represented on organisational decision-making bodies are more likely to have an impact. In particular, for CETLs that provide services at the central level and thus serve different disciplines and faculties, it is important that they are able to develop a cross-disciplinary focus.

CETLs also work more effectively if they have a clear mission and if teaching excellence is already important at the institution.

Hindrances to an effective functioning of CETL appear to be related to their implementation (Gosling & Turner, 2014). For those CETLs that are not aligned to existing cultures, practices and strategies nor connected to the prior planning of the institution, it is difficult to become accepted. This is also true for CETLs that were not established in a consultation process between university leadership and staff. CETLs that appear to not use their funding in an entrepreneurial way also do not seem to gain legitimacy. CETLs are also contested by staff if they lack clear goals or have a mission overload. Further, support of institutional leadership for CETLs must be in place. On the one hand, CETLs that do not act autonomously of the institutional leadership are often perceived with suspicion. On the other hand, a lack of support from leadership can make it also difficult for CETLs. CETLs that do not have strong leadership themselves are also often contested. Finally, those CETLs that cannot provide incentives or resources to promote activities which aim to improve the quality of teaching and learning also face difficulties.

CETLs as Networks of Teachers

At some higher education institutions, CETLs have been established as a teachers' network. They often function as a project, thus they have less formalized structures. Also their scope is limited: their activity area is often limited to a department or faculty. These projects also have their own staff who coordinate or support the Centre's activities. Responsibility and the major improvement activities, however, lie with the teachers who take different roles in the CETLs, for example as leaders of work packages that are part of the project. Mostly these centres provide teachers with the opportunity and resources to develop and conduct their own (innovative) teaching projects. These resources include time, i.e. teachers often receive an increase on the time they can spend for teaching. They thus have to spend less time on other duties. However, when doing their projects teachers need to use a 'scholarship of teaching approach', i.e. projects should be developed based on scientific evidence, an evaluation of the project should be done and results should be published. Within the project or Centre a regular exchange between teachers is facilitated by the Centre's staff. These CETLs also actively share project results with their host institution or with a wider audience through a variety of different media such as publications, websites and presentations.

This type of CETL resembles to some extent the so-called Faculty Learning Communities (FLC). At US higher education institutions, FLC are often initiated by Centres for Teaching and Learning that are located at the central institutional level (Beach & Cox, 2009; Cox, 2004). Such centres provide resources for the FLC such as facilitating group meetings or material to inform the group members. Mostly FLCs consist of 8 to 12 teachers who meet on a regular basis for a certain period to discuss issues around teaching and learning. FLCs can vary in composition.

They may consist of teachers from the same entry cohort (e.g. junior faculty) and some FLCs concentrate on one topic. Teachers participate in a FLC on a voluntary basis while the groups are led and supported by staff from the centre. Groups also build their own curricula. The group leaders support the teachers in dealing with the topic in a scientific or methodological manner, i.e. they promote scholarship of teaching and learning. Thus group leaders provide the members of their groups with background knowledge on student learning, teaching and learning formats as well as on student assessment. Teachers participating in those groups often develop and run teaching projects. Beside academic consultation, the groups provide the opportunity to reflect the projects and discuss outcomes. Studies run by Centres for Teaching and Learning that engage in FLCs revealed that teachers who were taking part in a FLC changed their teaching practices. Also for students a change in learning outcomes was stated. Within the groups a shared understanding and values of high quality teaching developed. Nonetheless, as the curricula of the group is developed in a democratic process, it might not meet the demands of all group members. Those teachers were less motivated to engage in the group activities as these are require resources such as time and the willingness to learn about new subjects. FLCs, however, also attract a certain type of academic staff. Mostly teachers who have a strong interest in teaching already engage in these groups (Beach & Cox, 2009; Cox, 2004).

Studies on FLCs also state that they are effective in changing teaching practices as well as in generating better learning outcomes for students. As these results are based on surveys among students and teachers, facilitating or hindering factors are mostly found at the individual level. In particular teachers' and students' attitudes towards teaching and learning were found to facilitate a stronger engagement and to change teaching practices significantly. The institutional context and the way FLCs engage teachers has not been researched in these studies. However, according to survey results, the institutional context, did not seem to matter as similar changes in teaching and learning practices occurred across all the surveyed institutions (Beach & Cox, 2009, p. 25).

TWO CETLS COMPARED[1]

The literature thus indicates some factors that may have an impact on how well CETLs can facilitate activities aiming to improve of the quality of teaching and learning. In the following section, two institutions that implemented CETLs will be studied in more detail. The first case is a German research university that has implemented a CETL as a department. The second case refers to a mono-disciplinary higher education institution in Norway that has implemented a CETL as a network of teachers.

The first centre under review is located at a German research university. The institution is rather large with more than 40,000 students and 5,000 staff members. The university is a comprehensive university. Due to its location and historical roots, the university attracts students from diverse socio-economic and ethnic backgrounds, i.e the student population has a high percentage of students with a migration background and also a lot of first-generation students. At this institution, the CETL (herafter, the Centre) has been established in the mid of the 2000. Currently it is a service unit that is located at the central university level. Its status, however, has changed in the recent years. The Centre is a follow-up unit of a former so-called higher education didactics centre whose major task was academic development. At the time of the survey, the Centre provided services in four major areas: didactical training for academic staff, professional development of early career researchers, development and implementation of a quality management system, in particular the implementation of a self-accreditation system, and as a cross-sectional task: the promotion of gender and diversity management throughout the university. The Centre reports to the Vice-Rector for Teaching and Learning as well as to the Vice-Rector for Development and Resource Planning. It engaged in supporting the university leadership in developing strategies, mostly in the area of teaching and learning but also around gender and diversity.

The Centre also coordinates a university-wide project funded by the German funding scheme 'Quality of Pact for Teaching' (*Qualitätspakt Lehre*). This project consists of a number of subprojects which aim to improve teaching and learning by either testing/experimenting with innovative teaching formats or providing preparatory classes for first year/first generation courses. These subproject are located at various levels at the university, e.g. at faculty level or at other service units. The majority of the Centre's staff are educational specialists who provide services in the different activity areas mentioned. They do not have other academic roles at the university or teach on the degree programmes. With regard to the university-wide project funded by the Quality Pact, a number of staff run these projects. Academic staff are 'clients' of the Centre. They can enrol in the Centre' courses and projects, which are considered as professional development activities. The Centre also offers individualized didactical trainings such as coaching of professors or other senior academic staff. It also supports teachers who would like to develop innovative teaching projects. Those teachers are supported by informing them about potential funding possibilities and helping them to write the bid for their project. The Centre delivers input to the project by pointing teachers to research literature and evidence available for similar teaching projects. Didactical courses are mostly offered for staff from all faculties, i.e. there are no discipline specific courses. The majority of course participants are early career researchers; senior academic staff attend the Centre's courses less frequently. New academic staff is informed about the Centre when they start to work about the university. The Centre, however, does not reach out to academic staff by advertising its services to the academic staff on a regular basis. Staff interested in academic development, improving teaching and learning activities have to make contact with the Centre themselves and ask for support. The Centre thus resembles the type of 'organisational unit' that has been described in the foregoing section.

The second case represents a Norwegian higher music education institution that has established a Centre for Excellence in Education (in the following CEE) in 2014. The institution is rather small, it has around 600 students following bachelor, master and doctoral training in instrumental teaching but also in related subjects such as music pedagogy or music theory. It also has about 400 academic staff with a high percentage of part-time instrumental teachers. The institution is highly selective, i.e. students have to pass a thorough selection procedure to get accepted. The CEE receives funding from the Norwegian SFU scheme. The CEE has three major objectives with regard to improving teaching and learning: Advancing music performance teaching, enhancing the quality of student's instrumental practice, in particular by cross-genre training, and to better prepare students for their later careers in the globalized music society (CEE application, p. 1).

The CEE is organized in a similar way to the Faculty Learning Committee model presented in a previous section. Thus, academic staff take roles and responsibilities in the project, staff involved in the project meet regularly to exchange about their work and experiences. The project is structured along the three major goals, i.e. for each goal work packages have been implemented that cover different aspects. The subprojects offer academic staff the opportunity to run their own small educational project for a limited period (e.g. for a semester). These projects are developed by the teachers themselves. To conduct the project teachers have to apply to the CEE. Selected project receive resources (in particular time) and support from the CEE. Teachers who run small educational projects meet regularly during semester and exchange their experiences. There is also an open-door policy; teachers are invited to attend the teaching of their peers. Teachers are also asked to document the outcomes of their projects; also here they receive support from the project leaders. Project outcomes feed into publications that are spread widely in the institution but also shared with other music education institutions and on the CEE's website. Project outcomes are also presented on a so-called 'Education Day' of the institution as well as on national and international conferences.

TEACHING AND LEARNING MICRO CULTURES

To learn about the institutional teaching culture, teacher interviewees were asked for their personal views on what quality teaching means to them and what kind of values they prefer when teaching. These questions were also raised in the interviews with Centre's staff and the university leadership. The analysis focused on to what extent interviewees discuss teaching in similar ways and in what context they developed their perspectives.

For the *German* case we found some common ground regards the definition of high quality teaching. The majority of teachers interviewed stated that good teaching should engage and motivate students as well as provide them with sufficient (theoretical) knowledge that is useful in their later professional life. Though converging for these aspects, teachers have strong individual ideas of what good teaching or quality in teaching is. Most of them developed these ideas throughout their own biography rather than when engaging with their colleagues or within the institution. Teaching is also regarded as an individual responsibility, i.e. problems in teaching were perceived as personal failures, acquiring teaching competences is perceived as an individual journey that is fuelled by a natural talent for teaching. Respondents also state very different challenges teaching and learning in higher education has to address. These challenges are often related to the context and problems respondents face in their everyday routines. The university's teaching and learning strategy has little importance in the teachers' perception of teaching and learning. The majority of them are not aware of the strategy or perceive it as having only little relevance for their teaching activities. Some of the teachers state that they agree with the values and goals mentioned in the strategy, but they do not feel well prepared to deal with them or to apply them in their teaching. Also a lack of resources to develop those competences is mentioned.

Teaching is also perceived as a strongly individualized task, i.e. preparing and running a course was frequently defined as a task for one person. When preparing a course most teachers did not have an elaborated didactical approach. Though the majority of teachers highly valued the idea that their teaching should engage and motivate students, they hardly addressed the question how students learn and what teaching could effectuate this. Most of them, in particular those who did not participate in any didactical training, state that the engagement of student is mostly dependent on how well or interestingly they present the knowledge in the classroom. To them a good teacher is mostly a good presenter that is more knowledgeable in the field of study than the students. Those teachers also did not recognize that there is pedagogical or didactical knowledge that could help them to run a class or a course. They mostly argued that they need to have elaborated knowledge of their field of study to be a good teacher.

The majority of teachers gained their teaching knowledge practices through 'learning by doing'. When they started their teaching career they were mostly thrown into this activity without any (didactical) preparation. Often they did not have colleagues with whom they could talk about different methods to run or prepare a class, a course or an assessment. These teachers mostly developed their teaching practices based on their experiences throughout their own studies. Some of them also stated that they have developed these practices in trial and error processes. Only very few teachers stated that they use a scholarship approach to teaching and learning, i.e. formulating learning goals and competencies, informing themselves about good ways how to engage students in adequate learning processes, how to assess students and how to research how effectively the teaching was.

Further, teachers also state they hardly exchange with their colleagues about teaching practices. There is, however, a lot of talk about teaching at different levels. In regular meetings at faculty or chair level teaching issues are addressed. Mostly the discussion of teaching addresses organizational problems such as overlapping schedules, lack of resources, planning of the teaching programme for the upcoming semesters or complaints of students. Teaching practices *per se* are not addressed and the majority of teachers consider these to be private issues. There are, however, also self-organized or informal meetings among teachers at faculty or chair level were teaching practices are discussed. Mostly, early career researchers who have a strong interest in developing their teaching competencies organise the meeting. Teachers participate in the meetings voluntary and frequently outside their paid working hours and they do not receive any resources or support.

Though there might be differences at faculty or department level, one can assume that a strong individualized teaching micro culture is prevailing at this university. Though teachers strongly engage in good teaching, the majority of them do not perceive teaching as a collaborative activity. Also, there is only limited awareness that there is pedagogical or didactical knowledge that could be helpful in preparing courses, classes and assessments. Thus, only few teachers were aware of any theoretical background about how students learn. To other teachers, motivating students to learn would be achieved by entertaining students or being a good presenter.

For the *Norwegian* institution we found a very high congruency of teacher answers when asking for their personal view on good teaching and what are important values in teaching. With regard to good teaching, the majority of respondents highlighted three major aspects. First good teaching should help the students to develop an ownership of or responsibility for their own learning. Second, good teaching helps students to define their own goals and to select where they would like to develop as musicians. Third, good teaching prepares students to be able to manage their own careers, i.e. to develop entrepreneurial competences to face the challenges of the changing music society. Shared values around good teaching include respect for the student, her or his knowledge and competences. The relationship between teacher and student is seen as needing to be trustful and with room left for the student to develop. Further, being open for collaboration and sharing with peer teachers is regarded as a very important competence for teachers. Interestingly, there was also a strong consensus about what are perceived as challenges to teaching. Here the majority of teachers stated that the student population has become diverse in the sense that they have nowadays more wide ranging goals concerning the direction they would like to develop as musicians. They also state that students' attitude has changed: students have become more self-confident and want to develop more freely. Also, the increasing competition in a more globalized music market is widely defined as a challenge that requires higher education institutions to better prepare their students for later careers. Also, overcoming the strong privacy prevailing in music education (one-on-one teaching; master-apprentice relationship) is identified as a challenge.

There was only very low variation with regard to perceptions of teaching across the different groups that were interviewed. The majority of the respondents referred to the aspects mentioned in a similar manner, some of them even used similar words when describing their personal view on teaching. There were also hardly any differences between teachers, managers/administrative personal and the institutional leadership. People who did not yet participate in the CEE's activities stated similar perceptions.

Looking at the content of the definitions reveals that these reflect an elaborated approach to teaching and learning. A student-oriented as well as a learning-oriented focus is strongly applied, and teaching is seen in a broader context, i.e. respondents are aware of the goals of teaching and the several purposes it should serve. The institution as well as the CEE were thus quite successful in developing a common sense about teaching and learning. Most teachers also stated that they developed their teaching practices in the context of the institution. Instrument teachers however stated their own experiences of being taught as a student had a strong influence on their ideas about teaching, but they were also aware of pedagogical and didactical knowledge that helps them to reflect and further develop their teaching practices.

The table below summarizes and compares the main features of teaching micro cultures.

Table 12.1. Comparison of teaching micro cultures

	The Centre (Germany)	CEE (Norway)
Definition of High quality teaching	No congruency among answers, frequently stated: • Engages and motivates students • Provides students with sufficient knowledge for their later professional life	High congruency among answers – common sense: • Students develop ownership for their learning • Helps students to define their own goals/how they would like to develop • Provides students with competences to manage their own careers
Teaching ideas and competencies developed...	At an individual level throughout biography, frequently in a trial- and error process	• At institutional level through exchange with other teachers and attending courses • In small teaching projects • At individual level through own teaching experiences
Relevance of institutional Teaching and Learning strategy for own teaching practice	Very low	Very high
Division of teaching labour	Highly individualized task, no sharing of ideas, division of labour hardly accepted by teachers	Strong collaboration, sharing of tasks
A good teacher	Is a good presenter/ entertainer	Supports students in finding their own ways

THE CENTRES' ENGAGEMENT STRATEGIES

At the *German* institution the Centre staff mentioned that they do not have an overall engagement strategy. As stated above, the Centre does not contact academic staff on a regular basis to inform about its activities. Rather, those staff interested in academic development have to request its support. While early career researchers frequently do so, the centre mentions that it is difficult to reach out to more senior academic staff. Senior staff requesting support are provided with individual coaching. Centre staff and leadership state that their promotion activities to engage teachers in quality teaching and learning do not have a strong impact and that have difficulties to promote a more collaborative teaching culture.

There are a number of factors that have contributed to this situation. In particular Centre staff stated that there are different layers of knowledge at the university and that it is difficult to bridge between them. On the one hand there is the layer of teaching knowledge that is presented by the Centre staff. This explicit knowledge is based on a more methodological approach on teaching and learning and includes for example basic didactical knowledge, learning theories and evidence on effective teaching methods. It thus represents a discipline of its own. On the other hand there is the layer of teaching knowledge as presented by the academic staff. This tacit knowledge is mostly based on the personal experiences of the teachers. It has very often been developed in a trial-and-error process, it also represents practices teachers have been experiencing themselves as students. This knowledge has been reflected also, but mostly in an individual manner rather than in a collaborative setting. Teachers themselves frequently do not relate their teaching competencies to this knowledge. To them being an expert in their field of study is much more important for good teaching. Bridging between these two knowledge layers is difficult in particular because the explicit knowledge base of teaching has already established an elaborated language, but there is hardly a language to express the tacit knowledge of the teachers. This makes it difficult for the teachers to communicate about teaching, either to identify potential problems they might experience in the class-room or to understand the educational professionals. Some teachers argued that they experience exchanges with the educational specialist as a threat because they perceive their support as a strong intervention in academic freedom. One teacher respondent stated that this perception is also motivated by a certain fear among teaching staff. Reflecting their own teaching practices and learning about alternative approaches would question their efforts and investment in establishing their teaching practices so far.

Another important factor is strongly related to the academic career system. Moving up the career ladder and in particular passing the bottleneck to move to a permanent position requires academic staff to strongly invest in their research performance. Investments in teaching performance are less important to academic staff as these do not usually have a strong impact on upward career mobility. Against this background, investments in teaching competencies appear to be ill-motivated.

The way the Centre promotes activities to improve the quality of teaching and learning often takes a strong individualized perspective. Training, coaching and supporting the implementation/development of innovative teaching projects is related to developing or professionalizing individual academics rather than engaging groups of teachers. There is also a strong idea that the Centre should provide academics with knowledge by transmission. Reflecting teachers' tacit knowledge about teaching practices as well as developing shared values of high quality teaching and learning through collaboration of teachers does not play an important role in the Centre's activities.

Another, but less strong factor is related to the lack of preparation of academic staff for teaching activities. In this study, the majority of 13 teachers believed that teaching requires excellent expertise in their field of study. For the design of teaching and learning processes, however, they considered their experience and intuitive knowledge as sufficient. This focus prevents teachers from reflecting on teaching and learning processes from a research perspective that would allow the identification of effective methods and practices.

Finally, the absence of formal time regimes hinders teachers who want to engage intensively in teaching practices or in developing (innovative) teaching projects. A major problem here is that employment contracts often do not define percentages of working time that have to be spent on research and teaching tasks. Though contracts sometimes include the number of week hours for teaching, they do not state how much time in total has to be spend on teaching (including preparation, etc.). This makes it difficult to provide teachers with resources, such as time, for the development of teaching projects, or to give them an incentive to pursue further training to improve their teaching.

At the *Norwegian* institution the CEE staff and leaders mentioned that when developing the Centre plan they were aware of the need to also develop an idea about how to engage teachers in its activities. They also were aware that they needed to promote central ideas and values underlying the work of the CEE.

The already existing institutional culture had a strong impact in this respect as it helped the CEE to bridge between knowledge presented by the CEE and the tacit knowledge of teachers. Unlike other music academies, the institution was already engaging in evidence-based educational development and also in research on music education or other music theory for a number of years. This provided the institution with expertise on educational development on the one hand. On the other hand interviewees also stated already knew how to carefully facilitate communication between instrument teachers and education developers. The composition of institutional leadership helped account for this: the team of leaders was always composed of staff from both the more theoretical and the more practical departments. Institutional leadership also paid high attention to bottom-up management. The leadership strongly promoted ongoing exchange and communication across the different groups.

The definitions of good teaching and learning and the preferred values for teaching and learning further strongly reflected the institution's strategy with regard to teaching and learning. This strategy was elaborated in a year-long bottom-up process involving the different internal stakeholders of the institution (staff, students, leadership). The strategy was written by a number of working groups, but there was also a steering group consisting of staff and students who worked together with an external consultant. Different versions of the strategy were discussed in meetings that were open to all staff and students. These meetings were attended by a quite high number of persons, and their feedback was integrated in the text. The strategy states clearly formulated development goals for a period of 10 years. However, the strategy also establishes mid-term reviews to evaluate achievements and adjust goals. The majority of respondents stated that the strategy had relevance for their daily teaching as they would share the values included in the strategy, in particular the importance of collaboration and sharing among teachers in the institution but also outside the institution. For the CEE too, clear objectives were formulated, which were known by all interviewees and were also supported by them. Most respondents found these goals relevant to their daily practice and also could see the benefits of the different projects run in the CEE. The university leadership also states that there is a strong alignment between the strategy and the CEE activities. CEE activities intend to support the implementation of the strategy. This is done by for example by testing different models of innovative teaching in order to promote more student-centred education activities.

The high degree of shared values and perceptions of teaching is also related to the fact that all teachers at the institution are obliged to attend a preparatory didactical course for their teaching activities. Most teachers stated that this course helped them to reflect their teaching activities/practice in a more reflected manner. Those persons who were involved in establishing the course find that the high acceptance of the teacher training was mainly related to the fact that the content has relevance for the music teachers as it clearly connects the educational knowledge to their practical work. Another success factor was that the course put high importance on the stimulating discussions and group work among teachers, also stimulating them to engage in small projects.

The principle to align the educational development as close as possible with the daily practice of the teachers is also used in the projects that are run under CEE's realm. Teachers who would like to participate in the projects can freely develop their own project idea. Their autonomy and competence is fully respected also by the CEE. To realize their project they receive support from the project leaders and their peers in the project. The CEE also provides them with financial and other resources to run the project. To develop and run their project the teachers also receive working time, i.e. part-time teachers receive an increase of their contract in terms of hours. For full-time teachers the percentages they have to spend on teaching or development work are changed, mostly their teaching load becomes decreased.

Dissemination of results in the institution itself as well as with national and international audiences is a main task of the CEE. A number of different channels to disseminate results have been established such as publications, a website and participation in international and national conferences. Besides publishing the results of the CEE project there was also a considerable effort to make the CEE as such, i.e. its goals and activities – well known among all staff and students. (Compulsory) staff days were dedicated to informing people about CEE activities. Also the selection of project leaders for the different work packages was done carefully. Mostly heads of departments were selected as work package or project leaders who informed their colleagues about the CEE in regular department meetings. Teachers who took part in the first round of projects were also chosen according to how well they were connected to the other teachers. This helped promote internal communication about the CEE. In order to open or broaden existing communication structures, project groups had teachers with diverse backgrounds (for example coming from different departments). This meant that teachers were forced to talk to colleagues they hardly met in the past. The regular meetings of the project groups serve to stimulate the reflection of the teachers on the projects carried out but above all also to encourage them to express their tacit knowledge. They are also asked to report on the project outcomes. Here they receive support from the project leader. The reports feed into printed publications that are distributed to each teacher in the institution. Dissemination however also benefitted from the existing vivid communication culture in the institution. Here, the interviewees pointed out that the institution has set up a wide range of committees, which involve teachers in various ways and give the opportunity to participate.

CONCLUSIONS: EFFECTIVE ENGAGEMENT STRATEGIES

Existing research suggests that promoting activities to improve teaching and learning is difficult to implement at higher education institutions. This is particularly true for CETLs as they frequently face difficulties in gaining acceptance and legitimacy among academic staff for the kind of knowledge they provide with their promotion activities. Recent research on UK funded CETLs stated that the lack of an adequate engagement strategy made it difficult for them to effectively promote their activities (Saunders et al., 2008). This research however did not address the various ways that CETLs are implemented at higher education institutions. Other research investigated to what extent teachers who participated in CETL activities changed their teaching practices. These studies revealed more positive results for the impact of CETL as those teachers frequently changed their teaching behaviour as well as student learning outcomes improved (Beach & Cox 2009; Bélanger et al., 2011). More recent research, however, noted a strong individualistic perspective, finding individual attitudes and motives of teachers the most important factors for the success of improvement activities. Other research highlights the role of teaching and learning micro cultures for engaging teachers in high quality student oriented teaching. Here stimulating communication and exchange between teachers about teaching practices is found to be fundamental to developing such micro cultures (Mårtensson & Roxå, 2016a; Mårtensson & Roxå, 2016b). Strong micro cultures, i.e. cultures where teachers share values, beliefs and knowledge about teaching, are able to orient teaching practices, support the development of a teacher identity and to effect changes in teaching practices. This research however does not explicitly consider the role of CETLs in stimulating and supporting these teacher networks, mostly networks that developed more naturally (e.g. Mårtensson & Roxå, 2016b).

Therefore in the previous sections, the engagement strategies of two highly contrasting types of CETL were investigated. The analysis focused on the extent shared beliefs, values and knowledge with regard to teaching and learning have been established at the two institutions and how CETL support these processes with their engagement strategy. It also addressed facilitating and hindering factors for these engagement strategies. Though one has to consider that this paper investigates only two highly contrasting cases, a number of preliminary conclusions are nevertheless drawn.

Comparing the two cases it appears that *CETLs that are able to bridge between explicit pedagogical knowledge and the tacit and implicit knowledge of teachers are more likely to successfully gain acceptance and legitimacy for pedagogical knowledge among academic staff.* Whilst the Norwegian institution had already established communication between education developers and teachers, this was still a difficult issue at the German institution. At the Norwegian institution the fact that teachers have to participate in didactical courses strongly supports the acceptance. Tailoring the courses to the everyday practices and routines of teachers is important here. This helped teachers to accept that the didactical knowledge helps them to do their teaching rather than assuming that the knowledge would replace their knowledge and teaching practices. Adapting to the teachers everyday routines and practices was rather difficult in the German institution. This is due to the central location of the CETL and its purpose to serve all faculties and disciplines. This makes it difficult for Centre staff to adapt to already existing cultures at faculty or department level or to have regular contact with academic staff. Also the Centre does not actively advertise its services to academic staff, rather academics have to request support and this approach does not smooth the communication between education developers and academic staff, as it establishes a slightly hierarchical relationship between the two groups.

Assigning the teachers an active role in and responsibility for improving activities taking place under the realm of the CETL also appears to stimulate a stronger engagement of teachers. Here the Norwegian case made clear that teachers very much enjoy the opportunity to develop their own teaching projects. Exchanging and collaborating with colleagues who work on similar tasks was reported as very helpful and inspiring. The fact that the CETL was able to provide appropriate resources, in particular time through the exemption from other activities, was considered a further important incentive. From the German case it became clear that only teachers who were strongly interested in developing teaching projects and who had found their own funding for that were engaging in these. For the majority of teachers the CETL was a service unit and they identified themselves as consumers of the services provided. Teachers thus had limited opportunities to develop their own projects and receive appropriate support. Also, stimulating networks and collaboration among teachers was not mentioned as an engagement activity by CETL staff. Only a very small number of teachers mentioned that they engage in such networks with their colleagues.

The scope and the size of the institution, however, also is an important factor. At the Norwegian institution the CETL was definitely more successful in developing a collaborative teaching culture simply because of the small institution size. This makes it much easier to promote the CETL, to select teachers who take responsibilities and roles in the CETL projects and to disseminate project results. An active outreach to teachers and promoting active communication is also crucial to successful engagement strategies. While the Norwegian Centre puts a lot of emphasis on

Table 12.2. Summary of engagement strategies

	The Centre (Germany)	CEE (Norway)
Bridging between implicit knowledge of individual teachers and pedagogical knowledge of Centre	Very difficult, because of: • Centre has to serve very different faculties, • No shared language developed/cross disciplinary focus difficult to achieve • Requesting support establishes hierarchical relationship between academic and centre staff	Made possible through: • Developing shared language through CEE by adapting to everyday practice of academic staff • No hierarchy between academic staff and educational developers
Roles in improvement activities/ Responsibility for improvement activities	• No active roles for academic staff, act as customers to the Centre. Centre staffs defines improvement of teaching and learning activities • No clear responsibility for improvement of teaching and learning	• Active roles for academic staff in improvement activities available • Shared responsibility for improvement of teaching and learning
Incentives	• Centre is not able to provide any incentives for enhancement activities	Centre is able to provide incentives such as time, money and support.
Implementation	• Individualized approach to academic staff does not help to establish an institutional focus on teaching and learning	• Network approach supports communication and exchange about teaching and learning and develop shared understandings • Projects give opportunity to develop own teaching idea
Scope and size of the institution	• Size and scope of the institution make it difficult to reach out to academic staff individually	• Personal contact with academic staff is possible.

actively outreaching to academic staff, the German Centre uses an passive approach requesting academic to search for opportunities themselves. *Defining the CETL as project that provides opportunities to develop and experiment in collaboration with others makes participation in its activities very attractive.* At the German institution, the CETL as a central level service unit is certainly more distant from the teachers. Also providing services rather than opportunities to actively engage in developing own teaching projects does not stimulate collaboration among teachers. Considering a *decentralized implementation of FLC at faculty level* could help to more strongly engage teachers in enhancement activities.

Table 12.2 summarizes and compares the most important aspects of engagement strategies for the Centres under review.

NOTE

[1] The two cases have been studied for the project CETLFUNK. In this ongoing project in total eight CETL in Germany, England, Norway and the Netherlands are researched with intensive case studies. The project seeks to understand how CETL support the university leadership when steering teaching and the CETL role in the discourse around teaching and learning. The two cases have been selected from the sample as they are highly contrasting in terms of the implementation of the CETL and the size of the institution. To address cultural biases that might result from the international comparative design the author took an relativist position towards the text provided in interviewees responses trying to reconstruct the respondent's meaning and perception while taking her or his cultural background into account. The project CETLFUNK is funded by the German Federal Ministry of Education and Research and led by the author (01PB14009 – CETLFUNK).

REFERENCES

Beach, A. L., & Cox, M. D. (2009). The impact of faculty learning communities on teaching and learning. *Learning Communities Journal, 1*(1), 7–27. Retrieved June 28, 2016.

Bélanger, C., Bélisle, M., & Bernatchez, P.-A. (2011). A study of the impact of services of a university teaching centre on teaching practice: Changes and conditions. *Journal on Centers for Teaching and Learning, 3*, 131–165. Retrieved July 01, 2016.

Challis, D., Holt, D., & Palmer, S. (2009). Teaching and learning centres: Towards maturation. *Higher Education Research & Development, 28*(4), 371–383.

Cox, M. D. (2004). Introduction to faculty learning communities. *New Directions for Teaching and Learning, 2004*(97), 5–23. Retrieved June 28, 2016, from https://cms.ysu.edu/sites/default/files/documents/Introduction_to_Faculty_Learning_Communities_by_Milt_Cox.pdf

Gosling, D., & Turner, R. (2014). Responding to contestation in teaching and learning projects in the centres for excellence in teaching and learning in the United Kingdom. *Studies in Higher Education, 40*(9), 1573–1587.

Kottmann, A., & Cremonini, L. (2017, in print). *Midterm report CETLFUNK.* Enschede, the Netherlands.

Kottmann, A., Huisman, J., Brockerhoff, L., Cremonini, L., & Mampaey, J. (2016). *How can one create a culture for quality enhancement? Final report.* Enschede, Ghent. Retrieved January 15, 2017.

Lieberman, D. (2005). Beyond faculty development: How centers for teaching and learning can be laboratories for learning. *New Directions for Teaching and Learning, 131*, 87–98. Retrieved June 28, 2016.

Mårtensson, K., & Roxå, T. (2016a). Peer engagement for teaching and learning: Competence, autonomy and social solidarity in academic micro cultures. *Uniped, 39*(2), 131–143. Retrieved June 26, 2016, from https://www.idunn.no/file/pdf/66873000/peer_engagement_for_teaching_and_learning_competence_auto.pdf

Mårtensson, K., & Roxå, T. (2016b). Working with networks, micro cultures and communities. In D. Baume & C. Popovic (Eds.), *The staff and educational development series: Advancing practice in academic development* (pp. 174–187). London: Routledge.

Pruvot, E. B., & Estermann, T. (2014). DEFINE thematic report: Funding for excellence. Brussels, European University Association.

Raaheim, A., & Karjalainen, A. (2012). *Centres of excellence in university education, Finland 1999– 2012: An evaluation,* from KKA – The finnish higher education evaluation council.

Saunders, M., Machell, J., Williams, S., Allaway, D., Spencer, A., Ashwin, P. et al. (2008). *2005–2010 centres of excellence in teaching and learning programmes: Formative evaluation report to HEFCE by the centre for study in education and training/institution of educational technology.* Retrieved from http://www.hefce.ac.uk/media/hefce/content/pubs/indirreports/2008/missing/2005-2010%20CETL% 20programme%20formative%20evaluation.pdf

SQW. (2011). *Summative evaluation of the CETL programme: Final report by SQW to HEFCE and DEL.* HEFCE. Retrieved from http://www.hefce.ac.uk/media/hefce/content.pubs/indirreports/2011/ RE,1111,Eval,of,CETL/rd11_11.pdf

Webler, W.-D. (2012). Vergleich von zentren für hochschul- und qualitätsentwicklung. *Personal- und Organisationsentwicklung, 7*(4), 130–133.

Wenger, E., McDermott, R., & Snyder, W. M. (2002). *Cultivating communities of practice. A guide to managing knowledge.* Boston, MA: Harvard Business School Press.

Andrea Kottmann
Centre for Higher Education Policy Studies
University of Twente

LIST OF CONTRIBUTORS

EDITORS

Rosemary Deem, Professor of Higher Education Management, Vice-Principal (Teaching Innovation; Equality and Diversity)and Dean of the Doctoral School at Royal Holloway University of London, UK. She is Chair of the UK Council for Graduate Education, co-convenor of the European Educational Research Association Network 22 (Higher Education) and a co-editor of the Springer journal *Higher Education*. R.Deem@rhul.ac.uk

Heather Eggins, Fellow Commoner, Lucy Cavendish College, University of Cambridge; Visiting Professor, Centre for Higher Education and Equity, School of Education and Social Work, University of Sussex; and Visiting Professor, School of Business, Leadership and Economics, Staffordshire University. H.Eggins@staffs.ac.uk

CONTRIBUTORS

Dominik Antonowicz, Associate Professor, Nicolaus Copernicus University, Torun, Poland. dominik.antonowicz@uni.torun.pl

Monia Anzivino, Post-doctoral Fellow, Department of Social and Political Sciences, University of Pavia, Italy. monia.anzivino@unipv.it

Vikki Boliver, Reader in Sociology, School of Applied Social Sciences, Durham University, UK. vikki.boliver@durham.ac.uk

Ellen Carm, Associate Professor, Institute for Internationalization and Interpreting, Oslo and Akershus University College of Applied Sciences, Oslo, Norway. Ellen.Carm@hioa.no

Frank G. A. de Bakker, Full Professor of Corporate Social Responsibility, Department of Management, IESEG School of Management, Lille, France. f.debakker@ieseg.fr

Harry F. de Boer, Senior Research Associate, Centre for Higher Education Policy Studies, University of Twente, The Netherlands. h.f.deboer@utwente.nl

Stephen Gorard, Professor of Education and Public Policy, School of Education, Durham University, UK. s.a.c.gorard@durham.ac.uk

Sandra Hasanefendic, Doctoral Student, School of Sociology and Public Policy, ISCTE-IUL, Lisbon, Portugal and Faculty of Social Sciences, and Department of Organization Sciences, Faculty of Social Sciences, Vrije University, Amsterdam, The Netherlands. s.hasanefendic@vu.nl

Myroslava Hladchenko, Associate Professor, Center for Higher Education Policy Studies, University of Twente, the Netherlands, and Faculty of Humanities and Pedagogy, National University of Life and Environmental Sciences of Ukraine, Ukraine. hladchenkom@gmail.com; m.hladchenko@utwente.nl

Tone Horntvedt, Associate Professor, Institute for Internationalization and Interpreting, Oslo and Akershus University College of Applied Sciences, Oslo, Norway. Tone.Horntvedt@hioa.no

Daniel Kontowski, Postgraduate Research Student, Department of Education Studies and Liberal Arts, University of Winchester, UK. daniel@kontowski.com

Andrea Kottmann, Senior Research Associate, Centre for Higher Education Policy Studies, University of Twente, Enschede, The Netherlands. a.kottmann@utwente.nl

António Magalhães, Head of the Department of Education Sciences, Faculty of Psychology and Education Sciences, University of Porto, Portugal and Senior Researcher, Centre for Research on Higher Education Policies (CIPES), Matosinhos, Portugal antonio@fpce.up.pt

Maria J. Manatos, Doctoral student, ISEG Lisbon School of Economics and Management, and Centre for Research in Higher Education Policies (CIPES), Matosinhos, Portugal. maria.manatos@cipes.up.pt

David Michael Kretz, M.A. Student in Contemporary Philosophy, Ecole Normale Superieure, Paris, France. david.kretz@ens.fr

Maria Teresa Patricio, Associate Professor, Department of Political Science and Public Policy, School of Sociology and Public Policy, ISCTE-IUL, Lisbon, Portugal. teresa.patricio@iscte.pt

Maria João Rosa, Assistant Professor, Department of Economics, Management, Industrial Engineering and Tourism, University of Aveiro, Senior Researcher at Centre for Research in Higher Education Policies (CIPES) and Researcher at GOVCOPP (Governance, Competitiveness and Public Policies), Portugal. m.joao@ua.pt

Michele Rostan, Associate Professor, Economic Sociology , Department of Social and Political Sciences, Rector's Delegate for Student Affairs, and Director of CIRSIS – Centre for Study and Research on Higher Education Systems, University of Pavia, Italy. michele.rostan@unipv.it

Cláudia S. Sarrico, Associate Professor at ISEG Lisbon School of Economics and Management, University of Lisbon and Researcher at CIPES , Matosinhos, Portugal. cssarrico@iseg.ulisboa.pt

Nadia Siddiqui, Postdoctoral Research Associate, School of Education and Applied Social Sciences, Durham University, UK. nadia.siddiqui@durham.ac.uk

Amélia Veiga, Assistant Professor, Faculty of Psychology and Sciences of Education, University of Porto, Matosinhos, Portugal. aveiga@cipes.up.pt

Pedro Videira, Researcher, Centre for Research on Higher Education Policies (CIPES), Matosinhos, Portugal

Sina Westa, Marie Curie Research Fellow, University of Ljubljana, Faculty of Education, Ljubljana, Slovenia. sina.westa@pef.uni-lj.si

Susan Wright, Professor of Educational Anthropology, Danish School of Education, Aarhus University, Denmark and Coordinator of the EU Marie Curie International Training Network 'Universities in the Knowledge Economy' (UNIKE). She co-edits *Learning and Teaching: International Journal of Higher Education in the Social Sciences*. suwr@edu.au.dk.